Inclusive Feminism

Inclusive Feminism

A Third Wave Theory of Women's Commonality

Naomi Zack

ROWMAN & LITTLEFIELD PUBLISHERS, INC.
Lanham • *Boulder* • *New York* • *Toronto* • *Oxford*

ROWMAN & LITTLEFIELD PUBLISHERS, INC.

Published in the United States of America
by Rowman & Littlefield Publishers, Inc.
A wholly owned subsidiary of The Rowman & Littlefield Publishing Group, Inc.
4501 Forbes Boulevard, Suite 200, Lanham, MD 20706
www.rowmanlittlefield.com

P.O. Box 317, Oxford OX2 9RU, UK

British Library Cataloguing in Publication Information Available

Library of Congress Cataloging-in-Publication Data
Zack, Naomi, 1944–
 Inclusive feminism : a third wave theory of women's commonality / Naomi Zack.
  p. cm.
 Includes bibliographical references and index.
 ISBN 0-7425-4298-X (cloth : alk. paper) — ISBN 0-7425-4299-8 (pbk. : alk. paper)
 1. Feminist theory. 2. Feminist theory—United States. 3. Feminism—United States.
4. African American women. I. Title
 HQ1190.Z3 2005
 305.42'01—dc22
                                                                        2004022278

Printed in the United States of America

♾™The paper used in this publication meets the minimum requirements of
American National Standard for Information Sciences—Permanence of Paper for
Printed Library Materials, ANSI/NISO Z39.48-1992.

To my sons, Alexander Linden Erdmann
and Bradford Zack Mahon

Philosophy is first of all a particular way in which the "rising class" becomes conscious of itself.

—Jean-Paul Sartre

Philosophy will not be able to bring about a direct change of the present state of the world. This is true not only of philosophy but of all merely human meditations and endeavors. Only a god can still save us. I think the only possibility of salvation left to us is to prepare readiness through thinking and poetry, for the appearance of the god or for the absence of the god during the decline; so that we do not, simply put, die meaningless deaths, but that when we decline, we decline in the face of the absent god.

—Martin Heidegger

If women ruled the world
It would be a good thing

—Joan Armatrading

Contents

Acknowledgments

I presented an overview of some of the main ideas of chapters 1–4 in a symposium on gender and race arranged by the American Philosophical Association (APA) Committee on the Status of Women at the March 2003 Pacific Division meeting in San Francisco. That paper was revised for a colloquium sponsored by the Philosophy Department of DePaul University in April 2003, after I was invited by Jason Hill; and it was further revised for the audience at the Pacific SWIP (Society for Women in Philosophy) meeting at the University of Oregon in November 2003. I thank all members of the audiences of those venues for comments and feedback, in particular Laurie Shrage, Sally J. Marcowitz, and Licia Carlson. Their comments informed the article I wrote, during the summer of 2003, for publication in the *Encyclopedia of Feminist Philosophy* edited by Eva Kittay and Linda Alcoff (Blackwell). Eva and Linda required explanations and clarifications of earlier arguments and ideas, which were very useful for the sake of that article and my work on the book. Also, my personal thanks to Helena Hershel, who read the first draft of chapters 1–3 in July 2003.

Collegial thanks to Scott Pratt for helping me clarify the logic of the definition of women that I propose in chapters 1–2, and to both Scott Pratt and Bonnie Mann for reading chapters 1–5 in an early draft during the fall of 2003. A shorter version of chapter 4 was presented at a feminist theory symposium at the Pacific APA in Pasadena in March 2004. I am grateful to the audience there, to Alice Crary and Inmaculada De Melo-Martin for their response papers, and to Elizabeth Potter for chairing the session. A short version of chapter 7 was presented at a University of Oregon Philosophy Department colloquium in April 2004, and a shorter version at the Pacific SWIP meeting at UCLA and then the longer short version again at the Philosophy

Department of Seattle University, both in May 2004. Thanks very much to Sandra Harding and Ann Garry, for hosting the SWIP meeting and asking probing questions, and to Jennifer Vest and Marylou Senna, for inviting me and organizing an engaged audience at Seattle University. Responses at those occasions, which did not result in direct revision, have nevertheless informed my final revision of the manuscript. The merits of the book were strengthened from all this early support, and I benefited from listeners and readers who encouraged the project.

I completed a draft of the book during the winter term of 2004, when I was on leave from teaching at the University of Oregon. I am very grateful to the Philosophy Department and the Dean's Office of the College of Arts and Sciences for that extra time.

Finally, the external readership for Rowman & Littlefield was invaluable for the final draft, especially Laurie Shrage's concerns, which led me to add what is now chapter 8. I am also grateful to Eve DeVaro Fowler for her speed and encouragement as Rowman & Littlefield's acquisitions editor in philosophy, and to Tessa Fallon, for her assistance. Thanks also to Matt Crum, a doctoral student in my department, for clerical assistance with the final manuscript. The book would not exist without Kärstin Painter's valiant efforts as production editor, and I thank her.

Thus a strong representation of feminists and friends of feminists have been friends to the manuscript. The remaining errors and distortions are the result of my own ignorance and stubbornness.

1

Beyond Intersectionality

No one is quite sure what is going on in academic feminism these days, in the early years of the twenty-first century. The foundation of second wave feminism collapsed during the 1980s and feminists did not unite to rebuild it.[1] Some decamped with key elements of the structure and created separate and unequal feminisms along divisions of race, sexual preference, or intellectual proclivity. Others remained close to the ruins and agonized over how it could be possible to talk about the subject of feminism—women. From an indeterminate distance, their bolder counterparts proclaimed that the idea of such a subject, requiring as it did a preformed woman's subjectivity, was an outdated conceit of masculinist modernism.

The result of this confusion has been a great deal of theory, as well as theory about how to do theory. Although well intentioned, the enterprise has not been effective, if the purpose of feminism is to create universal advocacy for women's interests. The most promising path to a new coherence runs through the sharpest criticism of second wave feminism—the claim that white middle-class feminists did not speak for all women. This claim presupposed the destabilization of biology as the physical cause of female gender. Female gender was no longer understood as a cultural and psychological effect of biological female sex, but rather as a cultural effect of male dominance or patriarchy. Women of color insisted that other cultural forces such as racism and classism were also determinants of female gender and that they determined it differently for white middle-class women, women of color, and poor women. At first, the feminist focus was "race, class, gender," and a popular equation was race + class = gender. Soon the theory and intellectual praxis of *intersectionality* became a leading feminist paradigm, and it now structures much feminist research and scholarship. In the social sciences, some feminists have

1

insisted that women of color experience multiple oppressions, resulting in unique identities of race, gender, and class, for instance, the identities of poor black women. It is thereby understood that race was always gendered and gender was always raced.[2] Intersectionality is believed to be democratic because women of color now have the authority, demanded by them and sanctioned by white feminists, to create their own feminisms. But, as a theory of women's identity, intersectionality is not inclusive insofar as members of specific intersections of race and class can create *only* their own feminisms.

The purpose of this book is to develop a new theory in third wave feminism that will be inclusive. Everyone will be understood to be able to work on the same general project, although they will retain their specific concerns. The purpose of this chapter is to explain the motivation behind intersectionality, explain the problems with intersectionality, and reclaim the idea that all women have something in common. I will propose that what women have in common is a relation and not a thing. Along the way, I will try to show where second wave feminists were too hasty in accepting the collapse of their edifice. But, because feminist work has always been generational, I think it is probably too late to reconstruct the old foundation. There is no reason to believe that all of the women who became feminists after the 1970s, especially those who were not born before then, would be interested in rebuilding the foundations that collapsed during their mothers' and teachers' generations. I therefore hope that all readers, of at least the two generations in question, will join me in constructing a new foundation.[3]

EXCLUSION AND INTERSECTION

There is no question that women are different. The questions are how different and how their differences due to race, sexuality, and class get constructed. The biggest question is whether such differences combined erase all commonality among women. If each difference changes all of the others with its addition so that the result is a distinct kind of woman, how does that happen? Of course, it is only on a theoretical level that differences can be first distinguished and abstracted, and then recombined, because people exist as integral totalities that are raced, gendered, sexualized, aged, socially ranked, and so forth. There has been much cathartic, charismatic, and metaphoric talk about these matters of intersection, but I do not think that the resultant theory and academic praxis has thus far been inclusive across varied points of "intersection." The turn to intersectionality was so fast that there was apparently no time for feminists to agree that their intellectual goal was inclusiveness. Perhaps part of the reason was that the protest from nonwhite and poor women (or on behalf of the latter, since the poor do not have a recognized voice in formal scholarship) arrived before there was a consensus among most feminists and other liberatory scholars that racial differences are culturally constructed without a basis in the very biological taxonomies that they are supposed to reflect.[4]

Now there is no such biological barrier to inclusive feminism. And there will need to be inclusive feminism in the third wave, if (to put it crudely) the third wave will be able to speak convincingly to the Third World (both within and without the United States). Perhaps even more importantly, third wave feminists need to be able to listen to Third World women.

As it stands, feminism, as practiced by academic women in the United States, has not become weaker as an academic subject since its historical and theoretical exclusion of nonwhite and poor women was affirmatively raised in the late 1970s. Even voices such as that of the Combahee River Collective in "A Black Feminist Statement, " which insisted on the moral dignity, human rights, and material aspirations of African American women, did not result in significant reconstruction of the second wave feminist project.[5] Neither was the internal intellectual trajectory of academic feminism redirected by the subsequent exploration of feminist exclusivity developed during the 1980s, for instance, by bell hooks in *Ain't I a Woman?* and Elizabeth Spelman in *Inessential Woman*.[6] To simply "allow" women of color to pursue their own feminisms, without real change within established and establishment feminism, does not constitute the kind of change that includes feminists who are women of color.

From my professional perspective, it appears that more philosophy students than ever are interested in feminism, more traditional philosophers than ever are recognizing its disciplinary legitimacy, and more graduate students than ever think they can succeed academically with concentrations in feminism. However, personal experience since 1990, backed up by broad, objective recent statistics (the faculty in higher education remains 90.4 percent white, a figure that has not changed since 1989), attest that the presence of nonwhites in the academy did not significantly increase toward the end of the twentieth century.[7] Neither have their numbers significantly increased among female philosophers or female feminist philosophers.[8] It would be misguided and misleading to claim that feminism is responsible for the overall whiteness of the academy or the field of philosophy, but the figures in higher education and the field of philosophy do support the assertion that feminist philosophers have not thus far, to use an old-fashioned term, integrated.[9]

Academic feminism in the United States has always been white in the sense that those with the leisure to pursue it have come mostly from the racially white, middle-middle and lower-upper middle classes. But more important than the demographics is the ways in which the intellectual content of second wave feminism preserved white middle-class exclusivity in its beginnings and continues to do so, even after the nonwhite protest.

Let me briefly summarize the substance of this protest, which has not changed in over twenty years because it has not yet been directly answered in theory or practice. [B]ell hooks reminded feminists that the nineteenth-century women's movement in the United States was a white women's movement. Only white women were acknowledged as participants by its white female leaders, and nonwhite women, particularly black women, were explicitly denied voice and presence. This exclusion extended to women's clubs, so that there were separate "colored" women's clubs in the late nineteenth century, and to the women's labor movement, when white female workers insisted on segregation by race in factories and sweatshops.[10] [H]ooks and others objected that when early second wave white feminists compared themselves to "blacks" in terms of oppression and disadvantage, they ignored the very existence of black *women*.[11] Black women's existence was ignored on the surface of the comparison because they were neither included in the group doing the comparing nor recognized as blacks. The white women doing the comparing did not say that they were treated as black women were treated (which they could not say because they often dealt with black women as subordinates or employees), and they did not seem to consider gender divisions among black people relevant in their comparison.[12]

The mid-twentieth-century comparison of being a woman to being black was insulting to blacks. It implied a special indignation that women should be treated as blacks were, as though the treatment of blacks were natural. Both theoretically and practically, in comparing the general category of women to blacks, the discourse implied either that all blacks were male or, in the absence of a stated androgynous ideal, that blacks as a group did not require making gender distinctions. Since gender distinctions were actively deployed by white feminists and valued by blacks, the result of the feminist comparison was an erasure of existing black women because it seemed to be assumed that all blacks were male. The comparison was insulting to black women because it pointedly failed to show them respect as women and slighted their femininity. Middle- and upper-class white women had a long history of taking such respect for granted, and white women of all classes were assumed to be feminine, even if some of them found femininity oppressive. Nonetheless, nineteenth-century black thinkers such as Gertrude Mossell, Anna Julia Cooper, Ida B. Wells, and the early-twentieth-century lawyer Sadie Alexander and her cohort had taken great pains to support the respectability of black middle-class women.[13]

The symbolic erasure of black women in the liberatory discourse of white women had economic and political analogues. Kimberle Crenshaw explained how the assumed maleness of blackness had a concrete form in work contexts when newly hired black women were the first to be fired in economic downturns. When they attempted to seek legal redress under the civil rights laws that applied to gender as well as race, they had no standing as plaintiffs. Both blacks and women were presumed to be already protected against discrimination and there was no basis on which black women could prove that they had been discriminated against, either as women who were black or as blacks who were women.[14] The law thus provided no means for identifying black women as a disadvantaged group in its own right, because white women who had been employed longer were protected by seniority rules, and black men by antidiscrimination laws. As women, the last hired, first fired black women did not in practice have the same protection as white women with longer employment. But the connection between being black and being the last to be hired was widespread enough to identify the intersection of black race and female gender as a distinct identity of disadvantage.

More recently, in *The American Dream in Black and White*, Jane Flax showed how Anita Hill's black female identity could not be represented in public discourse during the U.S. Senate hearings confirming Clarence Thomas as a Supreme Court justice. While the white senators could induct Thomas into their Horatio Alger mythology, Hill's femaleness excluded her from their utopian meritocracy, and her blackness rendered her female complaints of sexual harassment disreputable and dirty.[15] Hill's charges of sexual harassment against Thomas led to a national conversation about sexual harassment in the American workplace, followed by successful court cases and policy reforms. But the sad irony was that there was no discussion of the distinctive vulnerabilities attached to women of color as victims of sexual harassment, especially when they were harassed by men of color who would otherwise be expected to support them on the basis of racial loyalty or solidarity.

Hill presented herself as modest and ultrarespectable, and fourteen members of her family were present during her testimony. Her self-presentation was incongruent with representations of black women according to the premodern theory of gender that has been attached to women of color throughout U.S. history. This theory was retired for white women during the eighteenth century. It posited women, rather than men, as the unrestrained and predatory sex. The use of this premodern theory of female sexuality for women of color has always been convenient for oppressors.[16] It obscured the sexual exploitation of black female slaves, was used to vilify black "welfare mothers," and operates as a subterranean rationalization for the sexual harassment of women of color in the U.S. workplace to this day.[17] Had mainstream feminism been inclusive during the Thomas hearings in 1998, there might have been an opportunity to hear what women of color had to say about their distinctive experiences of both quid pro quo and hostile-environment sexual harassment at work.[18]

When black women protested their exclusion from feminism in the late 1970s, they emphasized their history of struggle for women's rights as well as racial equality. They objected that white feminists were preoccupied with the problems of white middle-class women, to the neglect of both the material conditions of poor women and the effects of white racism on nonwhite women. One of the racist effects was that women of color, unlike white women, did not experience patriarchy as their most pressing problem. Many black women claimed that white racism was their primary problem: if they were treated badly by black men, they believed it was an effect of how black men were treated by both white men and white women; and if they were treated badly by white men, they were treated worse than white women were. Moreover, and the feminist exclusion was just one more case in point, the broad consensus among black women was that white women did not treat them as well as they treated other white women. Furthermore, black women did not share the constraints of white housewives but had a long history of working outside their homes, often for white women in their homes.

By 1990, the lesson learned from the nonwhite protests against feminism was that the group calling itself feminist in the sense of speaking for all women did not speak for nonwhite or poor women.[19] And during the 1990s, after the collapse of the Soviet Union, U.S. feminists faced further challenges from East European women. Under communism, East European women had been expected to work both outside the home and within it in exploited subordinate positions; as a result of that experience, they were skeptical that communitarian political and social models advocated by First World feminists could serve their interests better than old-fashioned individualism and individual rights doctrines. Western feminists were also challenged by Third World women in traditional societies who did not have the opportunity or ambition to pursue liberation as a goal of equality with men. The result of these challenges was an intense uneasiness that the U.S. group calling itself feminist and purporting to speak, write, and think for all women on earth was regarded by women who were not white, affluent, American, or northern European as representing only itself and its own interests. The perceived exclusivity of second wave feminism destroyed its credibility as a political force. Feminism was not supposed to be exclusive, given the commitment of so many lefties, liberals, and even anarchists throughout twentieth-century women's movements, given the civil rights racial activists who supported 1960s women's liberation and given those (mostly white) lesbian feminists who understood being scorned and excluded.

These critiques of white feminism have resulted in segregated feminisms. But intellectual segregation is not a solution to inequality, any more than demographic segregation is. The white feminism that once saw itself as universal feminism has not succeeded in reconstructing an inclusive foundation, and as a result a crisis underlies all feminist efforts at this time. Feminism as a whole appears to be nebulously but alarmingly in decay, like a person suffering from a chronic low-grade infection that she hopes will go away and fears will erupt into a full-blown illness, an infection that continually saps her strength and clouds her mind. White feminists have been struggling with how *they* should think about the differences among women for over twenty years. They have their counterparts in a small number of academic feminists of color who struggle with how *they* should think about their differences. In contexts where thinking alone and only the written products of thought matter, the results have been tenure in institutions that barely change their demographics from one decade to the next. Hence, the underlying crisis of feminism has resulted in what Barbara Christian calls "a race to theory," with little change in the world for less privileged women who have no access to academic employment, or even a desire to obtain such access.[20]

The term "intersectionality" refers to multiple oppressions experienced by nonwhite and poor women in particular, but more generally to all women because differences in sexuality, age, and physical ableness are also sites of oppression. Ann Ferguson claims that the notion of intersectionality can include white middle-class women who wish to work against those aspects of their own identities that are oppressive.[21] However, Ferguson's suggestion does not make feminism inclusive because it provides no common ground on which privilege and underprivilege can communicate and work to correct privilege. Suggestions that white feminists continue to do their own good works as white feminists represent more rules for "parallel play."

In the paradigm instance of intersectionality, a black woman is understood to be not merely a woman in the white feminist sense, who is in addition black. No, a black woman is understood to be someone with a distinct identity of gender because *race is supposed to be a principal determinant of gender*: race + class = gender! Recourse to intersectionality is supposed to avoid essentialism, precisely because it allows for a theoretical ontology of different female genders. It does avoid essentialism which posits a sameness about women that can be derived from theories based only on the experiences of white middle-class women. But, as we shall see, avoidance of that kind of essentialism is not inclusiveness theoretically. Politically, it easily leads to a fragmentation of women that precludes common goals as well as basic empathy. The de facto racial segregation of both criticism and liberation along the lines of historical oppression sabotages present criticism and future liberation because women of color speak only to themselves. But they do not have enough power to liberate themselves as women without the help of white women, who continue to belong to the dominant and oppressive racial group. The general feminist presumption that women of color are adequately heard because they have opportunities to speak to themselves often results in individual experiences by women of color that they are excluded from the discourse of white feminists. As individuals, particularly in the academy, women of color are only able to breach this exclusion if they are willing to present themselves as representatives of this or that disadvantaged racial or ethnic group—they have lost the ability to speak to and be heard by white women *as women*.

Some feminist theorists, both white and nonwhite, have made of gender an all-encompassing kind of taxonomy that even includes biological sex. As a result, intersectionality may multiply essences because each different gender formed by specified intersections is a totally distinct category. Different kinds of female gender may be perceived to be so distinctive as to be virtually incommensurable, a condition exemplified in the insistence by some women of color that only they can speak and write about their problems with authority, and that white feminists defer to their insistence. This is simply too much ontological and discursive difference on a theoretical level. In practice, and on a level outside feminist theory, everybody knows that it makes sense to refer to white and nonwhite, rich and poor, straight and gay, and First, Second, and Third World women as *women,* and that there is something about those thus referred to which exceeds merely being symbolized by the same word. Even in theory, everybody knows that the *signifier* has a *referent*, that "women" refers to women.[22]

ESSENTIALISM, GENDER, AND COMMONALITY

The divergence between feminist theory and practical understanding can be resolved only after clarification about what is meant by essences and essentialism, as well as gender. Although no one course of clarification has the last word, what follows is a delineation of essences, essentialism, gender, and women that avoids the problems of incommensurability posed by intersectionality, while preserving its main asset of respect for differences among woman.

An essence can be something that all members of a group have in common, which is a necessary and sufficient condition for membership in that group. In this meaning, all women uncontroversially share the same essence that can be defined like this. Women are those human beings who are related to the historical category of individuals who are designated female from birth or biological mothers or primary sexual choice of men. Call this category FMP. The relation of women to the disjunctive FMP category is that of being assigned to the whole category or identifying with the whole category. This relation of assignment to, or identification with, the FMP category is a necessary and sufficient condition for being a woman, and there is every reason to view it as an essence shared by all women. However, this shared essence is not substantive and it is not an essence in individual women or in the group of women. The shared essential relation does not entail that all who are women are mothers or male sexual choices, or that they have been designated female from birth. Neither does it entail that female birth designation, heterosexuality, or motherhood are feminist values (or virtues). They are, rather, the historical conditions and facts that have made feminism necessary in a dual-gender system of men and women.

The advantage of positing such a relational essence of women is that it holds for all women in a universal sense. Poor or nonwhite women are not excluded, and the commonality posited does not impose the values of white middle-class European and American women on other groups. Relevant here is Spelman's distinction between two kinds of commonality. First, a dominant group may impose commonality with itself on subaltern groups in a way that ignores or suppresses the distinctive problems of subalterns, which are part of their oppression or result from it. Second, an oppressed group may claim commonality with a dominant group as a basis for ending oppression.[23] The commonality here claimed does not ignore or suppress differences because it is the basis on which difference exists, and what we implicitly refer to whenever we say that women are different. For example, poor black women may claim entitlement to prenatal care because, like rich white women, they have been assigned to, and identify with, the category containing mothers. And women of color who are feminists may claim participation in the (often now-segregated) discourse of white feminists.

The commonality of relation to a historical group can serve as a moral basis to end oppression by making liberatory efforts compelling to all women in their sameness, and such a moral basis can motivate political action and social change. Because they are all women, in this relation to the historical group of women, affluent American feminists should support women struggling against physical violence or famine in other parts of the world. Their commonality with American women makes it possible for Third World women to request political support or material assistance from those better off, on the basis of a moral entitlement. We are always morally entitled to the same treatment as those we are the same as, in a relevant respect. We are entitled to such equal treatment from those in positions to dispense it, and those who do not get what justice based on equality requires are entitled to help from those who do. The discourse and mechanisms of charity, which are always supererogatory on the part of benefactors and are reasons for resentment by recipients, can be replaced by an egalitarian discourse of duties and practical exchange. Assistance based on duties and claims constitutes real membership in a world that is unevenly advantaged. The practical exchange goes beyond the acquisition of ethnographic information about the disadvantaged into real information of benefit to benefactors' lives. The benefactors may be able to learn from those they assist, once they are able to relate to them as equals on the ground of the shared relation of being women. For example, subaltern women, unlike many Western white feminists, have extensive contacts of mutual dependence with kin, both fictive and biological. While this warmth of community may be oppressive, so often is the existential loneliness of the liberated Western middle-class woman, particularly if she is an academic. A mature and positive inclusive feminism will require a multiplicity of such comparisons and exchanges.[24] The alternative is increasingly hermeneutic theorizing within closed circles of privilege and increasingly specialized theorizing within groups lacking the privileges of those in the circle.

As mentioned, Spelman noted that difference ignored can lead to domination, as can difference postulated. However, she seemed to conclude (with considerable subsequent agreement within academic feminism) that the problems with difference ignored can result from *any* universalist project concerning human nature:

> The fact that hierarchical rankings are compatible with both the postulation of difference and the insistence on some kind of root similarity is closely linked to the promises and pitfalls of any attempt to provide an ahistorical, acultural description of "human nature" or "man's nature" or "women's nature."[25]

Spelman and other feminist critics of traditional universalism are right in claiming that universalist projects often mask generalizations from the particular circumstances of those who generalize, or that those who are privileged often generalize their circumstances as a paradigm which, without justification, is extended to the lives of those less privileged. Still, it does not follow from this that all universalism is pernicious, but only that overgeneralization from the circumstances of those privileged does not further the liberation of those not privileged. The universalism of first and second wave feminism was a false universalism, just as the universalism of Western political philosophers was false. The feminist universalism masked racial and class privilege, the philosophical universalism masked racial, class, and gender privilege. Of course, white middle-class men are not coextensive with all of humanity, and white middle-class women are not coextensive with all women. But this does not prove that the problem is with universalism as a theoretical goal, or with human nature or women as general subjects. It at most proves that the universalisms under criticism were false, incomplete, too hastily drawn from insufficient experience of human difference, of "life." It is an unfortunate irony that this very error of hasty generalization from insufficient experience is repeated in the feminist rejection of universalism itself.

Let's return to the concepts of essences and essentialism. The first meaning of "essence" as a necessary and sufficient condition shared by all members of a group does apply to all women, provided that what they are understood to share is not a thing but a relation to the historical FMP category. A second meaning of essence has connotations of determinism, such that an essence of woman would cause major aspects of what all women are, from which their social roles, experiences, and psychologies could be explained and predicted. Historically, this kind of deterministic essentialism has been used to justify subordinate roles of women in relation to men. There are no good reasons to believe that kind of essence exists, especially not in human biology. The essence that is the relation to the FMP category is not a cause of anything shared by all women, although in specific contexts, it may be understood as a cause of the distinctive experiences, social roles, or personhood of women in those contexts. Being a woman has different effects on social experience, emotional experience, and personhood because dominant agents in different historical contexts have had different understandings of the implications of being a woman and have assigned different social and psychological effects to it. Women have also actively lived their shared relation as women differently in different contexts.

These clarifications about what can and cannot be meant by "essence" point to a reconsideration of the problems with gender that led to the crisis in second wave feminism. The concept and term "gender" has been used to refer to the cultural and psychic dimensions of women's experience. In that sense, all women clearly do not have the same gender. But to the extent that gender has come to mean commonality in the sense that can be captured by "an essential definition of women," women do have the same gender. In this sense, as an all-encompassing term, "gender" means broad human identity in a dual system of men and women, and it includes both sex and sexuality in indirect ways by relation to the FMP category. It is an equivocation, a substitution of the broad meaning of gender that does not specify race, class, or sexuality for the meaning of gender that does, to claim that differences in race, class, and sexuality result in different genders in the inclusive sense of gender that refers to common women's identity.

This equivocation can have the theoretical effect of splitting women into theoretically incommensurable subgroups. Such splitting has little positive consequence beyond initial moments of invented and discovered, distinctive and valued identities. In the long run, the splitting symbolically reinstates the segregation of nonwhite and poor women from the vocal middle class, as was done in reality in the United States throughout the nineteenth century and much of the twentieth. Furthermore, such splitting of feminist discourse and efforts among lines of race, class, and sexuality reproduces within feminism the very social hierarchies that many feminists say they are committed to leveling. Divisions of human beings by race, class, and sexuality in society are not taxonomies of mere variety but grades of human worth and power. If distinctive genders in an all-encompassing sense are assumed to be built into the components of the hierarchies, the chances for egalitarian change shrink on the very ground of feminist theory. By contrast, if there is an accepted theoretical commonality among women across the hierarchical taxonomies of race, class, and sexuality, the hierarchy itself, along with its imputed ranking, stand a better chance of being abolished.

I propose that gender be understood as the different ways in which women act, think, and feel, given their historical circumstances, as well as the variety of roles, expectations, and limitations that are imposed on them. Included in this sense of gender would be different experiences and constraints of belonging to the FMP category. Gender, as a variable that always has specific, contextualized meanings, is clearly not something that all women share in the same way. There can be no essentialism of gender in this sense—except that all women have specific genders of one sort or another.

The theoretical confusion, or equivocation, in making the concept of gender encompass all that pertains to all women, and then using socially contextualized meanings of it to differentiate among women, is the result of an anxiety about universalism among white feminists. This anxiety about universalism has also resulted in a theoretical demarcation between white feminists generally and nonwhite and poor women. Too much is achieved theoretically by the supposedly liberatory willingness to question whether it is possible for feminists (read: white middle-class feminists) to talk about all women. And too much is lost in relinquishing an encompassing idea of women. White liberatory feminists should be willing to consider that it is possible to talk about all women, provided that one allows for the possibility that there are differences among women. Why should it be so difficult to accept the reality that there are women, and that all women do not have the same lives or the same problems, the same advantages, and the same disadvantages? Why should white middle-class feminists be so quick to retreat from the mere mention of difference into endless theorizing about their own fugitive and cloistered virtues?

Now, to return to the way in which Spelman and her colleagues have embraced difference, as either a foundation for feminist theory, or the reason why inclusive, grand, and universal feminist theory is impossible. As already noted, Spelman took second wave feminists to task for their belief that they could arrive at universal female gender by separating/filtering/subtracting race and class from everyone's gender. That method left them with an abstract notion of their own gender only, which they then assumed was the gender of all women. For instance, there was a time when white feminists assumed that black or Latina women were like them as women, but merely different in race or class. But if white women, as women, are oppressed by white men, it does not follow that they are oppressed in the same ways by nonwhite men, or that black women are oppressed by black men in the same ways white women are oppressed by white men, and so forth.[26] These objections are telling, killing. But exactly what do they rule out? Do they rule out a notion of commonality among women, or a somewhat quaint notion of an essence, as a same kind of thing that can be abstracted (or extracted) from all women and studied as such? Do they rule out any universal meaning of "women," or do they just rule out a false universal meaning? They do rule out the quaint essence thing and false universal meanings of "women." They do not rule out commonality among women or a true universal meaning of "women."

Greater than the error of thinking that white and nonwhite women share social and psychological gender is the error of ignoring what it is they do share. Nothing of social importance shared by all human beings is captured in a model of physical stuff, except for the part of the *Homo sapiens sapiens* genome that we all have in common or some of the chromosomal markers that accompany designations of individuals as male or female. Since there is nothing that we all have in common that is thick with social meaning, or even lucidly connected with ordinary phenomenological experience of our physical bodies, rejecting commonality among women as though they *could* share something like a quaint essence is an offensive against a nonexistent problem—hot air. Spelman's reading of Sojourner Truth's protest against nineteenth-century white feminists is very instructive in this regard. Spelman claims that when Sojourner Truth used the example of her own physical strength, labor, and appetite for food, she was locating her womanhood in a different gender from that of white women, in the sense that "gender" is an all-encompassing division among women.[27] A more obvious reading given Truth's rhetorical "Ain't I a woman?" is that she was asserting her womanhood despite her differences from white women, that she was claiming the same all-encompassing gender as white women, while at the same time referring to her differences from them. The obvious reading supports commonality among women. Indeed, since Truth brought attention to her difference in a forum in which women were demanding rights, it is unlikely that she meant her difference to set her apart from the group of subjects entitled to rights; she said nothing about a special claim for women as black working women or former slaves. Rather, it was the fact that as a woman she was not the fragile being those who persisted in denying women rights purported to protect, that her rhetoric served to support women's rights for both strong and fragile women. "Ain't I a woman?" can simply be understood as an attempt to dispel the stereotype that all women were fragile, a condition that would have disqualified them as subjects for the rights demanded, in the context Truth addressed. Truth was quite simply referring to her own strength to object to the generalization that all women were fragile, and her reference was meant to help the common cause of women. (The subtext that it was bold for Truth to insist that she was a woman because black women were not recognized as women is another issue, distinct from the point about rights for all women as women.)

The relational essence that women share is not a causal essence. Confusion between notions of causal essences and notions of noncausal commonality has led to a flight from universalism, which evades the problems

raised by the demographics and content of white feminism by avoiding the
noncausal commonalities that do unite women across differences in race,
class, and sexuality. The confusion stems from the assumption that if all
women have something in common, then it must be the case that what they
have in common *causes* a particular kind of common experience. Then,
when it is discovered that women have different experiences, their commonality is rejected. For instance, Linda Nicholson, in her introduction to
Feminism/Postmodernism, an anthology she edited in 1990, criticizes second
wave feminism for having universalized women in ways reminiscent of the
great errors in traditional white male philosophy. Nicholson writes:

> Modern philosophy has been marked not only by its universalizing mode but
> also by its strong belief in the independence of its pronouncements from the
> historical context of their genesis.[28]
>   . . . Therefore the postmodern critique has come to focus on philosophy and
> the very idea of a possible theory of knowledge, justice, or beauty. The claim is
> that the pursuit itself of such theories rests upon the modernist conception of a
> transcendent reason, a reason able to separate itself from the body and from his-
> torical time and place. Postmodernists describe modern ideals of science, justice,
> and art, as merely modern ideals carrying with them specific political agendas and
> ultimately unable to legitimize themselves as universals[29]
>   . . . Feminists, too, have uncovered the political power of the academy and of
> knowledge claims. In general, they have argued against the supposed neutral-
> ity and objectivity of the academy, asserting that claims put forth as universally
> applicable have invariably been valid only for men of a particular culture, class,
> and race. . . . Because feminist theorists have frequently exhibited a too casual
> concern toward history and have used categories which have inclined their the-
> ories toward essentialism, many feminist theories of the late 1960s to the mid-
> 1980s have been susceptible to the same kinds of criticism as postmodernists
> make against philosophy.[30]

So, according to Nicholson, who is here describing a feminist consensus
she shared with Nancy Fraser and others, in 1990, feminists were guilty of the
same kind of essentialization and universalization as white male philosophers. As quoted above, Nicholson's position avoids struggling further with
the question of whether there is something important that all who identify as
women do have in common. Her comparison of late-twentieth-century feminist self-criticism with earlier feminist criticism of white male philosophers
is, moreover, incomplete. Earlier feminists examined the psychological, social, and material conditions that advantaged white males to produce philosophy, and they compared those conditions with the general social and
material context of women during the same historical periods. The post–
second wave self-critical feminists have not turned an analogous lens on
their own social and material conditions that are concomitant with the *intellectual* exclusion or lack of recognition of nonwhite women. The requisite

lens would have to delineate details that are close up, details about the narrow academic and broader social context of what in all decency now has to be called white feminist philosophy. A focus on the academy would be an appropriate beginning for a self-examination of the material conditions of feminist privilege because it is a culture that many feminists already share on a daily basis. The academy is also the first culture that academic feminists ought to be committed to changing because it is their home. The academy has had even less success with racial integration than the wider society, particularly in philosophy departments. Although white feminists are not to blame for this situation, they are partly responsible since they seem not to have helped the situation, given their goals. Their responsibility may not be the full moral burden of deliberate acts of exclusion because in most cases, again, particularly in philosophy departments, white males retain controlling power. But it is a de facto responsibility insofar as white feminist philosophers individually benefit from continued racial segregation, now pointedly extended within gender. Such de facto responsibility is not easy to accept, and a certain amount of personal discomfort is inevitable. Acceptance of responsibility will require change by individuals in their own particular lives. Toward addressing that individual white feminist de facto responsibility in present academic philosophical culture, white feminists might consider things that can be done concerning disciplinary descriptions, student focus, and attitudes toward difference.

ACADEMIC PRACTICE

The division of academic disciplines pertinent to feminist concerns is still largely the taxonomy of "women and minorities." Thus many schools now have women studies programs, gender studies programs, Africana studies programs, and ethnic studies programs. Feminist philosophers quite often are recruited to serve on advisory committees connected to those programs or departments. Whenever possible, white feminists ought to remind their colleagues that this taxonomy literally ignores the existence of academics who are women of color. The taxonomy often carries over to search committees and graduate admissions committees, so that progressive members of those committees may support the hiring or admission of either women or persons of color, without noting that some women are also persons of color and some persons of color are also women. Feminists who serve on such committees ought to remind their colleagues of these humble facts, while at the same time discouraging them from believing that the inclusion of women of color counts as satisfying both racial and gendered requirements for diversity.[31] That assumption supports hiring or admitting, and subsequently overburdening, one woman of color to take the place of one man

of color and one white woman, according to the standard academic taxonomy. (For those who still find intersectionality theoretically useful, such double counting might be investigated as a new site of multiple oppressions.)
We need to remind our colleagues that if they are going to divide those who
are not white males into women and minorities, then they should not suspend this division to inflate whatever diversity has been achieved.[32]

The focus of students is perhaps easier to influence than the taxonomies
of colleagues. Most feminist anthologies are still either about gender, in
which the subjects are white women, or about race, in which the subjects are
black women, Latinas, or other women of color. Inclusive third wave feminists need to find ways of cutting through this bifurcation. It is not enough
to discuss the problems with white feminism, raised by women of color, beginning either with Sojourner Truth or the Combahee River Collective, and
throw in an excerpt from *Black Feminist Thought* by Patricia Hill Collins.
Needed are positive theoretical accounts of inclusive feminism, which are integral parts of the feminist curriculum. If a feminist professor starts a course
with the white feminists and assigns students the diversity feminism at the
end, she will have reinforced the standing divisions within feminism that
reinscribe persistent social hierarchies of race and class. This may not upset
white students or faculty, but it is a constant cause of frustration and anger
among students and faculty of color. One result is that the students of color,
who thought they were interested in feminist philosophy, leave that field for
Africana studies, ethnic studies, Native American studies or Hispanic studies.
Literally interpreted, intersectionality demands that women of color studying
philosophy abandon not only philosophy but also feminist philosophy, insofar as the feminism they encounter is written and taught by white women.
And that reinforces the long-standing division between women and minorities on college campuses, a division that ignores the presence of nonwhite
women. When female students of color leave philosophy in this way, philosophy remains overwhelmingly white (if not male), and feminism experiences further failures of integration. When I returned to academia in 1990, all
of the feminist work on race was done by women of color. Today, more and
more white feminists are doing work on race and their anthologies are an
excellent place to begin. Still, inclusive work on feminism and work on white
feminism by women of color ought to be in the curriculum. It is important to
educate graduate students about some principles of inclusive feminism, so
that white female graduate students do not assume that success in scholarly
careers requires that they concentrate on the work of white feminists (under
the tutelage of white feminist advisers), and so that nonwhite female graduate students do not experience a segregation of themselves and their research interests.

There is, furthermore, the question of individual attitudes. Most of the
women in the academy are white, but this is not to say that white academic

feminists have never encountered nonwhite women or poor women. Non-white and poor women are readily visible on the street or at the mall, in restaurants, as housecleaners and janitorial staff, nannies, clerical staff, and in all manner of nonprofessional service occupations. Nonwhite and poor women are portrayed in the media and their problems are discussed in the newspapers. Many of their occupations are still stereotypical, exploitative, and personally demeaning. This nonpeer contact and information often results in distinctive images that are inconsonant with middle-class aspirations. No middle-class person likes to think of the young female members of her family maturing into women who clean toilets for wages. Academic feminists do not live outside the social order, and it should not be assumed that their impressions of the members of groups less advantaged than their own in the broader social hierarchy are, in the absence of serious reflection, privileged toward liberation. In academic contexts where white feminists are committed toward liberation, they ought simply to suspend such images and make as few assumptions as possible about the nonacademic backgrounds and experiences of nonwhite women colleagues and students. Even the most casual and well-meaning remarks associated with such images have the ability to personally damage nonwhite women in the academy and impede their academic progress.

This is a matter not just of pure attitude but also of attitude that expresses material life habits outside the academy. For example, most of the senior academic white feminists I know can afford to have other women clean their houses. So one may ask, Who cleans their houses, and what do they, the feminist employers, know about the broader social, economic, and political factors that influence who is likely to seek work cleaning private homes in the geographical areas in which they live? Do they connect their work in feminism with this issue of who cleans their houses? How does the connection or failure to make it affect what they do in the academy?

The woman who cleans your house is visible. Unseen are the women abroad who assemble your gadgets and make your clothing. It is very convenient for First World women that the struggles and suffering of these unseen women are not evident in the products of their labor. Deference for difference or relegation of the problem to its relevant intersection (postcolonial studies perhaps?) is neither a practical solution to such "division of labor" nor a moral justification of the continued invisibility to white feminist philosophers of women of color, be they continents away or ensconced in their offices down the hall.

I suggested at the beginning of this chapter that intersectionality provides a way to address the collapse of second wave feminism. This collapse is not the effect of intersectionality alone. The specter of quaint-thing essences has haunted attempts to define women in any one intersection or race-class group. Linda Alcoff definitively surveyed that problem in 1989. She observed that for feminists to break free of erstwhile masculinist descriptions of women, they must take care not to base their identities on biology. But if culture is understood to be the basis of female gender, this can facilitate a perspective of social determinism that does not allow for individual autonomy or political change. A true theory about the cultural construction of gender can be just as deterministic as a false theory about biological foundations. But a notion of an autonomous "female" subject of politics may evoke a notion of preformed modernist essences. Alcoff proposed that women create strategic identities for political change, based on common circumstances.[33] Alcoff's strategic identities would presumably be intersected identities. Thus far, intersectionality has not borne impressive political fruit. Once identities become distinct, their associated circumstances tend to be problematized as belonging to those identities only. Those who might help others less advantaged are not motivated to do so because the recognition (or invention) of racially different women's gender identities has already created and circumscribed separate domains of assistance and cooperation. However, the problem is not with the idea of common circumstances as a basic component in feminist social and political theory (an idea I will support in chapter 4), but with the reification of intersections as incommensurable identities.

The difficulty of defining women within any one intersection, as well as across intersections, should now be viewed as the result of looking for the wrong kind of defining property. Once women are defined by their relation to the historical FMP category, the problems with either biological or cultural determinism are avoided and there is no hidden and illegitimate substance needing further explanation. Still, more needs to be said about the nature of the relation between women and the historical FMP category, a subject that will occupy chapters 2–3 and motivate the rest of this book.

NOTES

1. I am following customary usage among feminist writers by calling the thought and practice of feminism after the challenges from nonwhite women in the late 1970s the "third wave," with the understanding that the "second wave" refers to the period beginning in the early 1950s, following publication of Simone de Beauvoir's *The Second Sex* and Betty Friedan's *The Feminine Mystique*. The "first wave" began with Mary Wollstonecraft's *Vindication of the Rights of Women* and other writings at the end of the eighteenth century, and it ended when women received the right to vote in the United States and England, by 1920. This leaves the period between 1920 and 1950 uncovered—a time of socialist writing and activism, the heyday of intellectual Marxism, when gender was believed to be subsumed under issues explicitly understood to be matters of social class.

2. Irene Browne and Joya Misra, "The Intersection of Gender and Race in the Labor Market," *Annual Review of Sociology*, August 2003, 487–513.

3. Most intellectual fields are generational. A cohort reaches a consensus and makes it the basis of its life's work until retirement, when new people and sometimes new ideas take over the field. This is especially true of feminism insofar as it is tied to specific historical periods that reinforce generational difference in the life history of individuals. Most professional philosophers form their major, career-enduring ideas as they write their dissertations or, for feminist philosophers who are trained in traditional, prefeminist philosophy, in reaction to that training. It is difficult for people to change their first main ideas as they mature and achieve success based on those ideas, and such change may not be rewarded professionally. One is rewarded for what one has already done, and with the rewards come expectations that one will continually re-present that material (like a comedian with just the one joke). The flip side of this is resistance to new ideas. As Thomas Kuhn said about the physical sciences, the adherents of an old paradigm, once in control of a field, have to leave the field before a new paradigm can be fully persuasive. However, I am not suggesting that present feminist leaders, in philosophy and the rest of the academy, need to retire before a new paradigm is possible. I am optimistic that some of the argument and discussion about subjects raised in this book will be useful to the upcoming generation of feminist philosophers who are just starting their academic careers, and also that the "old guard" (who are for the most part a few years younger than I am, even though they have been at this longer than I have) will remain flexible.

4. Naomi Zack, *Philosophy of Science and Race* (New York: Routledge, 2002), 1–9, 103–19.

5. Combahee River Collective, "A Black Feminist Statement," in *The Second Wave: A Reader in Feminist Theory*, ed. Linda Nicholson (New York: Routledge, 1997), 63–70.

6. bell hooks, *Ain't I a Woman?: Black Women and Feminism* (Boston: South End, 1981); Elizabeth Spelman, *Inessential Woman: Problems of Exclusion in Feminist Thought* (Boston: Beacon, 1988).

7. Robin Wilson, "A Kinder, Less Ambitious Professoriate," *Chronicle of Higher Education*, November 8, 2002, 10–11.

8. Naomi Zack, ed., *Women of Color and Philosophy* (Malden, Mass: Blackwell, 2000), 1–22. My guess is that at the beginning of the 2003–2004 academic year, fewer than twenty women of color were employed in tenure-track positions in philosophy departments and that fewer than ten of them concentrate on work related to either feminist or racial issues. And yet there are about 15,000 academic philosophers in the United States, and since the early 1990s about one-quarter of all new philosophy Ph.D.s have been female.

9. It's a slight misusage to say that parts of the academy that remain almost all-white are segregated because the term "segregation" suggests that there is a nonwhite group doing the same thing someplace else. In fact, the problem with the almost all-whiteness of the academy is that it also contains all of the nonwhites in the academy.

10. hooks, *Ain't I a Woman?* chaps. 4–5.

11. hooks, *Ain't I a Woman?* chap. 5.

12. Sometimes a male black experience was appropriated in defense of feminism. For instance, Toril Moi in 1985 quoted Ken Ruthven's concern that feminist critics of feminism would be considered the "female equivalent of the 'white arsed nigger' of separatist black rhetoric," a concern that he offered as a reason for him, a man, to

write critically about feminists. Toril Moi, *Sexual Textual Politics: Feminist Literary Theory* (New York: Routledge, 1985), 174; from Ken K. Ruthven, *Feminist Literary Studies: An Introduction* (Cambridge: Cambridge University Press, 1984), 14. Neither Moi nor Ruthven seemed to notice that at the time when such black rhetoric was resonant, the subject would have been male. So self-absorbed were white feminists, their critics, and the critics of their critics, that they did not notice that the first "black equivalent" of a white female would have been a black female. Had Ruthven written the "white female equivalent of the 'white-arsed female nigger,'" his witticism could not have been presented as an innocent appropriation of widely recognized black rhetoric. As it is phrased, Moi seems to read the appropriation as innocent, insofar as her stated concern is with Ruthven's condescension toward the white feminists he is trying to protect from other white feminists.

13. Kenneth W. Mack, "A Special History of Everyday Practice: Sadie T. M. Alexander and the Incorporation of Black Women into the American Legal Profession, 1925–1960," in *Critical Race Feminism: A Reader*, ed. Adrien Katherine Wing (New York: New York University Press, 2003), 91–100.

14. Kimberle Crenshaw, *Demarginalizing the Intersection of Race and Sex: A Black Feminist Critique of Antidiscrimination Doctrine, Feminist Theory, and Antiracist Politics* (Chicago: University of Chicago Legal Forum, 1989).

15. Jane Flax, *The American Dream in Black and White: The Clarence Thomas Hearings* (Ithaca, N.Y.: Cornell University Press, 1998).

16. Naomi Zack, "The American Sexualization of Race," in *RACE/SEX: Their Sameness, Difference, and Interplay* (New York: Routledge, 1997), 145–56.

17. The idea of women of color as hypersexual can also work as a lightning rod for widespread public backlash against sexual permissiveness, as it did during the public outcry against the exposure of Janet Jackson's breast on national television on Super Bowl Sunday in 2004.

18. Consider, for instance, distinctive forms of flirtation practiced by white men on women of color; resentment by men of color expressed as sexual entitlement directed to women of color only; overt hostility toward women of color by white women in reaction to the sexual attention women of color get that they do not; and the poisonous competition among women of color which becomes race based because their sexual harassment is race based. Because women of color are presumed by men of color, white men, white women, and even themselves to be "highly sexed," offenses have to be more inappropriate to get the same amount of attention as offenses against white women. ("The Woman of Color in the Workplace," particularly in high-status jobs, perhaps in academia, is a text waiting to be written.)

19. Social class has always been mentioned in mainstream feminist descriptions of post-intersectionality gender, but its theoretical treatment remains shallow and meager.

20. Barbara Christian, "Diminishing Returns: Can Black Feminism(s) Survive the Academy?" in *Multiculturalism: A Critical Reader*, ed. David Theo Goldberg (Cambridge, Mass.: Blackwell, 1994), 168–77. See also Barbara Christian, "The Race for Theory," *Cultural Critique* 6 (1989), reprinted in *Making Face, Making Soul/ Hacienda Caras: Creative and Critical Perspectives by Women of Color*, ed. Gloria Anzaldúa (San Francisco: Aunt Lute), 335–45.

21. Ann Ferguson, "Resisting the Veil of Privilege: Building Bridge Identities as an Ethico-Politics of Global Feminisms," in *Decentering the Center: Philosophy for a*

Multicultural, Postcolonial, and Feminist World, ed. Uma Narayan and Sandra Harding (Bloomington: Indiana University Press, 2000), 189–207.

22. I say this in disagreement with Judith Butler's theoretical "liberation" of women, which she accomplishes by "disconnecting" the symbols representing women from women (*Bodies That Matter: On the Discursive Limits of "Sex"* [New York: Routledge, 1993], 67–72). There is no evidence that such a move would liberate existing women (or even that the most august and Olympian of feminist theorists would have the power to pull that plug). Would disconnecting the word "slave" from slaves have freed American slaves? Does the disconnection of the term "domestic violence" from domestic violence create safety for the victims of domestic violence? Can we help pregnant women suffering from malnutrition by "disconnecting" the signifiers of maternal and fetal malnutrition from the actual pregnant women who do not get enough food?

23. Spelman, *Inessential Woman,* 10–15.

24. Why haven't affluent feminists started a "being a friend" program with poor women in the Third World and in their own nearby urban and rural neighborhoods? Such a program would not only help poor women but would also enlarge the vision of affluent feminists.

25. Spelman, *Inessential Woman,* 12.

26. Spelman, *Inessential Woman.*

27. Spelman, *Inessential Woman,* 14.

28. Linda J. Nicholson, ed., *Feminism/Postmodernism* (New York: Routledge, 1990), 2.

29. Nicholson, *Feminism/Postmodernism,* 4.

30. Nicholson, *Feminism/Postmodernism,* 5.

31. Even the current cultural coinage of "diversity" in higher education is problematic because it lumps all students or faculty of color together as a something that can be added or increased. Discourse about "diversity" in this sense is another way of assuming that race can simply be added into a context, while at the same time remaining separate. It is another form of segregation. A full discussion of this issue is beyond the present book, but please see my forthcoming *The Passion of Race in Higher Education.* (Seriously.)

32. How should the standing divisions be revised? An easy answer is that more categories should be added to correspond to ignored "intersections." But then the problem arises of where to stop in the multiplication of entities, not to mention how to finance the expanded curriculum. Furthermore, the addition of more categories could result in further numbers of isolated scholarly groups who do not talk to one another even though they have common goals. Needed are new comprehensive theories that will affect scholarship within standing disciplines, so that they can keep up with demographic changes in society. The social demographic changes are already changing institutions outside academia, such as global corporations and the military. The time may have come when academia itself must be viewed as a conservative force because its main function is to train those who will occupy privileged positions of leadership in the world as it is, rather than train those who will change the world. At a time when public institutions of higher education are increasingly dependent on funds from private sources, they may no longer be in a position to assume positions of social leadership that oppose the ideologies of their most generous donors. This is a challenge

of moral leadership for academic provosts and presidents, who will eventually have to reeducate those donors (or find new ones) to fulfill their stated commitments to racial diversity on college campuses, particularly in graduate schools.

33. Linda M. Alcoff, "Cultural Feminism versus Post-Structuralism: The Identity Crisis in Feminist Theory," in *Feminist Theory in Practice and Process*, ed. Micheline R. Malson, Jean F. O'Barr, Sarah Westphal-Wihl, and Mary Wyer (Chicago: University of Chicago Press, 1989), 295–326.

2

The Identity of Women

The purpose of proposing a universal definition of women is to formally support an identity that everyone can recognize. A universal women's identity can also be understood to have a dimension of common selfhood. For both senses of identity, the definition of a woman is someone who identifies with or is assigned to the historical category of human beings who are designated female from birth, biological mothers, or the primary sexual choices of men. What does it mean to be a kind of human being or have a kind of self that is constituted by a relation to a category? Such a relational identity is not a substance or an essence in individuals, and neither does the category itself have substance or essence because as a category it is a social construction. The relational nature of women's identity entails that the womanhood of all women is located somewhere outside each woman. What all women share is no more than this constructed identity. Even the term "womanhood" is misleading because it connotes a common substance, which is precisely what does not exist and what women cannot share.

What good can such an identity do for anyone interested in changing the world or understanding and empowering herself? The answer is that the relation of being a woman is sufficient for social existence in a dual woman–man (or man–woman) system. It is not necessary for existence in a dual woman–man system because one could be a man. But it is necessary for social existence in such a system that one be either a man or a woman. Thus the relation of being a woman is a social identity. Assignment to the FMP category constitutes the external identification of human beings as women, and their identification with the category constitutes their subjectivity as women.

In this chapter, I will explore some of the philosophical aspects of this relational identity of women. I will begin with the imagined nature of both women and the FMP category and then briefly address the problem of universals for any definition that could apply to women. I then consider the logic of any definition of women, partly agreeing with Marilyn Frye's critique of Simone de Beauvoir's claim that women constitute an "other" relative to men, but adding considerations from traditional logic to Frye's attempt to construct women as a "positive" logical category. Next, I return to de Beauvoir's definition in order to make sure that it has been properly understood and not dispensed with too quickly. Through a discussion of a current situation involving an American's adoption of a female orphan from India, I suggest that the indistinct subject of this situation, a three-year-old named Haseena, provides reason to reclaim de Beauvoir's definition of women as Other as an accurate description of the situation of some women.

THE IMAGINED NATURE OF WOMEN AND THE FMP CATEGORY

The whole category of being designated female from birth or being a mother or being the primary sexual choice of men is *imagined* because its disjuncts are abstractions. Almost all women who have existed have lived out one or more of the disjuncts in concrete ways, but the totality of the disjuncts as a basis of women's social identity is vague. It is deliberately and necessarily vague as a definition, and necessarily vague as a description of the historical social practice of sorting human beings. By the same token, the group of women does not and can never exist as a concrete aggregate at the same time, in the same place. This is obvious because some women are dead and others have not yet been born. But even if all women were alive at once, they could not all assemble together at the same time, or if they could, it would be unlikely to happen. However, that something is imagined does not mean it is imaginary. Both horses and unicorns are imagined but unicorns are imaginary and horses are real. One can imagine something real when parts of it are known to exist or to have existed, even though it is not experienced and may never be. If what was previously imagined comes to be experienced, it might also turn out to be different from the way in which it was imagined. But, again, this does not invalidate the faculty of imagining what is real. Imagining real things is a corrigible, faulty process, but for many kinds of things, it is the only way we can think about them as aggregates. The ability to imagine the aggregate, in this case all women, is based on having experienced only some of them, but such limited experience is all that is necessary to develop an understanding of the social significance of the group.

It is a broad fact of recorded human history that human beings designated female at birth, recognized biological mothers, and recognized primary sexual choices of men have constituted a whole identity to which any given woman is assigned, or which she accepts as her own. The broad historical fact would ground any practical project of inclusive feminism because in the background of such projects there is always at least a vague understanding of what the word "women" refers to, in ordinary usage. But, and of course, ordinary usage is problematic because it is substantialist. A woman is someone who is assumed *to be* female, *to be* a mother (or a potential mother), and *to be* a heterosexual partner (or a potential or past one). Even those who are not feminists realize that not all women are all of these things. Feminists now realize that some women may be none of them, and that even if they are one or more of them, that because of their oppressive histories, it is appropriate for them to reject identification with femaleness, motherhood, or heterosexuality, even if it requires rejection of a woman's identity overall. Clearly the problems with being a human female, a mother, or a heterosexual partner have made feminism, as advocacy for the well-being of women, necessary. Furthermore, past beliefs that there exist inevitable causal links between the FMP disjuncts—for example, beliefs that being female is a sufficient condition for being, or wanting to be, a mother, or a sexual choice of men—now represent contingencies for many woman. This is precisely because some female designees are neither mothers nor male sexual choices and because transsexual male-to-female women have not been designated female from birth. Many women are now at liberty to choose whether they want to be human females, mothers, or female heterosexuals, and if they do choose to be those things, they can choose how to be them. Even women who do not have such liberties, because of cultural constraints or other circumstances, now have the potential to acquire them. There is also the paradoxical possibility that some men who are not transsexuals may be women. This possibility is given in the severance of all necessary connections between being a woman and being female, a mother, or a sexual choice of men. There is nothing to exclude some men from being women through an identification with the FMP category, which informs their life choices and behavior. The question of whether such men would still remain men and whether some women, who might be men through an analogous identification with the socially constructed category of men, would also remain women, cannot be answered until more is said about the logical nature of the category of women.[1]

THE CATEGORY OF WOMEN AS A UNIVERSAL

The group of women cannot be experienced, but imagined only. Each disjunct of the FMP category is also imagined only, due to the kinds of practical impossibilities in experiencing all human female birth designees, biological mothers, or men's sexual choices. Thus the FMP category is vague as a whole and its disjuncts are each vague. Still, for existent women, their attributes of being female from birth, being biological mothers, or being the sexual choices of men are distinct and real. What many feminists have thus far failed to do in their quest for a universal definition of women (or subsequent abandonment of such a quest) is draw the very distinction that is necessary to get a viable universal definition started, namely, the distinction between universals that can be imagined only and particulars that can be directly experienced because they are real. We know that each individual woman who has ever existed, exists now, or ever will exist, is real. And we know that the term "women" does not refer directly to the collection of all of those individual women, as individual women, because they are not and cannot all be known as individuals. Even if they were all alike, they could not all be known as individuals, so this is not yet an issue of diversity among women. Rather, the universal term "women" refers to the group of all those individuals as we can imagine it, and the word "woman" refers to any individual member of the group as we imagine her. The word "woman" also refers to any and every individual existent woman, past, present, or future, without the intermediary of the imagined universal. That is, the words "women" and "woman" can refer to both universals and to real, existing individuals. These are things that can be said about "women" and "woman" as abstract general nouns.

We know that abstract general nouns refer successfully to relevant groups of things, even though we may not know how their reference can be justified. Consider Thomas Nagel's queries about meaning in the case of the general noun "tobacco" in *What Does It All Mean?*:

> All of us have seen and smelled tobacco, but the word as you use it refers not just to the samples of the stuff that you have seen, or that is around you when you use the word, but to all examples of it, whether or not you know of their existence. . . . You might think that the universal element is provided by something we all have in our minds when we use the word. But what do we all have in our minds? . . . The mystery of meaning is that it doesn't seem to be located anywhere—not in the word, not in the mind, not in a separate concept or idea hovering between the word, the mind, and the things we are talking about. And yet we use language all the time and it enables us to think complicated thoughts which span great reaches of time and space.[2]

Applying Nagel's intuition to women, we can say that individual, existent women are real and that the problems for second wave feminists in trying to explicate women as a universal subject did not lie with the word "women" or with exactly how that word refers to individuals. Rather, those second wave problems arose from the difficulties in trying to construct a concept of women, trying to state the meaning of the word "women," or trying to find the right way to imagine women, which could work as a universal intermediary between the word "women" and existent women. In old-fashioned philosophy speak, "women" *refers* unproblematically and there is thus no problem with its *denotation*. The problem is all in the *connotation* of "women." While for practical purposes, as Nagel points out, the word "tobacco" is adequate without an explicated concept (i.e., without connotation), the word "woman" as a theoretical term requires conceptual explication, or connotative meaning.

In the case of tobacco, Nagel seems to assume that an adequate concept could be constructed, and he is perplexed by how the word and/or the concept can apply to all existent tobacco.[3] Feminists quite properly have not been obstructed by the humongous philosophical problem Nagel is gesturing toward, the question of how words and concepts connect to the world—the problem of reference. Rather, feminists have been perplexed by what the word "woman" *means,* by how to construct the concept of woman, or how to imagine "a woman." They do not doubt that there are women or that the word "woman" can be successfully used to refer to a person. They have been constrained to come up with a definition of women that will express the diversity among women. However, insofar as a definition is about what members of the group have in common, as imagined, it cannot do this. Definitions cannot capture diversity even when simple stuff like tobacco is being defined. In the case of the complex aggregate of half of the human species, the best that a definition can do is allow for known differences within the group in two ways. First, any distinct trait not shared by all women should not be part of the definition, and, second, the definition should not exclude any distinctive traits that some women may have.

Feminist theoretical perplexity about the right definition of "women" arises from a century of women's advocacy that has exactly rendered contingent those previous definitions of women that expressed theories of biological or social determinism, through the media of common essences that were posited as things present in each and every woman. However, there is an enduring historical legacy of these determinisms, which cannot be overlooked even as third wave or postmodern feminists strive to construct a discourse about women toward conclusive disruption of the remnants of this legacy. We do not know what women can become in the future (we do not even know what many women who are different from feminist theorists have already become today), and all exciting, creative, and productive possibilities must be left open on a theoretical level. This is why inclusive feminism now requires a syntactic shift from a substantive–essentialist mode of women's identity to a relational one. This shift does not require either a disconnection between discourse and reality or an abandonment of women as a universal subject of feminism, although the old syntax is recalcitrant. Beliefs that each woman had a substantive essence that determined her toward a few prescribed sexual and social roles, as well as mothering, are difficult to relinquish. There is a strong, persistent impulse to fix the substance so that it can shoot through a few special gaps in biological causation and social determinism, gaps that (now that they are acknowledged) do not merely permit but necessitate a nonsubstantive definition and relational identity of women. But such fixation is not necessary once the connection between women and the determining biological and social forces is understood to be no more than the intentional processes of assignment to, and identification with, an abstract category.

THE RIGHT DEFINITION OF WOMEN

The right definition of "women," insofar as it is liberatory, cannot merely be nonsubstantive but must leave room for women to continue to break out of the oppressive ways in which they have historically been defined and socially constrained. In the focus on women's oppression, feminists have too often concentrated on analyzing how past essentialisms were related to women's oppressions, at the expense of considering how new essentialisms will serve their ongoing liberation. Simone de Beauvoir, in her canonical definition of woman as Other, failed to support a liberatory dimension from the very beginning.[4] In her introduction to *The Second Sex*, de Beauvoir poses this question: "If her functioning as a female is not enough to define woman, if we decline also to explain her through 'the eternal feminine,' and if nevertheless we admit provisionally that women do exist, then we must face the question: what is a woman?"[5]

Her answer is surprisingly swift. Except for a footnoted reference to Emmanuel Levinas[6] there is no well-developed historical, intellectual, or philosophical justification for her claim that woman is Other:

> The bond that unites her to her oppressors is not comparable to any other. The division of the sexes is a biological fact, not an event in human history. Male and female stand opposed within a primordial *Mitsein*, and woman has not broken it. The couple is a fundamental unity with its two halves riveted together, and the cleavage of society along the line of sex is impossible. Here is to be found the basic trait of woman: she is the Other in a totality of which the two components are necessary to one another.[7]

De Beauvoir's answer to her own question is not systematic because she did not tell us what the requirements for an adequate definition of woman would be. Moreover, it is not a feminist answer because it does not allow for the further development and liberation of women. It is a sociological or anthropological descriptive definition of women, theoretical only in its abstract quality, for woman as Other is something that can be imagined only.

The feminist problem with de Beauvoir's definition of woman as Other is that it assumes the perspective of those to whom she is the Other, the perspective of men, which de Beauvoir identifies as an egocentric, gendered perspective that is at the same time assumed to be neutrally human.[8] Thus "she is defined and differentiated with reference to man and not he with reference to her; she is the inessential as opposed to the essential. He is the Subject, he is the Absolute—she is the Other."[9] De Beauvoir relates the way in which human males view females to a more general human tendency to construct us–them, ingroup–outgroup distinctions that privilege the identity of the parties constructing them. But, in her examples of tribalism, racism, and even the attitude of three occupants of a train compartment, she does not make distinctions between men and women. She assumes that the general exclusionary human tendency is gender-neutral, which in her own terms would be masculine: "The category of the Other is as primordial as consciousness itself." In her own discourse this has the effect of excluding women from the domain of those who are conscious, if consciousness requires that one be a subject.

Thus de Beauvoir defines woman in a way that describes her oppression from the perspective of her oppressors. Woman is Other *for* man, as well as Other *than* man. While her subsequent analysis of how the biology of human reproduction has framed the social condition of woman does answer the question of why women have not been able to successfully resist their oppression, it does not theoretically advance her initial claim that "the functioning as a female is not enough to define woman." Instead, her analysis takes a step backward from that claim about biological constraints to an assumption that all women are females. She does not say that they are designated females or identify themselves as females but implies that they *are* female in the old essentialist way, the way in which biology determines, because biology is destiny. The sense of paralysis that overhangs much of the text in *The Second Sex* is perhaps the result of de Beauvoir's contradictory position: she identifies herself as a woman as she defines and analyzes the nature and situation of women as the biologically destined captives of the only ones who can be on the inside of a group that defines those who are Other to it. But, and here is the other side of the contradiction, she pursues this project of consciousness while conscious of the fact that her identification as a woman precludes her being a subject. Of course, Simone de Beauvoir was an exceptional woman who eluded the common biological destiny of her gender. What would have theoretically redeemed her from the arrogance of that position, as well as saved the group of women as she imagined it from their biological determination, would have been a positive definition of women. But de Beauvoir is caught here between her belief that women are females, which she knows is not an adequate definition of them, and her protest against what has been made of women-as-females. It is understandable that she chooses to define women in terms of what she is protesting against, but inevitable that such a definition turns out to be problematic in liberatory terms.

THE LOGIC OF THE CATEGORY OF WOMEN

A positive definition of women needs to be a definition that is not completely relative to the perspective of men in a historically grounded, dual man–woman or woman–man social system that privileges men. I partly agree with Marilyn Frye that it is in a logical sense, and not a normative one, that such an independent definition needs to be positive. Frye translates de Beauvoir's self/other model of men and women into a logical schema of A and not-A, where A stands for men and not-A stands for women. Frye avers, "I would displace the A/not-A dichotomy with a genuine plurality. Let there be two categories, two subjectivities, A:B. . . . Make that arrogant A *share* the universe."[10]

Frye is right to emphasize that a positive definition of women needs to address the logical status and relations of the group of women as a subject of liberation and not as an object of oppression.[11] She is right that a positive definition cannot be masculinist. De Beauvoir's self/other model is masculinist because it defines women from the perspective of men. But, by a logically positive definition, Frye seems to mean one that is semantically independent of the definition of men. Therefore, any logically positive definition of women would have a built-in normative factor because women would no longer be defined from the perspective of men, which in the history of gender domination and oppression has been the dominant perspective. Defining women as not-men also provided a definition of what men are not, for if men are A and women are not-A, A is not not-A. Nonetheless, historically the logical symmetry did not always hold up because men were assigned attributes that women simply lacked. So, any logically positive definition of women would also have to be normatively positive in comparison to the logically negative not-A definition. Still, neither a purely logically positive definition, which is what Frye thinks she is providing, nor a logically positive definition with its positive normativity made explicit can succeed in defining women as a category that is completely independent of a definition of the category of men, because both categories are historical categories that have always existed together. Men are indeed the only other historically recognized category with which women share a dual woman–man or man–woman system.

In traditional logical terms, Frye is proposing that women no longer be understood as the *contradictories* of men but as their *contraries*, although she does not seem to be aware of the relevance of this distinction to her proposal, a lapse that is costly to the cogency of her analysis. Two classes are contradictory if an individual cannot be a member of both and must be a member of either. Two classes are contraries if an individual cannot be a member of both but need not be a member of either.[12]

As it stands, Frye's proposal to cease viewing women as the contradictories of men is very helpful to feminist theory because it relaxes traditional gender boundaries. Thus, if men and women are contradictories, then everything in the universe (or in this case the domain of gender) is one or the other, but not both and not neither. The contradictory definition posits women and men as logical opposites. The contradictory definition also makes it impossible for there to be individuals who are neither men nor women, such as intersexuals, and it also makes it impossible for there to be individuals who are both, such as hermaphrodites. However, if men and women are contraries, then they can have different traits that are not opposite. Also, if men and women are contraries, allowance is made for the existence of intersexuals (although not for the existence of hermaphrodites). To answer the question posed earlier, if men and women are contraries, then men who become women cannot also remain men, and women who become men cannot also remain women. (Although, as stated, neither could anyone be both a man and a woman if men and women were contradictories.)

Instead of referring to traditional logic and explicitly positing women as the contrary rather than the contradictory of men, Frye tries to wrest the category of women from that huge multiplicity of kinds of things that can be called "not-men," a category that she realizes includes everything in the universe except men.[13] Frye proposes that the positive category of women be constructed to include undetermined variations in circumstances and subjectivities, and she thinks that this can be done by positing women as a kind of thing that cannot have a contradiction. Frye wants to avoid a "B/not-B" schema, where "B" stands for women, as well as avoiding the A/not-A schema where "A" stands for men. She writes:

> If identity is related to social category, and social categories are constructed, performed, or thought of as A/not-A structures, it is not easy (and perhaps impossible) to think in one thought/moment of an individual as a member of more than one category. . . . But if the category of women is constructed as a positive self-supporting category not constituted by universal exclusive relation to the-absence-of-it but by self-reliant structures of differentiation and relation, the identity or subjectivity associated with it has no built-in exclusivity or closure against other identity categories, no analytically built-in hostility to multiple category memberships and subjectivities.[14]

In terms of traditional logic, this is a difficult passage to understand. As noted, Frye does not want the category of women to be defined as the contradictory of the category of men. So far, I have seen no problem with that stipulation. In addition, Frye does not want the category of women to be the contradictory of any other category, and, conflated with this, she does not want the category of women to have any contraries within it because she believes that will preclude differences within the category of women. However, the category of women would have to be a contrary of the category of men, by her own demand that "arrogant A share the universe." Also, if there is a positive, inclusive category of women, then differences within that category would not be the kinds of things that could be contraries of the whole category. There are, for example, many different kinds of pedigreed dogs and an animal may be dog and a Collie or a dog and a Dachshund, but neither Collies nor Dachshunds, nor any of the other kinds of dogs, are contraries of dogs.

Perhaps Frye is implicitly suggesting that the category of women cannot have subcontraries? According to traditional logic, classes can be subcontraries within a larger class if some individuals can be members of the larger class and also members of one of the smaller classes.[15] Thus, "Some dogs are Collies" and "Some dogs are not Collies" are subcontraries. White women and Latina women are subcontraries of the class of women, as are poor women and middle-class women. But one would have to further divide the subcontraries to allow for membership in more than one group of women, so that a woman could be both Latina and middle class, for example.

The difficulty with Frye's passage stems from the fact that she is trying to posit a logically positive category of women but doesn't want it have any traditional logical restrictions, perhaps because she wants to have both the item that all women have in common and an ability to accommodate the kind of intersectionality that precludes commonality among women. She seems to be hoping that the positive definition will ensure commonality across varied intersections. However, a positive definition of women, in contrast to men, cannot by itself determine the logical relations among different kinds of women. There is no reason why the positive category of women cannot have contradictories and contraries outside of it, and subcontraries within it. Traditional logic is a friend to a feminist inclusive category of women, if understood as an external set of rules. Any proposition can have a logical contradictory and any category of things can have a contradictory category, a contrary category, or contain subcontrary categories. The contradictory category of women is all things that are not women; men are a contrary category of women, within the domain of gender; white women and Latina women are subcontrary categories within women. Being the contradiction, contrary or internal subcontraries of something is not an inherent property of any thing or group of things, but a contextualized relation. The world can be divided into many different categories based on purposes, interests, and prior divisions into categories. The divisions themselves are neither absolute nor completely given by what is believed to be the nature of the things being divided because making the divisions requires prior commitments to the context of classification, as well as to systems of classification.

It does not make sense to define women as the contradictory of men because the contradictory of men is too broad a category ontologically, as Frye herself states.[16] (The category of not-men includes stars, shoes, and cabbages, as well as women.) There should be a positive category of women and it should allow for diversity within women. The definition I have offered of women as belonging to the historical FMP category accomplishes the requisite commonality in a way that allows for diversity, provided that diversity exists on the prior ground of commonality. The interesting question is not whether women and men ought to be accepted as a contradictory pair. That would divide the world into men and women-as-not-men, which does not distinguish women from all of the other things that are not-men, while it at the same time unfairly privileges men (assuming that it is independently known what men are). Rather, the interesting question is whether men and women should be imagined as a contrary pair. Insofar as it is impossible to imagine the group of women without also imagining the disjunctive attributes of the FMP category, which have all been historically associated with women, and insofar as those attributes of female sex, motherhood, or heterosexuality each involves relations to members of the group of men in human social history, as well as species history, women and men are a contrary pair.

DE BEAUVOIR'S OTHER RECLAIMED

Women should be understood as contraries of men, but not Other to them because they are, or should be, more than Other for men. But maybe Frye and I have too quickly rejected de Beauvoir's notion of women as Other, in rejecting her notion of women-as-Other-for-men. Maybe there is something decisive in the history of human existence and thought that permits us to say the following. Granted, it is arbitrary to divide the world into men and not-men, but within the domain of gender, in the confines of a dual man–woman or woman–man system, which is the system that has characterized human history and thought, each attribute believed to be distinctive of women can be understood as the contradictory of an attribute distinctive of men.

Let's therefore return to de Beauvoir and examine her reasons for positing women as the Other in this more detailed, but still apparently contradictory, sense of Other. Directly after posing the question, What is a woman? de Beauvoir writes that stating the question suggests "a preliminary answer" because "a man would never get the notion of writing a book on the peculiar situation of the human male."[17] De Beauvoir then writes that if she wishes to define herself, she must first of all say, "I am a woman." And she explains this by launching into her theory of woman as Other:

> In actuality the relation of the two sexes is not quite like that of two electrical poles, for man represents both the positive and the neutral, as is indicated by the common use of *man* to designate human beings in general; whereas woman represents only the negative, defined by limiting criteria, without reciprocity. . . . Just as for the ancients there was an absolute vertical with reference to which the oblique was defined, so there is an absolute human type, the masculine. Woman has ovaries, a uterus; these peculiarities imprison her in her subjectivity, circumscribe her within the limits of her own nature.[18]

What de Beauvoir here asserts is indeed deeply peculiar and distressing, truly mesmerizing, so it is not surprising that two or three generations of feminists have been unable to snap out of it. Nonetheless, we should note that de Beauvoir's preliminary answer to the question, What is a woman? presupposes her final answer. In asking the question, she sees herself as entering into a discourse dominated and normalized by men, so that before being accepted into the discourse (if indeed she can ever be accepted), she has to identify herself as an unusual participant in the discourse. In other words, a woman is someone who is not usually permitted to speak seriously among men. And it is a short distance from that to this: "She is defined and differentiated with reference to man and not he with reference to her; she is the incidental, the inessential as opposed to the essential. He is the Subject, he is the Absolute—she is the Other."[19]

Now, let's return to the A–not-A schema rejected by Frye as her interpretation of what de Beauvoir meant in defining woman as Other. Is being the Other of the Absolute A the same thing as being the contradictory of A? Logically, it is difficult to see how Frye's reading could be correct. In order for women to be the contradictory of men, they would have to be the detailed logical opposite of men, based on the attributes of both men and women that could be compared. Being excluded from the domain of masculine activities precludes such comparison. One would have to say that for de Beauvoir, in logical terms, if the universe is our domain, woman is some kind of contrary to man. As a logical contrary, she is no different from myriad other contraries, such as cabbages, slugs, and God, such that there are things that are neither man nor his contrary, woman, but no things that are both man and his contrary, woman. However, and this is important for a contextualized interpretation of de Beauvoir, we are here restricted to the domain of gender. The very condition of exclusion from masculine activities, which precludes that detailed comparison between men's attributes and women's attributes, allowing women to be defined as not-men (i.e., as the contradictory of men), would also block the possibility of woman being included in the same context as man so that she could be a contrary to him. In other words, the problem with how women are traditionally understood, according to de Beauvoir, is not yet a logical problem. Rather, the problem is the deeply ethical one that women are so devalued within the domain of gender that they cannot be properly categorized using logic.

If de Beauvoir is taken at her word, woman is not part of human ontology. She is not an "absolute Other" as Frye reads it[20] but instead, as de Beauvoir herself proclaims, "he is the Absolute—she is the Other."[21] The problem described by de Beauvoir is thus an ontological rather than a logical one, not ontological in pertaining to the being of women, but ontological in the sense of being admitted into the domain of what is recognized to exist. In order for the category of women to have logical relations to that of men, it must be possible for women to have some independent characteristics so that all of their characteristics are not completely dependent on the characteristics of men. All the more reason that a positive definition of the category of women is required, although it cannot be a merely formal definition as Frye explicitly proposes, or even a normative formal definition as I suggested Frye might implicitly have in mind, but a definition with semantic content. A positive definition of women requires the assertion of positive attributes that make it possible for the category of women to have the logical relations of being contradictory or contrary.

However, I am not ready to dismiss de Beauvoir's notion of woman as Other based either on its circularity or its failure to meet the requirements for logical relations in a system of categories. Circularity is not a serious problem in a phenomenological analysis, which posits and describes figure and ground together, as an experienced integrity. The apparent failure in logic points to something very important in studies of oppression because de Beauvor's notion of an Other precisely captures the dimension of the absence of relations that characterize a category of beings whose attributes are not considered. I do not think that adult women universally suffer from being Other in this sense, at least not today, but this does not mean that others may not still suffer from the condition.

HASEENA

Consider Haseena, the indistinct subject of a story about foreign adoption in India, which appeared in the *New York Times* on June 23, 2003. The title of the story is "A Challenge in India Snarls Foreign Adoptions," and it has a sidebar, "One woman claims corruption, and another waits to take a child home."[22] A companion article on the same page is titled, "For Poor Families, Selling Baby Girls Was Economic Boon."[23] In the main article, Gita Ramaswamy, "a long-time union-organiser-turned-book-publisher," is described as having disrupted the foreign adoption system in the state of Andhra

Pradesh. Ramaswamy was at the time trying to obtain a nationwide moratorium on foreign adoptions because she claimed that the system was corrupt and encouraged the sale of baby girls, in some cases for as little as twenty dollars. In the companion article, Rukkibai, a young mother, states that she sold her fifth daughter for that amount over the initial opposition of her husband.[24]

For fifteen months, Sharon Van Epps, an American woman, tried to adopt three-year-old Haseena. Ramaswamy halted Epps's adoption process, although it was not evident that Haseena was "trafficked." The Indian Central Adoption Resource Agency prefers to place children with Indians, but they had no objection to Haseena's adoption by Van Epps and her husband, John Clements ("a partner in a major accounting firm"), because Haseena had been born with "mildly deformed feet" and another agency reported that Indian parents could not be found for her. In response to publicity about the case, an Indian couple came forward to adopt Haseena, but the director of the state agency for Women Development and Child Welfare wrote a letter to the court claiming that the husband of this couple did "not come out of love and affection for the child." On May 28, 2003, Haseena was removed from the Tender Loving Care orphanage, where she had been since the age of six months, and the authorities then placed her in a state-run orphanage. Van Epps was not allowed to see her there, although she had already bonded with the child and at the time the article was written went to the state-run orphanage daily, hoping for a change in policy.

In the article, Ramaswamy says of Van Epps, "Her faith in the power of the color of her skin, and the superpower status of her country is so strong" that she is convinced "she must win." Van Epps is reported to have an album of pictures of Haseena. "When I open it now," she says, "I just cry."[25]

We should note the biases in this reporting. Foremost, the story is presented as though the challenges of corruption in foreign adoption in India are new, and based solely on Ramawamy's activism. In fact, a superficial Internet search reveals that the problem of the sale of female infants for foreign adoption was covered by the Indian press at least as early as 2001, when it was presented as a "racket" that the Andhra Pradesh state government was attempting to check.[26] The headline, "A Challenge in India Snarls Foreign Adoptions," implies that foreign adoptions are a normal right of Americans. The sidebar "One woman claims corruption, and another waits to take a child home" implies that Van Epps's home in the United States is already Haseena's home. And finally, the title of the second article, "For Poor Families, Selling Baby Girls Was Economic Boon," exaggerates the value of twenty dollars, even for a couple so poor that their combined earnings were about two dollars a day for field labor.

Ramaswamy and the mother interviewed in the second article are presented as the villains of the story. Van Epps describes herself as a "test case" in the struggle between Ramaswamy and the Indian government. Ramaswamy is quoted as arguing that the Indian government allows foreign adoption as a partial solution to the poverty and degradation of many women in India. But the statistics are remarkable because in 2002, out of a population of 1 billion people, there were only 1,200 in-country adoptions and 800 by Americans and Europeans. Evidently, any form of adoption is a very partial solution to conditions of poor women in India and the offensive mounted by Ramaswamy seems unlikely to have significant impact on the condition of poor women in India. Without further information about internal political issues, the *Times* article makes Ramaswamy appear misguided, if not perverse.

From a liberatory feminist perspective, the real subject of the story is the innocent victim, Haseena. In the article about Rukkibai, who sold her fifth daughter for twenty dollars, it emerges as a subtext that only female infants are sold because male infants represent more hands to produce food for their families. Born into poverty, female, and not considered adoptable within her culture because of her "mildly deformed feet" (whatever that denotes), Haseena is an indistinct object with an uncertain future and no autonomy. Her only listed positive attributes are "rich black hair and dark eyes," attributes that as stated serve only to objectify her. She is, moreover, silent, both literally in that she does not talk (or did not when Van Epps first met her) and symbolically in that she has no say, no voice, in the situation that is about her. Even Rukkibai, who is symbolically the beneficiary of Ramaswamy's activism, has a future bound up with her husband and remaining seven children, as well as sufficient autonomy to have sold a child against her husband's wishes. Ramaswamy not only has autonomy but also sufficient clout to create a vexing public controversy and bring grief to at least one American. Van Epps is presented as a victim because of her thwarted desire to mother an orphan, but she is persistent and sufficiently powerful to have gotten two U.S. senators to write letters on her behalf, the U.S. embassy to make an inquiry about the case, and the *New York Times* to write her story.

It is Haseena, therefore, who is Other in de Beauvoir's sense, and it is not necessary to compare her to male children born into poverty in order to apprehend this. She is Other to Van Epps, who expresses no concern about the long-term consequences of removing Haseena from her natal culture. And she is Other to Ramaswamy, who ignores her existence as a concrete individual in claiming, "We are not working on Haseena not going abroad. We're working for change in the system."[27]

In terms of logic and theory, if it is not insensitive to return to those considerations now, the story about Haseena shows that it would be precipitous to dispense with de Beauvoir's definition of woman, although one might say that women-as-Other are a subcontrary of the group universally defined as identifying with or assigned to the FMP category. That is, some women are Other and some women are not Other. Furthermore, the subjects whose actions and attitudes determine that some women are Other are variable. Historically, they have been men, but they may also be women. While de Beauvoir can now be read as overstating her case, especially since she claimed the condition of Other for privileged European women such as herself, at this time a large percentage of the world's population does start out as Other on the basis of gender. While it may sound odd to include children in the FMP category, FMP is a disjunction and children are designated by sex at birth. Also, all human children who mature into adult men and women do so within the constraints of sexual designations at birth, which determine the gender category that will constitute their identity as adults.

Haseena, rejected within her natal culture as a valuable female object and centered in an international drama in which she is further objectified, is a startling example of someone who fails to have the kinds of attributes enabling her to be compared with others in her situation. These would be legal attributes of autonomy and perhaps rights of nationality. While it is easy to dismiss Haseena's lack of legal attributes on the grounds that she is a child, there are many children who cannot be so easily transplanted and have adult advocates authorized to represent their autonomy. Still, if it is correct that Haseena is an Other, it is important to realize that what makes her an Other is not something inherent in her but her circumstances. Adult women who suddenly lose their families, social position, or worldly assets as a result of natural or social disasters might also be Others in this sense. And so might many men and boys. The point is that the ontological restrictions in de Beauvoir's notion of Other as applied to women (i.e., the inability of someone who is Other to be compared to participants in a domain of human activity or discourse) are floating parameters of oppression. Insofar as women are usually contraries to men and can therefore be imagined as constituted by their relation to a category that has logical relations in an ontology of categories, those women who are or become Other fall off the map of discourse. Without political standing, or rights, they are not qualified to receive formal justice, but it is important to remember them as subjects of feminist care and concern.

NOTES

1. Men could be preliminarily defined as those who are assigned to or identify with the whole category of human beings who are designated male at birth or biological fathers or those who are the primary sexual choices of women. However, such a definition would probably not be sufficiently descriptive of the asymmetries in the attributes of men and women in human history.

2. Thomas Nagel, *What Does It All Mean?* (New York: Oxford University Press, 1987), 39, 42–43.

3. I might be misreading Nagel. He could mean that even without a definition, "tobacco" is the proper name of all tobacco, or even that "tobacco" is not a proper name but nonetheless mysteriously attached to all tobacco. But I want to avoid those issues here.

4. Marilyn Frye takes up this exact problem, from a political perspective, although her claims about logic are idiosyncratic, as I will soon show. See Marilyn Frye, "The Necessity of Differences: Constructing a Positive Category of Women," *Signs*, Summer 1996, 991–1010.

5. Simone de Beauvoir, *The Second Sex*, trans. H. M. Parshley (New York: Knopf, 1952), xvii.

6. De Beauvoir, *Second Sex*, xix n. 8.

7. De Beauvoir, *Second Sex*, xviii.

8. De Beauvoir, *Second Sex*, xviii.

9. De Beauvoir, *Second Sex*, xix.

10. Frye, "Necessity of Differences," 998.

11. Frye seems to assume that logic is unproblematically about the world, rather than about propositions. Although many contemporary logicians would question this assumption, it has a respectable history in philosophy and it does not lead to errors in the current discussion about membership in only two classes (women and men). For the older view that logic is about the world, see Morris R. Cohen and Ernest Nagel, *Introduction to Logic and Scientific Method* (New York: Harcourt Brace, 1934), 16–21.

12. Irving M. Copi, *Introduction to Logic* (New York: Macmillan, 1961), 42–43. The reference to Copi provides an application of this concept that would shift the discussion to the truth or falsity of propositions asserting that individuals are men or women.

13. Frye, "Necessity of Differences," 1001–6.

14. Frye, "Necessity of Differences," 1004.

15. Copi, *Introduction to Logic*, 143.

16. Frye, "Necessity of Differences," 1004.

17. De Beauvoir, *Second Sex*, xvii.

18. De Beauvoir, *Second Sex*, xviii.

19. De Beauvoir, *Second Sex*, xix.

20. Frye, "Necessity of Differences," 993.

21. De Beauvoir, *Second Sex*, xix.

22. Raymond Bonner, "A Challenge in India Snarls Foreign Adoptions," *New York Times*, June 23, 2003, A3.

23. Raymond Bonner, "For Poor Families, Selling Baby Girls Was Economic Boon," *New York Times*, June 23, 2003, A3.

24. Bonner, "For Poor Families," A3.

25. Bonner, "Challenge in India," A3.

26. See, for instance, Ravu Sharma, "Children as Commodities," *Frontline: India's National Magazine*, May 12–25, 2001.

27. Suppose that Haseena were only a month or two old. Would the attitudes of Van Epps and Ramaswamy that I have claimed "Other" her, have the same effect? This depends on your theory of development, your belief about the age at which human beings acquire inalienable rights, and whether you think that the undisturbed inheritance

of one's natal culture is such a right. I myself do not have answers to these questions. My intuition is merely that a three-year-old does have some inalienable rights and that undisturbed inheritance of a natal culture deserves serious consideration as one of those rights. Still, being loved is a tremendous benefit to a child that could outweigh being summarily deprived of a natal culture.

3

Female Designation, Culture, and Agency

The idea that women are female human beings, and that their femaleness is given as a fact about them, obscures the process of identity formation in a woman–man or man–woman gender system. No child would be capable of inventing and creating its identity as a man or a woman on its own, or even capable of typing itself as male or female, from its earliest days. Female identity starts out as a primary item of the social equipment of infant care, external to the child and imposed on her as instruction and management of mind, body, and behavior. Human infants are designated male or female at birth, and individual identities as men or women develop after that designation in a dual-gender system. The designation itself is merely a matter of words: "It's a boy!" or "It's a girl!" However, the words do more than note a biological fact. The words announce and direct the trajectory of the individual's psychological and social development. A child that remained an "it" following birth could not become a recognizable social agent in a dual-gender system.[1]

In a dual-gender system, the ontological domain is circumscribed so that an adult is either a man or a woman, but not both and not neither. Within that domain, classification proceeds as though men and women were logical contradictories of one another, even though each has attributes that are recognized to be more than mere negations of the attributes of the other. As I explained in chapter 2, men and women are logical contraries of each other, so that the man–woman gender division can be understood as analogous to a taxonomy of fruit that contains only apples and pears, and not a taxonomy of fruit that contains apples and antiapples. That there are believed to be *only* men and women gives each group the appearance of being the contradictory of the other because any human being must be either a man or a woman, and not both.

41

A newborn becomes either a man or a woman, an outcome set at birth by the designation as male or female. The newborn is thus given a presumptive male or female gender at birth, along with the presumably biological designation as male or female. From the fact that a newborn is designated female, historically it has been presumed that she may become a sexual choice of heterosexual men and that she may become pregnant and give birth to children, who she will rear. In the history of the dual man-woman system, female designation has been a necessary condition for heterosexual female roles and mothering roles. But even in the most traditional or oppressive (to women) instances of such a system, it is not sufficient. Female birth designation does not automatically lead to heterosexual and maternal roles, and if biological essentialism is toned down (which it is more and more in Western culture, as well as feminist theory), we can see that it does not even automatically lead to being a human female in society. However, both the expectations of adult femaleness that are imposed on a child and the active part of her own social development are consequences of her female sex assignment at birth.

Most infants can easily be designated male or female at birth because they have genitalia that are typically male or female. The epistemology of sex designation breaks down when a baby has ambiguous or incongruent genitalia because then a decision is made about how to type the child, based on available surgical and chemical procedures and an assessment of which sex designation will be less harmful psychologically.[2] These exceptions to easy sex designation prove that the either/or male–female taxonomy is not purely biological. Even given the exceptions, the majority of human beings seem to accept exclusive male–female sex distinctions from birth as a basic fact of human life. However, the either/or male–female sex typology is a twofold cultural paradigm. Male–female sex differences are cultural, first, because they are not the sole options provided by biology and, second, because after the biological exceptions are ignored, being a human male or female is a condition imposed, accepted, learned, and performed within a particular culture.[3]

Parents might have personal reasons or specific cultural traditions that delay naming a child, and such reasons can usually be explained to others within their social communities, with a high probability of acceptance. But it would be inappropriate, if not irresponsible, to delay a sex designation (even if a baby were biologically intersexual) in most social communities. Some people in nontraditional subcultures might consider analogous identity deferral admirable if religious affiliation were at issue, and a smaller number might tolerate it for racial identity if parents were of different races. But imagine parents announcing, "Our baby is two months old but we are not going to label it as male or female until our child is old enough to understand what these categories mean and can make an independent and informed choice to be male or female."

Uncommon as intersexed individuals are, and inappropriate as deliberate sex-gender designation deferment would be now, both of these examples establish that given the known facts about the cultural contribution to sex assignment, it is possible for children not to be designated either male or female at birth. Also, in the future some cultures might become egalitarian and pragmatic about gender traits and sexual preference. Those same cultures, or more traditional ones, might accept the development of artificial wombs or uterine transplants, which would make it possible for men to experience and fulfill the physical obligations of pregnancy. There is also the possibility of in vitro gestation. All of these cultural and techno-physiological innovations could result in a deep sexual and gender androgyny. In deeply androgynous cultures, it might be inappropriate and irresponsible to describe a child as male or female from birth. It is also possible that infants with ambiguous genitalia will at some point be openly designated as intersexuals, without social stigma and in the absence of other radical social androgyny.

Such possibilities illuminate the gap between being born with certain genitalia and being designated female. For human beings, sex designation is not a purely biological description, but a social description that in the past has been believed to be directly and unproblematically based on biology, but which now appears to be far more complicated. Social gender descriptions need not be based on the biological structures they have been based on and, strictly speaking, should society be different, they need not be made at all. Furthermore, between being born with genitalia designated female and becoming a human female, there occurs a rich, complex process of development, imagination, and individual choice and agency. Feminist theorists who have focused on intersectionality have paid little attention to what can be known and said about the structures of such development that are true for all women. And before intersectionality, second wave white, middle-class feminists, who critiqued the oppression of women in Western societies, often lost sight of what children designated female at birth themselves contributed to the development of their female gender.

To develop into a woman, based on female designation at birth, is to join the group of women, according to what is expected and imposed in one's immediate social context, in combination with what is distinctive or unique about one as a developing individual. It is not only that one becomes a woman but that one becomes a human female in a social and psychological matrix. I proposed in chapter 1 that feminists define women as human beings who are assigned to or identify with the FMP category (female birth designees or heterosexual men's choices or biological mothers). In chapter 2, I examined some of the logical characteristics of the group of women. Once it is understood that there is nothing substantive, no psychically or physiologically inherent thing, present in all women that makes them women, it becomes necessary to further understand how some human infants become women in society. This was Simone de Beauvoir's great contribution to feminist theory, even though there are strong legacies of biological determinism in her own account of how one becomes a woman or of how women are made.

In this chapter I will reexamine the cultural nature of what confronts and envelops an individual who is assigned to the FMP category via female sex designation at birth. I am adding two things to the standard feminist answer to de Beauvoir's implied question of how one becomes a women. The first is a perspective on female gender development, which posits the components of that development as external to the psyches of those who develop into women. The second addition is an emphasis on the aspect of individual agency in that development, which I believe has been neglected in second wave feminist theory. It is now socially intelligible that some female humans may not become the heterosexual choices of men or mothers. Becoming and being female should therefore be understood as distinct from becoming or being a heterosexual choice of men or a mother. This distinction can be made on a theoretical level, as well as in many real situations, notwithstanding lingering substance essentialisms that continue to derive femaleness, female heterosexuality, and motherhood from either physical biology or metaphysical and imaginary notions of womanhood or femininity.

GENDER DEVELOPMENT AND AGENCY

Imagine again Haseena, the three-year-old Indian orphan who was the subject of the *New York Times* story mentioned in chapter 2. At the age of six months, Haseena was brought to the Tender Loving Care home by her illiterate, unmarried mother, who could not endure the social stigma of an illegitimate child. Haseena had "mildly deformed feet," which adoption authorities later claimed made it difficult to find Indian parents for her. Sharon Van Epps began to visit Haseena when she was about eighteen months old, and although Haseena was not verbal, she physically clung to Van Epps. The *Times* story emphasized Van Epps's devotion to Haseena and Haseena's emotional attachment to her.[4] This is all that we know about Haseena, but it is sufficient to illuminate some general facts about female gender development, even in the absence of information about whether Haseena will become a woman in Connecticut or Andhra Pradesh. Haseena was designated female at birth, presumably unproblematically. The adults in charge of Haseena would have, at various times and in various ways, envisioned a specific cultural location for her as an adult. Whoever raises Haseena will influence her development into a woman based on some vision of her as an adult. For instance, if she stays in India, she will likely be trained in a craft so that she can support herself, as poor women in India are required to do, whether or not they marry.[5] If she is adopted by the American couple, attention will be paid to the quality of her education because she will be expected to have meaningful work for herself or to offer intellectual and cultural resources to her husband and children, should she marry. In both situations, she will be taught how to care for and groom her body, and some part of this practice will be specifically related to the fact that she is female. She will be guided into the cultural practices appropriate to her gender, and her bond with Van Epps is a recognizable motivation for her cooperation in such a project. That these claims can confidently be made about Haseena implies that at age eighteen months, she is past the point of no return in gender development toward being a woman, although she is only at the beginning of the process.

That gender identity in children may be fixed at the age of two or three, or even earlier, does not tell us how such identity is developed by individuals. We know that the kind of gender identity a child designated female acquires is partly imposed, but we also know that the child must cooperate. We need a sufficiently general account of how children designated female acquire an identity that will be acceptable to others, insofar as it is appropriate to their sex assignment. Without evidence that gender identity is innate (and, given its many different forms, much positive evidence that it is acquired), we have to assume that from the inside out, people learn to see themselves in ways that express their gender, and that how they see themselves more or less conforms to how others expect them to see themselves. First a child's body is typed and then the child is expected to develop a mind or some aspect of a mind that conforms to what others imagine to be the right kind of mind to go with the kind of body she has. Parents and other caregivers are generally not content that a child go through the motions or in a detached way perform a certain kind of gender role. Rather, they require, however they may communicate the requirement and verify its fulfillment, that the child have certain thoughts, feelings, and desires. The girl is expected to have a girl's self that corresponds to the fact that she is female.

Before assuming a sexual or maternal role, the girl must learn how to be a human female. If she assumes or enacts sexual and maternal roles later on, her female self will coexist with them or combine with them. If she lives past these roles or never assumes or enacts them, her female self will endure, although it will change over time. Psychology can tell us how gender development takes place and what its stages are in any given culture. And history and cross-cultural contrasts can provide descriptions of the different forms of female gender. The contribution of inclusive feminist theory should contain a phenomenological perspective based on the first person, which is sufficiently abstract to account for a range of external oppressions. Second wave feminists provided many useful analyses of the ways in which kinds of female gender expressed the oppressed position of women in the man–woman system. Some of these oppressions, particularly those applied to the physical development of female children, became weaker during the twentieth century. Needed is a phenomenological account of female development that bridges oppression and relative nonoppression in the recent history of the West, as well as oppression and nonoppression across cultures today.

Many second wave feminists critiqued the oppression of women based on a philosophical account of consciousness and the body, which was derived from the writings of Sartre, de Beauvoir, and Merleau-Ponty. A standard and stripped-down version of the account would begin with Sartre, who posited consciousness or human awareness as uncaused or transcendent, the source of choice, agency, and action. Things other than consciousness, including an individual's body, were understood to be caused, immanent, chosen, or acted on. Consciousness was the subject and all else was the object.[6] Building on Sartre, de Beauvoir first defined woman as Other, not only to man as a gendered being but to man as a universal human being who was consciousness in Sartre's sense; she then showed how women failed to achieve complete transcendence as choosing, doing, acting, conscious beings.[7] Merleau-Ponty emphasized the location of free and active consciousness in the movement and action of the body, so that the body itself was to be understood as the locus of a person's self. He seemed to be talking about the body of a man rather than a woman in European society.[8]

Second wave feminists variously adjusted and applied this account to explain how much of what appeared to be natural about women until the second half of the twentieth century could be better understood as the effects of oppressive cultural norms on their social gender. But often the second wave critique failed to focus on how women could overcome their social location as Other or develop more active selves as subjects. That oversight in turn obscured instances in which women already exercised agency under oppressive conditions.

Consider Iris Young's widely read essay, first published in 1980 and reprinted by her in 1990, "Throwing Like a Girl: A Phenomenology of Feminine Body Comportment, Motility, and Spatiality." Young makes three gender-specific observations and claims: women tend to move with their limbs close around their bodies in self-protective postures, resulting, for example, in carrying books against the front of their bodies, while boys and men carry books at their sides; women occupy less space relative to men; women view themselves as positioned at a fixed point in space rather than viewing space as something they are free to move around within. Young speculates that women and girls exhibit a conflict between regarding their bodies as objects and living their bodies as free subjectivities, in Merleau-Ponty's sense of "I can." This results in awkwardness in activities such as running, throwing a ball, or fording a small stream. Young is careful to separate her claims from either a view that women are biologically determined to move in these ways or a claim that such movement expresses a "feminine essence."[9] She concludes: "Women in sexist society are physically handicapped. Insofar as we learn to live out our existence in accordance with the definition that patriarchal culture assigns to us, we are physically inhibited, confined, positioned and objectified."[10]

Western society changed for girls during the last decades of the twentieth century, and the female bodily constraints that Young described as typical in 1980 are not typical today. After 1980, girls became more widely engaged in sports, old women who climbed mountains got their pictures in newspapers, and women of all ages began to engage in practices of physical fitness, such as running and weight lifting. Girls and women no longer cradle their books, but, like men and boys, carry them in backpacks or briefcases. Athletic footwear, jeans, shorts, and sweatshirts appear to have freed women from defensive and fearful bodily postures. Star female athletes are highly acclaimed in the mass media and, glass ceilings notwithstanding, women in positions of authority, power, and leadership are regularly visible on magazine covers. Of course, this bodily freedom is not true of all girls and women, but it is true of enough of them in the West to challenge the physical stereotypes of Young's 1980 account.

There has also been sufficient social change to disrupt the Sartre–Beauvoir–Merleau-Ponty picture that women typically lack the kind of subjective agency that could motivate physical mobility and freedom. At the same time, the increasing agency of girls relative to boys is not prevalent all over the world or even in the West. Unless we posit different female bodily genders and then explain how a person could change from one into another, a feminist theorist of girls' bodily experience needs to dig deeper to see if there is a common dimension of agency underlying the range of bodily oppressed and bodily liberated cases.

At the end of her essay, Young notes that it is unknown whether girls have the same limitations of movement when engaged in activities that are specifically assigned to them on the basis of gender. This is a crucial question because all of Young's examples of physical movement in which girls are awkward or ineffective pertain to activities that were not typically "feminine" at the time she wrote the essay. But Young also provides a clue for the kind of bridging phenomenological analysis that I am suggesting is necessary: "When I was about thirteen, I spent hours practicing a "feminine" walk, which was stiff and closed, and rotated from side to side."[11]

In practicing a feminine walk, no matter how constricting the walk itself, the person practicing it would have to have the kind of confidence and "I can" subjectivity about her body that is not evident when girls throw like girls. Sitting modestly while wearing skirts, walking confidently in high heels, modulating one's voice, eating delicately, removing bodily hair, applying makeup; all of these disciplines of female middle-class physicality, and many others, require an active subjectivity, which on the level of acquiring and displaying the desirable female gender trait, would have to be just as free, deliberate, active, and confident as the way boys throw balls.[12] It would be perverse to posit in the victim of oppression for the sake of justifying the oppression, the conscious bodily agency derived from the Sartre–Beauvoir–Merleau-Ponty positive human account. However, awareness of the agency of those oppressed in complying with oppression serves two important liberatory purposes. First, the necessity of the existence of such agency to satisfy the requirements of oppressors that one have a self appropriate to the sex type assigned to one shows how thorough oppression (in this case, gender oppression) is. Mind control is part of the oppression because the mind is objectified as a thing to be controlled, and also because oppressors have "theories of mind" according to which specific intentions, motivations, and desires need to be present for certain actions and behaviors to occur and to count as compliance. Second, the same agency deployed in order to comply with oppression can be redeployed to resist oppression and, beyond that, to live a more liberated bodily life once the oppression eases. If traditional girls and women believe that their identity as female is not harmed if they increase their bodily movement, then they will become more mobile. The recent near-universal shift in Western women's clothing from skirts to pants is evidence of that. The broad theoretical use of recognizing active subjectivity in women who are oppressed is that it provides a coherent basis for political action and other forms of empowered change.

WOMEN'S SELF-OBJECTIFICATION

That women in Western culture became more athletic and mobile in less than a generation supports the view that when they "threw like girls," they did not lack the agency and individual subjectivity implied by their description as Other. The agency may now be viewed as having been misdirected by women earlier, perhaps toward an objectification of their own bodies as merely decorative and sexually attractive, instead of outwardly toward the world, through bodily movement. However, the objectification of one's own body need not in itself preclude agency because the acquisition of many skills requires a kind of self-objectifying discipline. The relevant factors are what parts of the body are being objectified and to what ends, and what is being relinquished in the process. One can objectify one's body toward health as well as disease, toward proficiency as well as ineptitude. Unfortunately, second wave feminists often wrote as though objectification is in itself sufficient proof of dehumanization. The error comes not so much from a misreading of Sartre and de Beauvoir as from confusing the negative value or self-limiting effect of a practice with the active component of the practice itself. There is now a well-received feminist tendency to dismiss the component of constructive individual effort in women's projects of beautification.

As an example of the dismissal in question, Thomas Martin attempts to apply Sartre's account of sadism to the ways in which individual women work at living up to female beauty ideals:

> In the issue of female beauty ideals it is the continual and pervasive nature of the ideal, or messages transmitting it, in conjunction with the persuasive nature of general attitudes toward it, that cause women to experience their bodies as objects, often even as the preeminent object of their consciousness. It is this that parallels the sadist's infliction of pain upon the other's body, as a way to make the body, as flesh, demand the attention of their consciousness. In short, female beauty ideals parallel the procedures of Sartre's sadist in that both result in women, on the one hand, and the sadist's victim, on the other, experiencing their bodies as objects of their consciousness.[13]

Martin suggests that when the individual woman focuses on a part of her body as problematic, she objectifies its physicality in the same way an observer renders the physicality of another person obscene, according to Sartre. Let's look at Sartre's account:

> The *obscene* appears when the body adopts postures which entirely strip it of its acts and which reveal the inertia of its flesh. The sight of a naked body from behind is not obscene. But certain involuntary waddlings of the rump are obscene. This is because then it is only the legs which are acting for the walker, and the rump is like an isolated cushion which is carried by the legs and the balancing of which is a pure obedience to the laws of weight. It can not be justified by the situation; on the contrary, it is entirely destructive of any situation since it has the passivity of a thing and since it is made to rest like a thing upon the legs. Suddenly it is revealed as an unjustifiable facticity; it is *de trop* like every contingent.[14]

Clearly there is a double detachment here. The observer is detached from the obscene rump and for the observer, the obscene rump, as obscene, is momentarily detached from the body to which it belongs. Both detachments are missing when a woman problematizes part of her body because it does not conform to a beauty ideal. First, the woman is concerned about the part of her body in question as a part of her. And second, she aligns her identity with the perceived flaw, perhaps too closely, which is a lack of detachment. Such too-close identification may in pathological cases result in immobility, but usually, even in that most beauty-obsessed of cultures which is our own, women do something about their perceived flaws, that is, they act. Although Martin concedes that the ideals women are now exhorted to emulate are often athletic and physically healthy, he insists that the objectification of one's own body needed to realize these ideals inhibits a "bodily activity toward objects in the world."[15] Does he mean that women cannot act in the world in spite of the knowledge of their perceived flaws? Are we as good feminists to deny that women ever have flaws in their appearance, or that beauty ideals are always bad? Are they bad because beauty is bad or because all ideals are bad?

Absurdities aside, women do act in the world not only when they think they have flaws, but often because of, and upon, those very flaws. Imagine that Jane, a forty-five-year-old American woman, sees an ad or watches a movie that features a woman in her twenties who has a thin, athletic body. Jane first admires the image, compares the image's abdomen and upper arms to her own, and decides that she wants her abdomen and upper arms to resemble those of the woman in the image. She takes up tennis, walks, swims, or lifts weights over a period of time, and chooses and follows a nutritionally balanced diet that has fewer calories and more protein than she used to consume. Jane acts in ways directed toward objects in the world and she is motivated by the desire to change the appearance of her body toward a mass media beauty ideal. Some feminists might say that Jane was being tyrannized by a mass media beauty ideal that is beyond the reach of most middle-aged women. But imagine that Jane never saw the image of the younger woman, and that after a yearly physical checkup, her doctor told her that she had the kind of "apple-shaped" body that predisposes middle-aged women to heart problems, and advised her to follow exactly the same regimen that she would have pursued to emulate the image. Could the same feminists who saw the emulation project as a form of internalized oppression disapprove of the health project? They might say that for theoretical purposes it is Jane's motivation that counts for or against her liberation. But why is a desire to look better, if beauty is always believed to be in the eye of the beholder, a wrong desire? Is there a difference in quality of effort in the two cases if the results are the same? At some point, the final criterion ought to be whether Jane is better off. I submit that Jane is better off if she becomes physically healthier under the tyranny of beauty ideals than if she ignores those ideals and makes no changes. It might be best for Jane to pursue her health for its own sake, but in an imperfect world, good results from impure motives are often better than no results from pure motives. Furthermore, it would be needlessly ascetic to insist that virtue requires Jane taking no pleasure in the effects of healthier habits on her appearance.

However, Sandra Lee Bartky identifies the very component of individual effort in the construction of a culturally valued female body as a challenge for radical feminism:

> While its imposition may promote a larger disempowerment, discipline may bring with it a certain development of a person's powers. Women, then, like

other skilled individuals, have a stake in the perpetuation of their skills, whatever it may have cost to acquire them and quite apart from the question whether, as a gender, they would have been better off had they never had to acquire them in the first place. Hence, feminism, especially a genuinely radical feminism that questions the patriarchal construction of the female body, threatens women with a certain de-skilling, something people normally resist: Beyond this it calls into question that aspect of personal identity which is tied to the development of a sense of competence.[16]

Bartky here acknowledges the skill developed by women in their disciplines of cultural female body construction, but she problematizes it as a mistaken investment of human capital from the perspective of a radical feminism that would greatly alter present heterosexist culture. She sums up: "Femininity as a certain 'style of the flesh' will have to be surpassed in the direction of something quite different, not masculinity, which is in many ways only its mirror opposite, but a radical and as yet unimagined transformation of the female body."[17]

What Bartky may mean by the "female body" does not exist in a way that can be experienced or described outside of culture. It is women's bodies of particular styles that need to be transformed if Bartky's sense of what has to happen comes to be widely shared (after someone figures out how to imagine it). Such transformation would not be brought about by spurts of rebellion but by sustained disciplines of health (if not beauty) practiced by individual women. In other words, the old skills need to be deployed in new ways, at least at the beginning of a revolution in the cultural form of women's bodies as female. Entrenched skills, be they cosmetic, sartorial, or athletic, which are called for in conformity to current mass media ideals, need to be redirected. This is an issue of "retraining" rather than redundancy, as Bartky seems to assume.

Some women have already accomplished part of this redirection (and within that group, some may also continue to instantiate received ideals of female beauty). But all women have not constructively redeployed old skills, and many who have not suffer further insofar as they do not reflect the new bodily ideals. The new ideals of beauty, health, strength, and athleticism have not been wholly created by women liberating themselves but also by capitalist interests that continue to objectify women's bodies, even, or exactly, when they are displayed in their greatest glory. However, this is not completely a case in which capitalist interests are to blame for further women's objectification or for appropriating discoveries about women's physicality made by others. Rather, the objectification may still be necessary to make a more active female physicality a desirable goal for millions of women who continue to hold traditional notions of constraints on women's physicality. Weak female physicality may be shifted to strong female physicality, beginning with a change in what women objectify about themselves.

This change from objectified weakness to objectified strength is clearly beneficial to women in ways that feminists should not overlook out of disdain for self-objectification. A woman who is physically healthy and strong is that much closer to realizing ideals of psychic empowerment traditionally denied to women.

Nonetheless, a description of women and girls as deficient in primary human subjectivity and agency, which is based on how they have been regarded and treated by boys and men, is neither a critical description nor a liberatory one, and it obscures the human agency of those oppressed. Oppression sometimes robs people of their humanity by thwarting their agency. When oppression is severe, complete apathy may result along with an inability to function. To be fair, the traditional female, sexual, and maternal roles of women have not stifled human functioning on that primary level but instead pruned, directed, and controlled it in ways that depend on and perforce preserve the enduring humanity and continuing agency of girls and women. Otherwise, there would be nothing about female physicality that could be a subject of change for radical feminists, without reliance on a false biological essentialism or belief in the existence of an untouched femaleness or womanhood enduring through the dehumanization of existent women. As radical academic feminists continue to critique the poses of fashion models, they should be distracted from neither the ongoing commodification of women's bodies nor the individual energy invested in these commodities by both models and consumers. Moreover, what is true about the existence and persistence of women's agency within and beyond women's sexual and aesthetic objectification is even more compellingly evident in the activities and internal structures of "women's work." Housework requires physical stamina, patience, discipline, and a great variety of skills. The care of children and other forms of family work is an unending series of complex and robust "I can's." The objectification and exploitation of women as wives, mothers, and simply "women" in their assignment to such tasks is to a large degree external to the skills required. From the perspective of women who value their abilities to perform in such roles, the external objectification may be a minor problem.

THE CULTURAL SEX-GENDER SYSTEM

The way in which a human child becomes a human female depends on external social directions. One is told what to do, one sees others doing it, and one joins the group of those who do those things. The first-person impetus toward being female consists in a willingness or desire to join the group of other women. The felt impetus cannot be understood as a biological effect of having female genitalia, gonads, or chromosomes, for two reasons. First,

there is no evidence that biology determines the assumption of specific social roles of femaleness because the social roles need to be taught and are
geographically and historically different. Second, insofar as children become
aware of male–female taxonomy, their awareness and ability to type others
is not based on biological differences because those differences are usually
not evident in clothed society.[18] (It is indeed ironic that human beings are assigned a sex at birth based on biological structures and that those structures
are not salient for a child's own understanding of gender assignment or typing, and may not even be relevant for identity.) Even if the relevant biological structures caused the desire to be female, they would not in themselves
be sufficient to cause an understanding of the logic of the social taxonomy
(i.e., that one must be male or female) or of its constancy once one sees oneself as male or female.

Psychologists are expected to explain how individual children develop
into men or women. They should also tell us what the process of gender development contains and the kind of process it is. However, such psychological accounts presuppose the prior existence of the sex-gender system as any
child's initial social environment. The term "sex/gender system" was first
used by Gayle Rubin in "The Traffic in Women: Notes on the 'Political Economy' of Sex" (1975). Rubin wrote, "I call that part of social life the sex/
gender system, for lack of a more elegant term. As a preliminary definition,
a 'sex/gender system' is the set of arrangements by which a society transforms biological sexuality into products of human activity, and in which
these transformed sexual needs are satisfied."[19]

Rubin's term captures what I'd like to emphasize, but with an emphasis on
"system." On my view, the sex-gender system is a cultural system that can be
understood wholly on the side of culture because the notion of biological sex
that is salient in culture does not correspond to biological sex in biology. In proposing an inclusive commonality of women, I am presupposing the prior existence of the cultural sex-gender system for any given child. The sex-gender system has a history long and well entrenched enough to be the core of gender
definition, and perhaps identity development also. (The oppression of women
over human history anchors the liberatory dimension of feminism and the sex
typing and roles historically characteristic of the group may ground contemporary identity.)

The question of whether human biology was the cause of the sex-gender
system in our early species history is not relevant to gender, liberation, or
identity, as we need to understand them today. Individuals have for so long
been born into the dual-gender system that children do not reinvent the system through their development; rather, they adjust to it given the specific culture in which they mature. Humans are of course biological beings, but it is
no longer possible for any individual or group of individuals to live on the
basis of culturally unmediated biological realities. We do not even know, or

have the means to determine, what such biological realities might be, especially those that concern sex and gender.

The human sex-gender system in all its variety would take more than a lifetime of concentrated intellectual and empirical study to fully understand. Most individuals have only a partial understanding of the sex-gender system in their culture, and their suspicion of their own ignorance about a subject that they believe is of primary importance is probably part of the reason for the insecurities specific to each gender, and for continual curiosity about how other people practice the system. Any nonessentialist study of sex role development therefore needs to avoid projecting aspects of the system onto the child before she has learned them and to include an ability to imagine the psychic condition of the child before she has learned those aspects of the system, which are the subject of study.

No one has succeeded in demonstrating that any particular sex-gender system is too complex to be learned to the degree that individuals are able to function within it with socially recognizable identities. A demonstration that individuals could not learn the parts of the system necessary for their social functioning and gender identities would be the basis of an empirical hypothesis that the sex-gender system is innate, not in its links to biology but *as a cultural system*. It is possible that all particular cultural sex-gender systems are the result of a general innate capacity to acquire a culturally specific male or female sex, develop sexuality, and reproduce or nurture young, but that no particular system is innate. Although there is no conceptual necessity to posit the general sex-gender system as innate, the universal prevalence of particular sex-gender systems could be considered strong empirical evidence for the innateness of a general system. Counting against the innateness of a general sex-gender system is the fact that individuals do not require an implicit knowledge of the principles of the system to be able to function socially as human males or females.

In contrast to sex-gender social functioning, individuals seem to need implicit understanding of grammar in order to participate in a particular linguistic community. As Noam Chomsky has presented the case, it would be impossible for children to acquire this understanding based on the limited experience that is apparently sufficient for them to use the language in new ways—ways in which they have not yet been taught. Children are able to use language according to grammatical rules before they have been taught the rules underlying their usage or have had sufficient experience from which to infer the rules on their own.[20] However, to practice their sex and gender, individuals only need to develop a social identity as male or female that enables them to function socially in their local sex-gender system. It seems obvious that the ways in which children begin to do this are not as complex or creative as the ways in which they begin to use language.[21]

A particular sex-gender system is partially learned in relevant ways during childhood and adolescence, and practiced in adulthood. The male or female identities of individuals accompany them into old age, while over time their sexual and reproductive roles attenuate. This age dependency of sex-gender systems can be largely explained by the close connection of the systems to biological reproduction, if we assume that human societies have had an enduring interest in supporting human biological reproduction. Given the asymptotic increase in *Homo sapiens sapiens* populations (from about 10,000 to 6 billion) since modern humans first appeared about 100,000 years ago, the sex-gender system has been stupendously successful in supporting human reproduction.[22] Whether the planet can sustain this success is an open question. That this success has come at the cost of women's opportunities to flourish for their own sake is indisputable historically and underscored at present by the fact that areas of the world with the greatest population momentum are also areas in which women appear to be least liberated (from a Western perspective). However, the important theoretical point is that sex-gender systems have been more closely tied to human reproduction than to any other outcome for *Homo sapiens sapiens* as a biological species. As a total cultural system, sex-gender systems support biological reproduction while perpetuating themselves on a cultural level. Not surprisingly, there is an analogy between cultural mothering and cultural sex identity as female. Cultural sex identity as female is projected onto the biological structures of some human beings, and cultural mothering is projected onto biological reproduction by human mothers. In both cases, physical structures and processes are falsely imagined to necessitate social roles that are better understood as components of a nonphysical imaginary structure—a symbolic structure. The human species invented the systematic study of its own biology and then used that study to posit biological foundations for culture. Biology has been overextended in modern cultural projects in confused ways that benefit dominant interests. And on the basis of that overextension, humans have in turn shaped what they understand to be their biology. Although biology continues to be used and reused as a justification for the cultural project of sex-gender, feminists cannot afford to forget that the problems which make feminism necessary are not biological but cultural.

NOTES

1. With the present uses of ultrasound imaging during pregnancy, the consequences of sex designation may precede birth, in forms of acculturation that could affect a late-term fetus, and also as a reason to abort a fetus (usually female) if parents have strong sex preferences.

2. Such choices are now made as soon as possible after birth, often resulting in surgery to construct genitalia appropriate to the chosen sex and remove tissue assumed to be inappropriate to that sex, followed by hormone therapy. Such medical treatment may lead to recurring physical problems as well psychological distress. Some adult survivors of this kind of intervention have begun to advocate against invasive treatment through organizations such as the Intersex Society of Aotearoa/New Zealand (ISNZ) and Intersexual Society of North America (ISNA). See Myra J. Hird and Jenz Germon, "The Intersexual Body and the Medical Regulation of Gender," in *Constructing Gendered Bodies,* ed. Kathryn Backett-Milburn and Linda Mckie (New York: Palgrave, 2001), 166–78. The legal question of criteria for being male or female has not yet been addressed in the courts, although as intersexual advocacy becomes more widely known (it is conservatively estimated that one infant out of 2,000 births has ambiguous or incongruent genitals), it is difficult to see how sex assignment can remain an ad hoc and quasi-secretive medical issue. See Julia Greenberg, "The Law's Failure to Recognize Intersexuals and the Transgendered: A View through the Lens of Therapeutic Jurisprudence," *Congress Abstracts,* www.pfc.org.uk/congress/abstract/abs-027.htm. See also Katherine A. Mason, "Intersexuals Fight Back," *New Haven Advocate,* April 3, 2001, www.alternet.org/story/html?StoryID=10672; and Suzanne J. Kessler, "The Medical Construction of Gender: Case Management of Intersexed Infants," *Signs,* Autumn 1990.

3. Sex as male or female is not wholly created or invented by culture or language because there is a biological substratum that is given meaning through male or female designation at birth, and girls and boys do develop *physically* as male or female. Still, culture is projected onto biology and shapes it. American girls, for example, begin to menstruate several years earlier than their mothers and grandmothers did. See Joan Jacobs Drumberg, *The Body Project: An Intimate History of American Girls* (New York: Vintage, 1997), 3–25. However, there is a biological reality that exists outside culture and language, including birth designations as male or female. Therefore, I agree with Toril Moi's criticism of Judith Butler's extreme position of social constructivism regarding sex in *Gender Trouble.* See Toril Moi, *What Is a Woman?* (New York: Oxford University Press, 1999), 40–57. I disagree with Moi that there is a Wittgensteinian solution to the varieties of sex or gender, which she advances in response to what she reads as Butler's nominalism. Philosophically, Butler and others who would derive physicality from symbolic structures are not nominalists but *idealists.* Nominalism, in John Locke's sense, held that matter is real (and the human body is a special arrangement of matter) but that how we classify it is an effect of thought and language. See John Locke, *An Essay Concerning Human Understanding,* ed. Peter H. Nidditch (Oxford: Oxford University Press, 1975), 3.5.S13-S22.436–51. Idealism, by contrast, is the philosophical position that denies the existence of any reality outside of ideas, language, or "symbolic discourse."

Depending on how prevalent and otherwise biologically healthy intersexual individuals are—which is not known because of the physical ways in which intersexuality has been reconstructed—the dual-sex system is either ruthlessly nominalist in ignoring intersexuals in its taxonomy or moderately nominalist in dealing with exceptions. At worst, the dual sex system is nominalist because every nominalist system has rules for constructing categories, applying the system to reality, and dealing with exceptions. To say that a system is nominalist is not the same thing as saying that it is arbitrary. Human racial classification is an interesting contrast to male/female sex classification in this regard because there are no reliably variable *phenotypical* traits of race that could support common social taxonomies, in the way in which those taxonomies purport to be supported by reliable variations, as well as a scientific foundation. On why racial categories are not nominalist, see Naomi Zack, "Race and Philosophic Meaning," in *RACE/SEX: Their Sameness, Difference, and Interplay* (New York: Routledge, 1997), 29–44; and Zack, *Philosophy of Science and Race* (New York: Routledge, 2002), 111.

 4. Raymond Bonner, "A Challenge in India Snarls Foreign Adoptions," *New York Times*, June 23, 2003, A3.

 5. Martha C. Nussbaum, *Women and Human Development: The Capabilities Approach* (New York: Cambridge University Press, 2000), 67–68, 280–81. An interesting fact in Nussbaum's book is that most women in India now work. Even those employed in the most menial tasks or overburdened by domestic duties have access to networks of other women who can inform them about their rights and assist with domestic and business problems. Throughout India, one effect of the lack of a corporate business structure dominated by large firms, and of the undercapitalization of small firms, is that many women who would otherwise be on the lowest rung of a labor sector have self-employed status because they are independent contractors.

 6. Jean-Paul Sartre, *Being and Nothingness*, trans. Haxel Barnes (New York: Philosophical Library, 1952).

 7. Simone de Beauvoir, *The Second Sex*, trans. H. M. Parshley (New York: Knopf, 1952).

 8. Maurice Merleau-Ponty, *The Phenomenology of Perception*, trans. Colin Smith (New York: Humanities, 1962).

 9. Iris Marion Young, "Throwing Like a Girl: A Phenomenology of Feminine Body Comportment, Motility, and Spatiality," in *Throwing Like a Girl and Other Essays in Feminist Philosophy and Social Theory* (Bloomington: Indiana University Press, 1990), 153.

 10. Young, "Throwing Like a Girl," 156.

 11. Young, "Throwing Like a Girl," 156.

 12. The equipment and techniques of female self-presentation are more exhausting to list than to assemble and practice. Susan Brownmiller did a pretty good job at chronicling the equipment for women's skin care in 1984. See Susan Brownmiller, *Femininity* (New York: Fawcett Columbine, 1984), 127–68. However, skin care is no longer in the sole province of female gender. A television show that debuted on Bravo in July 2003, *Queer Eye for the Straight Guy*, features skin care products and practices (including a mud body wrap at a spa visit in the first episode) in makeovers of "straight guys" by five gay style experts. The show has a subtext that gay men know more than straight men about issues of aesthetics and personal style, which have been traditionally restricted to women. As a result, the show positions gay men as intermediaries between women and straight men in such matters. Presumably this bridge role of gay men is less of an assault on masculine identity than would occur if women were presented as the experts,

or if the sexual orientation of the show's authorities on cooking, interior decorating, grooming, and so forth, were not mentioned, much less emphasized. The acceptance of the authority of gay men by straight men suggests that both types of men are able to distinguish between sexual orientation and male sex gender, so that straight men trust the gay authorities because they share the latter with them. In fact, the gay men are presented as helping the straight men (who are slobs) become more attractive to women. The assumption here is that women must be aesthetically pleased by men in order to find them sexually attractive. Romance materializes between aesthetics and sex; the spruced-up men are better able to create a romantic atmosphere and then achieve their romantically guided sexual goals. *Queer Eye* was preceded by a British and American version of a show called *What Not to Wear*, in which women were given fashion makeovers to minimize natural "flaws" and enhance natural "assets." All of these makeover shows represent monetary expenses that are part of a larger consumer culture, so that being able to buy the right clothing or beauty products and services may surpass a willingness to conform to beauty ideals as a necessary condition for living up to the ideals. More recent is a show called *Extreme Makeover,* in which chosen contestants, who are usually women, are given cosmetic and reconstructive surgery to increase their attractiveness, thus raising the financial bar. In all of these makeover shows, the person who has been transformed reveals the new self (or "other") to an admiring group of friends and relatives. Such "reveals" (a noun introduced in *Extreme Makeover*) create a dimension of approval within an immediate community, which puts a final stamp of respectability on projects that might otherwise appear to be vain, superficial, self-indulgent, extravagant, or even unsociable or selfish. The subjects of these transformations, even though they may be passive recipients of expert technique, are depicted as decisive, brave, and strangely self-empowered.

13. Thomas Martin, "Sartre, Sadism, and Female Beauty Ideals," in *Feminist Interpretations of Jean-Paul Sartre*, ed. Julien S. Murphy (University Park: Pennsylvania State University Press, 1999), 99.

14. Sartre, *Being and Nothingness*, 520–21.

15. Martin, "Sartre, Sadism, and Female Beauty Ideals," 102.

16. Sandra Lee Bartky, *Femininity and Domination: Studies in the Phenomenology of Oppression* (New York: Routledge, 1990), 77.

17. Bartky, *Femininity and Domination*, 78.

18. Jaipaul L. Roopnarine and Nina S. Mounts, "Current Theoretical Issues in Sex Roles and Sex Typing," in *Constructing Gendered Bodies*, ed. Kathryn Backett-Milburn and Linda Mckie (New York: Palgrave, 2001), 7.

19. Gayle Rubin, "The Traffic in Women: Notes on the 'Political Economy' of Sex," in *Toward an Anthropology of Women,* ed. Rayna R. Reither (New York: Monthly Review Press, 1975); reprinted in *The Second Wave: A Reader in Feminist Theory,* ed. Linda J. Nicholson (New York: Routledge, 1990), 28.

20. Noam Chomsky, "Recent Contributions to the Theory of Innate Ideas," *Synthese*, 1967, 2–11. Reprinted in *Minds, Brains, and Computers: The Foundations of Cognitive Science*, ed. Robert Cummins and Denise Dellarosa Cummins (New York: Blackwell, 2000), 452–57.

21. In comparing language learning and performance with gender learning and performance, it becomes evident that the two interact. The child uses language to learn about gender and gender, identity may in turn affect further language learning and usage.

22. The increase in population accelerates. There were 1.7 billion people in 1900 and 5.9 billion in 1998; 8 billion are projected for 2025. *U.S. Census Bureau World Population Profile: 1998- Highlights*; www.census.gov/ipc/www/wp98001.html.

4

Inclusive Feminist Social Theory: Requirements and Methodology

In chapter 1, motivated by the need for an inclusive third wave feminism, I proposed that all women shared assignment to, or identification with, the historically defined category of human beings who are designated female from birth, biological mothers, or primary sexual choices of men—the FMP category. Chapter 2 examined the logical nature of category FMP. Chapter 3 extended the analysis of chapter 2 and showed how culture is related to female sex designation at birth; I also introduced the importance of a concept of first-person agency for ideas of social change. Chapter 3 was thus the beginning of a feminist theory of gender development and difference, based on the ideas of a nonsubstantive commonality of women proposed in the first two chapters. Since specific or local women's genders can be viewed as variables that are culturally contexualized, it makes sense to extend the analysis of women's genders, insofar as it is an analysis of women in society, to feminist theories of the social sciences, history, and political theory and politics. This chapter is about requirements for inclusive feminist theories of culture or feminist social theory(ies). Inclusive feminist social theories can provide contexts for understanding specific sex-gender systems in which children develop or acquire their gender. On the basis of such contexts, the psychology of gender development can then be understood. Therefore, chapter 5 is about feminist theories of psychology. Because my distinctions between feminist social theory and feminist psychological theory are critical of other feminist theoretical work, chapter 6 is a discussion of the connections between feminist social theory and feminist psychological theory. Chapter 7 continues the analysis of women in society, based on their commonality, into the question of how women might become a real historical subject or a force in history. Chapter 8 applies that discussion to feminist political theory and feminist politics.

Psychologists would be expected to provide an empirical account of how existing individuals develop into men or women. As a reference for feminist theory, this account could not posit biological causation of culturally relative constructions of gender. Individuals do not become women or men, or even human females or males, as a direct result of their biology alone. Some still believe that biological structures such as gonads, secondary sexual traits, chromosomes, and DNA constitute biological sex and determine its physical development in an individual. But such beliefs have cultural components. In no culture are male and female gender based solely on biology, and in a contemporary dual-sex system, the widespread extirpation of biological intersex with medical techniques shows that the *taxonomy* of biological sex is partly determined by nonbiological, cultural factors. If even sex type is partly an effect of culture, and if within culture beliefs that gender is determined by sex can be rejected as partial or false, then gender taxonomies should be understood as projected onto sex taxonomies that are themselves projected onto biology. This underdetermination of sex and gender by biology is one reason for the importance to feminist theory of sociological and anthropological accounts of gender identity and difference, assuming that sociology and anthropology are the sciences of culture (and that in historical studies they can be applied to the past as well as the present). A second reason for the importance of sociological and anthropological accounts is that individual psychology and biology combined are not sufficient to account for gender difference and identity as a dynamic process of development. Always, the child becomes a woman or a man within the norms and expectations of a culture.

The lines between the social sciences are not always sharply drawn in established disciplinary practices. The social sciences have been combined deliberately by feminist writers undertaking cultural analyses of psychology and psychological analyses of culture.[1] Nevertheless, I am going to begin by assuming that anthropology and sociology are sciences of society and that psychology is a science of individuals. This assumption will be justified in the analysis of the normativity of feminist social theory in this chapter, and by concern for the circumstances of existent women in my critique of feminist psychoanalytic theory in chapter 5. The justifications amount to this: if social theory is presented as psychological, it precludes social change; if psychological theory is presented as social, it precludes individual change.

From a developmental or existential perspective, the sociological and anthropological accounts of gender ought to come before the psychological ones. Any child can be assumed to begin life within a specific culture that is ordered by its specific version of what we understand to be the general sex-gender system of modern *Homo sapiens sapiens*. This perspective of the child learning its own gender and gender relations within its cultural system also allows for a first-person phenomenology that includes individual choice and agency. Individual choice and agency are part of any respectful account of human nature, but as I indicated in chapter 3, they need to be addressed in order to understand change in a given sex-gender system that benefits women as the group historically oppressed in such systems. Individual choice and agency also need to be motivated in order to effect change in such systems.

REQUIREMENTS OF INCLUSIVE FEMINIST SOCIAL THEORY

I propose the following requirements for inclusive feminist social theory. First, because feminism in its most general sense is a critical theory that is motivated by goals of better lives for women, feminist social theory should be unapologetically normative. Second, feminist social theory should be grounded in facts about the existence of real women who can all be defined by their common relation to the FMP category. Third, feminist social theory ought to explain how women are oppressed in society. Fourth, feminist social theory ought to be comprehensive and address oppressions of women that are apparently distinct from gender, such as racism and classism. And fifth, feminist social theory ought to be methodologically distinct from feminist psychological theory so that political action is possible.

Normativity

Sandra Harding in her 1983 anthology edited with Merrill Hintikka, *Discovering Reality: Feminist Perspectives on Epistemology, Metaphysics, Methodology, and Philosophy of Science,* posed the question that is also the title of her article in the volume: "Why has the sex/gender system become visible only now?" Harding views the sex/gender system as an irreducible organic force in human societies, an underlying causative reality and not an imaginary construction. She defines it in terms of male dominance:

> Sex/Gender is a system of male-dominance made possible by men's control of women's productive and reproductive labor, where 'reproduction' is broadly construed to include sexuality, family life and kinship formations, as well as the birthing which biologically reproduces the species.[2]

Harding does not undertake to answer her question but to show that it is a reasonable and neglected question that could not have been posed before second wave feminism, in traditional epistemologies that were based on assumptions that all knowledge and discoveries are independent of the social conditions of knowers and discoverers. Marxist epistemologies would have allowed for social contexts of knowledge, but Marxists did not traditionally believe that the oppression of women was a general social

condition independent of class oppressions—Marxists would have reduced gender to class if they could.[3]

Here is an intellectual answer to Harding's question. Although the sex-
gender system in Harding's realist sense can be assumed to have existed
throughout recorded history, it would be anachronistic to speak of people
being aware of it as such before the 1970s. This is because the discovery of
the sex-gender system required clear intuitions (if not conclusive scientific
evidence) that female gender—the roles assumed by women in society—is
not fully determined by biology.[4] If women had the capability to function
beyond their traditional submissive social roles of passive females, male
sexual objects, and stay-at-home mothers, and if women did not freely
choose those roles, then it could be concluded that there was something
wrong with the roles. Not wrong in that the roles were mistakenly assigned
in innocence, but morally wrong insofar as the roles thwarted the development of women as human beings (they would have had the same effect on
men had they been assigned them), and further wrong insofar as women
were confined to those roles and punished for rejecting them or choosing
other roles. This moral wrongness of traditional women's roles led to feminist explorations of the general social conditions that generated the roles
and the eventual theoretical discovery of an underlying social structure that
could be called a sex-gender system.[5]

It is important that Harding posits the sex-gender system as something real
in the world because this makes moral judgment possible and grounds it as
reason for action. Harding's claim that the system is real also reminds us that
women are oppressed in material—economic and physical—circumstances.
If the sex-gender system were a model or a hypothesis so that Harding instead said, "Much of what we know about human history has taken place *as
though there were* a Sex/Gender system," feminists would be obligated to
determine whether there was a sex-gender system before moral judgment
and its attendant action could be envisioned and justified.

To posit a real sex-gender system is to claim that men unjustly control the
lives of women, and the implication is strong that all men and only men do
this. To take into account societies in which some men do not control the
lives of women, as well as individual lives and situations in which women
are free of the control of men, suppose that something else instead, which I
have been calling the "sex-gender system," is posited. The sex-gender system consists of the assignment of male or female sex to human beings at
birth, together with the expectation that they will belong to the correspon-
ding group that has male or female gender, of which there are many different types, depending on time and place. Suppose that the sex-gender system
is not defined in terms of male dominance. Would feminist social theory that
depends on positing a sex-gender system still be normative? Yes, if female
genders in society were believed to be enacted in ways that disadvantaged

women compared to men, without good reasons for doing so. And yes, if it were believed that the cultural determinations of gender were based on a sexual taxonomy that purported to mirror biology but failed to do so because of presently unknown numbers of individuals who were and are born biologically intersexed, and that the accepted either/or taxonomy were unjust for its omissions.

As a posit of feminist social theory, I prefer the weaker "sex-gender" system that does not have male dominance built into it, to Harding's stronger "sex/gender" system that does.[6] The weaker usage allows one to talk about female as well as male dominance. Many poor and nonwhite women and girls are dominated and exploited by other women, often white women of greater privilege, but not always. While such situations can often be reduced to larger social structures of male dominance, in some cases the reduction may be implausible or too far removed from the instant situation of oppression to be meaningful. The last would be true in situations where women have had direct control over the lives of other women and girls, for instance in all-female institutions, in homes where mothers are the main authorities over daughters, in separatist lesbian communities (as well as nonegalitarian lesbian relationships), in homes or workplaces where women employ or supervise other women for service labor, and in unfair and unprincipled situations of competition among women. There are also unjust practices of dominance among feminists themselves.[7]

Furthermore, it is useful to consider the dominance of men by men in situations where women are not direct participants, such as traditional wars, all-male professional contexts, business, politics, men's prisons, and so forth. While it could be argued that such male–male dominance requires the support of women outside the field of action, or that it relies on dominant males symbolically turning their subordinates into women, this needs to be shown on a case-by-case basis. (There is also a persistent intellectual tradition to dismiss male–male dominance as an effect or expression of evolutionary biological factors, such as male display and male sexual competition for females, instead of viewing it as a cultural phenomenon in its own right.)[8] Same-sex dominance, of men by men or women by women, may occur in the ways distinctive of male or female genders, which are otherwise formed in a sex-gender system, but it may also depend on a certain amount of gender switching, blurring, or simply erasing. Furthermore, there is the possibility of a system of male and female gender without male dominance. Given these considerations, if one posits the weaker "sex-gender" system, then male dominance or men's control over the lives of women can be viewed as a variable with a range of oppressive intensity. The weaker posit is the general system that is universal. Congruent with the universal sex-gender system and its variable of male dominance, there is a race/ethnicity system and a wealth/class system. Sometimes a specific race/ethnicity system will dominate a specific sex-gender system, for instance, when women of color experience racism as more oppressive than sexism. Other times, the wealth/class system may dominate both the other systems, for instance, mothers in sudden extreme poverty would view getting enough food for their children as more important than resisting either racism or classism.

Recognition of either the sex/gender system or the sex-gender system as a real dynamic in society is a way of conceptualizing the injustice of women's places in society. Such injustice can be identified by feminists (as they do in many different ways) because feminism itself is a critical theory. There was extensive discussion of the nature of political critical theories during the twentieth century, as well as significant reflection on how feminism is a critical theory or on what feminist critical theory should be.[9] The result is several requirements for critical theory, which can be distilled as follows. First, the material context of what some types or classes of people believe about other types or classes in society should be understood by the theorist, so that the ways in which practical interests are connected to beliefs, or to myths that mask beliefs, can be made evident. Second, the critical theorist is expected to address situations of oppression or other social ills, using the insights gained from the connections between material interests and beliefs. Third, in addressing oppression, the critical theorist must have something at stake in the outcome, or convincingly speak from the perspective of the oppressed. Fourth, theorists need not require that their beliefs about what is happening in society be accepted as true by either the majority of oppressors or those oppressed. (Although if the critical theory has a strong moral dimension, there may be an optimistic assumption that if participants could view their actions as theorists do, then they would behave differently.) Fifth, insofar as critical theories are about real social conditions, they are capable of revision as social conditions change.

Feminism is evidently a critical theory given these requirements. First, feminists claim that men believe women are passive, relational, nurturing, and intellectually inferior, and that these beliefs justify and protect men's material interests through the exclusion of women from important endeavors, the exploitation of women's labor, and the manipulation of women's emotions and sexuality. Second, feminists show that the stereotypical beliefs men hold about women are false and they explain how men use them to benefit themselves by exploiting and dominating women. Third, feminists are women and those men who advocate for women's interests and support the work of women feminists. Fourth, feminists understand that those who oppress women through ongoing repetitive practices in their daily life will not initially recognize that they are oppressive, and that women who are oppressed will often resist descriptions of themselves as oppressed. And fifth, feminism is presently pluralistic; different views and goals have changed in response to changing social conditions, along with the personal and intellectual growth of theorists and as a result of feminist discourse itself. Feminism is therefore critical theory, and so is the feminist subfield, feminist social theory, which has largely consisted of analysis and criticism of the Western forms of the sex-gender system that treat women unjustly.

Moral outrage at injustice is not the only kind of normativity that motivates feminist social theory. After women realized that they are capable of doing and having more than their traditional roles afforded, many feminists simply wanted more power for women. (The impatience that many female undergraduates express with first and second wave feminist texts comes from their belief that the moral battle has been won; they now want to be taught about greater empowerment for themselves.) Feminist social theorists motivated by desires for power and informed by perceptions of power imbalances are not likely to be as optimistic as are morally motivated theorists that people will change once they become aware of what they are doing. Force, rhetorical persuasion, legal action, and the manipulation of images may take the place of moral argument as preferred strategies for such theorists. A third kind of normativity in feminist social theory is care or concern for the well-being of other women, together with a belief that such altruistic modes are common in human nature within or across genders. And there are also religious or spiritual normativities.

Factuality

There is presently a "rationalist/empiricist" divide in feminist social theory, although practitioners on both sides would probably reject this philosophical terminology. Perhaps a "textual/factual" divide is a more appropriate description. Scholarly work on the textual side is presented as deriving from the thought of writers such as Marx, Freud, Foucault, Sartre, Lacan, Derrida, Wittgenstein, and others whose primary intellectual concerns did not include advocacy for the well-being of women. Feminists who derive their own ideas from the ideas of such nonfeminist thinkers often announce that they are "appropriating" the work of their forebears (perhaps because the rudeness of "appropriation" is believed to erase dependence on patriarchs). A more polite form of textual feminist theory is presented as "influenced by" the work of canonical feminists such as de Beauvoir or Chodorow (where the appropriate influences legitimate new work without precluding its originality). In contrast to these daughters of text, factual feminists proceed from existing social problems, statistics, or striking situations—they attempt to look out at the social world directly before theorizing. Rich and interesting as the textual work is, both in itself and as a vital contribution to the developing intellectual culture of feminism, without the addition of relevant facts or descriptions of existent social problems faced by women, it fails to be a live form of critical theory, and it is not useful for changing the world. For instance, if the social subject is motherhood, texts that idealize deep and primordial bonds between mothers and infants cannot by themselves be used to explain how working women with infants in day care have problems that are the result of the present sex-gender system in the United States. Neither are such texts useful for understanding the situation of young women who angrily oppose and defy the values and gender of their mothers because they are maturing in a society with different female gender norms than the ones in which their mothers became women. If the subject is the problems of contemporary black women, a text-based theory about connections of ideas of blackness to Christian notions of sin and ugliness is not useful for addressing intellectual discrimination against black women or their underrepresentation in the mass media. Similarly, text-based analyses of the sexual exploitation of black women during slavery are not directly relevant to the difficulty contemporary educated black women have in finding suitable mates among black men, or the reasons why black "welfare mothers" were particularly despised by white conservatives during the twentieth century.

Another example of texts versus facts can be found in contemporary abortion discussions. Relevant social theory about abortion no longer turns on the question of whether women ought to have access to abortions (if a feminist opens this discussion then she must be prepared to discuss whether *Roe v. Wade* ought to be reversed) but on the conditions under which abortion is a good choice. And yet, as Laurie Shrage explains in *Abortion and Social Responsibility*, the feminist establishment remains fixated on defending abortions in any trimester, as though any restriction on abortion violates the right of choice.[10] Opposed to the feminist establishment are conservative "pro-life" groups fixated on defending the life of fetuses at any stage of pregnancy. In the middle is the American public, which largely endorses a pro-choice position on abortion and accepts the legality of early-term abortions. Indeed, most abortions are performed during the first trimester of pregnancy. What the public does not accept is public funding for the abortions of poor women, partly because the plight of the poor with unwanted pregnancies does not fascinate it and partly because its attention is captured by the ping-pong of the debate: *Late-term abortions are always permissible choices* versus *No late-term abortions are ever permissible*. If establishment feminists, in the academy and the leadership of national U.S. women's groups, acknowledged that most abortions are performed during the first trimester and that public funding for abortions could be easier to secure if abortions were restricted to the first (and sometimes second) trimester of pregnancy, they might then agree to some restrictions on when abortions can be performed so as to enable abortion funding for poor women. The ongoing fixation on an absolute right to abortion at any time during pregnancy may be justified by relevant texts, but it does not generate political positions that are helpful to poor women with unwanted pregnancies. This is not to say that theoretical feminism is irrelevant to social concerns. For instance, tolerance by feminist leaders to the contradiction between a defense of abortion based on privacy rights and requirements that teenagers seeking abortions get parental consent may be a pragmatic political compromise.[fn] But it adds the privilege of adulthood to that of class, making abortions an unobtainable luxury for those who may need them most—poor teenage women from conservative families. Conflicts between text-based theory and political exigencies may always require ad hoc resolution, but so far there has been very little feminist discussion of the tension itself.

I am not suggesting that feminist social theory should always be "applied" with a primary concern for those most disadvantaged in specific situations. But I do want to emphasize that some important theoretical work may not be based on canonical texts. The text/fact divide in feminism is not a theory/practice divide, and those who derive professional and personal esteem from their attachment to certain texts ought not to be indulged on the grounds that their work is "higher" or more intellectually sophisticated than those who theorize reality. Again, the textual theories are interesting, and the interests of relatively advantaged women ought not to be ignored. However, past charges that feminism was not inclusive derailed the second wave project because feminism had neglected the circumstances of those relatively disadvantaged. Complete immersion in text-based theories continues the same kind of exclusion, albeit with more privacy, since the text-based feminists rarely even try to make their ideas known to women outside their literary and scholarly circles.

Theorists must know what the current conditions of different kinds of women are. Facts, furthermore, have a force in argument that is directly connected to the possibility of action. This is not merely rhetorical force but the logic of an Aristotelian practical syllogism that has a description of a current situation and a normative statement as premises, with live action as its conclusion. The motivation for school breakfast programs are an example.

Description: "Children come to school hungry."
Normative statement: "Children's hunger is a social wrong and it impedes their ability to learn."
Conclusion: Breakfast is served to schoolchildren. This is not a statement that breakfast ought to be served to schoolchildren—the "ought" is already contained in the normative statement; food is physically made available to hungry children.

Virginia Woolf practiced fact-based feminism in *Three Guineas*. In addressing an educated man who had asked her opinion on how war could be prevented, she wrote from the perspective of the upper-middle-class women whom she called the "daughters of educated men."

We need not have recourse to the dangerous and uncertain theories of psychologists and biologists; we can appeal to facts. Take the fact of education. Your class has been educated at public schools and universities for five or six hundred years, ours for sixty. Take the fact of property. Your class possesses in its own right and not through marriage practically all the capital, all the land, all the valuables, and all the patronage in England. Our class possesses in its own right and not through marriage practically none of the capital, none of the land, none of the valuables, and none of the patronage in England. That such differences make for very considerable differences in mind and body, no psychologist or biologist would deny. . . . Though we see the same world, we see it through different eyes.[12]

Woolf explicitly defends fact-based feminist social theory here. She eschews psychological or biological explanations of gender difference and instead, well aware of traditional social class distinctions, distinguishes between men and women in the same class, based on their different educational, economic, and social histories. She calls men and women different classes. Whether or not one agrees with her about that, it is an interesting theoretical hypothesis backed up by the kinds of differences, in education, wealth, and social power, which are used to distinguish social classes in the traditional sense that includes men and women in the same class.

In a different but related vein, Pierre Bourdieu has recently argued that the invariance of male dominance revealed in ethnographic studies of gender relations in particular societies requires an understanding of real social mechanisms and institutions. He claims that realization of this point may lead to the "formulation of strategies aimed at transforming the present state of the material and symbolic power relations between the sexes." Bourdieu also claims that the invariance of male dominance does not exist principally or primarily in the domestic sphere, but in public agencies and institutions such as the school and the state. He concludes that with this recognition "a vast field of action is opened up for feminist struggles."[13] I interpret Bourdieu to mean here that feminists should take action against specific social institutions.

To be sure, Woolf and Bourdieu are problematic feminists. Bourdieu relies on his 1960s study of the Berbers of Kabylia, whom he calls "exotic," for understanding late-twentieth-century European male dominance *as a social construction*.[14] The use of the word "exotic" suggests that a "primitive" or "immature" culture is an early stage of development still foundational for a familiar/French/advanced culture.[15] Virginia Woolf, writing in 1938, was intent on describing the exigencies of her own relatively privileged "class" of women, with no stated regard for poor women or women of color.[16] Nevertheless, the factual orientation of both these writers underscores how the empiricist strain in feminist social theory can thrive independently of the kind of positivistic, objectifying, or quantitative social science analysis that most feminist social theorists would properly reject.

Furthermore, the requirement of fact-based analysis for feminist social theory need not be restricted to a theorist's own time and place. Indeed the most interesting fact-based analyses are often anthropological and historical, provided that care is taken with assumptions relative to the theorist's time, place, and social position. While feminist leaders in privileged societies are less likely to be expected to effect change in other cultures, they may help women who can effect such changes. An understanding of past oppressions and exclusions in one's own society is useful for understanding present conditions that can be changed because sometimes the past lives on only as tradition. For example, many women who are the first members of their families to attend college are changing a tradition that is no longer held in place by external conditions.

Explainability

Feminist social theorists should be able to explain why a given social practice or structure is oppressive to women and what keeps it in place. To do this they need accounts of women's autonomy and flourishing, against which something can be seen to be oppressive; of women's motives, goals, and intentions, to explain what situations of oppression mean to them; of how their culture assigns women to institutions and otherwise trains them in ways that perpetuate oppression.

Suppose, as Susan Bordo implies, that female anorectics are oppressed. As Bordo describes them, anorectics are self-denying young women who derive egotistical pleasure from suppressing their hunger for food.[17] Although Bordo implicitly recognizes that women suffering from anorexia nervosa are, through practices of extreme self-discipline, oppressing themselves, she interprets this phenomenon as a "crystallization of culture." This implies that a successful psychological analysis of the anorectic "type" could work as a kind of hermeneutical indictment of the culture in which this type lives. What the anorectic gains through what I am calling her self-oppression is a feeling of superiority to other women who cannot achieve her thinness. For Bordo's crystallization of culture hypothesis to be true, the anorectic has to be correct in perceiving women's thinness to be a cultural value. The anorectic is correct because most women upheld as beautiful in the mass media are thin (although not usually as pathologically thin as the anorectic, who may be starving to death) and women who are fat are (often but not always) presumed unable to be beautiful. Bordo, many other feminists, anorectics, and other women believe that beauty is not an objective property but a value that exists only when others say or think of someone, "She is beautiful."

Bordo also assumes that the anorectic wants to be thin so that men, who dominate the culture and from whom the anorectic believes the main goods of life flow, will pronounce her beautiful. However, the competition with other women implied in the anorectic's feelings of superiority to them suggests that male domination may not be a direct factor in the psychology of anorexia nervosa. The anorectic may compete with other women in contexts where male approval or admiration is irrelevant to success, for instance, in women's colleges. Contemporary anorectics are usually (although not always) young women who have some measure of autonomy and opportunities to secure the goods of life independently of male desire or generosity. And anorectics are a numerical minority in such contexts. The female anorectic in contemporary America is often discussed by feminists as living out a wider cultural oppression of women by men. But that analysis ignores the distinct motivating factors for anorectics, an oversight that extends to discussion of other harmful pathologies (e.g., abuse of cosmetic surgery) that are motivated by desires to conform to mass media beauty ideals, also in competition with other women.

What is needed for a complete explanation of the tyrannical effect of mass media beauty ideals on the lives of some women are additional hypotheses that social norms have a greater influence on those women than on other women and men. Perhaps some women in contemporary American society are still, despite liberatory gains, more likely to try to conform to beauty ideals. If so, the factor that would have to be changed to correct the tyranny of those ideals over the lives of these women is not the inaccessibility of the beauty ideals, but variable gender-based tendencies to conform. It remains to be shown exactly what the remaining social institutions and practices are that impose different conformity standards within and across gender.[18] Such an approach might address the ultimate causes of anorexia nervosa, and as a result explain how women's physical appearance is more objectified than men's in U.S. culture.

Once disabused of the reflex to protect women from beauty ideals in ways that simplify the relationship of women to those ideals, feminists might address more prevalent weight-related problems such as obesity. Not all women who fail to conform to beauty ideals have unerring instincts that guide them toward maximum health, and it is an empirical question whether women who are sensitive to such ideals as a group are in worse physical and psychological health than women who ignore the ideals in their daily practices.

Comprehensiveness

The comprehensiveness of a feminist social theory is the range of causes of women's oppression that it is able to coherently address. A sufficiently comprehensive theory will be inclusive because the variables according to which some women are different from the theorist will be among the recognized causes of oppression. If "intersectionality" is used to achieve comprehensiveness, then all of the groups in society who identify as women and suffer from distinct oppressions have to be included as subjects of inquiry in feminist social theory. While this encourages the flourishing of "difference feminism(s)," if each group speaks only for itself, there is no unified feminist social theory other than a disjunctive list of all of the distinct social theories that arise from each different "intersection."

As noted in chapter 1, intersectionality is the view that race, class, sexual preference, ethnicity, religion, nationality, ableness, and anything else combine in individuals or groups to result in distinct women's genders. Intersectionality was posited to solve the problem that second wave feminism was an overgeneralization of the experience of white, middle-class women. Both pre-intersectionality feminism and post-intersectionality feminisms share the assumption that there are three primary factors in feminist social theory: sex, gender, and oppression. Usually "sex" refers to female biology, "gender" to cultural constructions, and "oppression" to male dominance. I have argued thus far that sex, beginning with sexual designation at birth and extending through social identity as a human female, is influenced by culture and that oppression need not always be male dominance. Most important, however, is this theoretical release that comes after women are defined by their relationship to the FMP category: *the biological-cultural/sex-gender distinction no longer need be a starting point for feminist social theory because women are not defined by their common female sex.*

Feminist social theory begins in the relationship between individuals designated female and their local sex-gender systems. There is no need to posit female sex as something that all women share in order to have a coherent social theory and no need to give up the possibility of a coherent theory because a universal notion of female sex cannot be posited. Neither is it necessary to abandon the possibility of a coherent social theory that is an integral whole, which results in having to make do with a series of disjunctive theories for disjunctive identities. It also doesn't matter whether female sex is a matter of biology and culture, or culture only. Even more generally speaking, feminist social theory does not start from specific women's identities, either as impossibly generic women or large numbers of kinds of women. Identities are imagined as things in women, even when they are reduced to practices or performances that render the identities dispositions to behave in certain ways. Feminist social theorists themselves have varied identities, which can be described by all of the permutations permitted in intersectionality, but the new theoretical perspective is not a standpoint from a given identity. Rather, there is examination of the external conditions accompanying given identities, either one's own or someone else's. For a feminist social theorist, identities are not things in theorists or other women insofar as the identities are oppressive (and critical theory is about what is oppressive) but circumstances and situations that theorists try to understand, with goals of changing them.

Feminist social theorists may continue to describe, compare, and criticize all manner of intersected identities, but the problematic identities should be understood as capable of change. Without a fundamental assumption that problematic identities are mutable, social change and political action are foreclosed. Here is an example. The standard account of black female gender in the United States is to posit it as an identity first formed under conditions of slavery and persisting in black women today. It is assumed that the gender of black women is historically stable because without this assumption, feminist social theorists who think that women have attributes that make them black women could not address the current plight of poor black women as a legacy of slavery. But suppose we forget about identities and just consider the fact that during slavery in the eighteenth and nineteenth centuries, it was convenient for white slave owners and other white men to apply a premodern theory of sexuality to black women, a theory that was no longer applied to white women. This was a monosexual (as opposed to a dual-sexual) theory based on a biological view that female genitalia were the same as male, but turned inside out within the body. According to that (basically Aristotelean) theory, women were the aggressive and lascivious sex and their maternal obligations were not part of what was important about them as women. Thus the older theory of sex and gender did not posit the psychic side of maternity as an integral part of women's nature.[19] I have argued elsewhere that this premodern theory of female gender and sexuality served to conveniently naturalize the economic relations of whites to the sexuality and reproductive capacity of black women.[20] During slavery and segregation, white slave owners and later landlords and employers counted the children of black women as a financial asset because they represented desirable, free, or cheap labor. The sexuality of black women could be exploited by white men without guilt because it was viewed as unrestrained, and this exploitation was ultimately profitable if it resulted in black offspring.

During the late twentieth century, poor black women became objects of contempt sparking "welfare reform" because their children were a liability in an economy that did not need to exploit their labor (there were no jobs for undereducated black youth). Over the same time period, except for entertainment media images, black female sexuality lost its desirability as an economic "resource" for white men to exploit, although it was still considered unrestrained. Over both time periods, the premodern theory of sexuality as applied to poor black women made it possible to first encourage their "breeding" and then try to constrain it, in both cases by slighting their maternal feelings and obligations.[21]

This kind of analysis refers in both historical cases to an otherwise discarded theory of female gender, which downplays maternity but either values or devalues reproduction, depending on the economic interests of oppressors. It is possible only if one views individuals as real, but their identities as external and situational. Indeed, it is only when identities have this kind of distance from human beings that individuals can change their identities. Because the stereotypical cultural descriptions of black women's race and sex can be explained as the outcomes of economic calculations profitable for dominant interests, it is not surprising that black women who enter the middle class are reassigned to the gender theory that was previously reserved for white women only—the modern theory that incorporates women's experience of maternity into their gender. As a result, the maternity of middle-class black women can be taken seriously by whites as something that black women themselves value. As wives or heads of middle-class nuclear family consuming units, black women can be presumed to be "good mothers" because they are now able to buy the housing, clothing, appliances, medical care, and education that their children require, and to discipline themselves appropriately as consumers of those products.[22] (It is also expected that their children will be trained as consumers, thereby guaranteeing future profits for the purveyors of consumer goods.) But we know very well that female black slaves and black "welfare mothers" also had the feelings and obligations of "good mothers."

It is therefore not identities that change as black women change social class, but rather their material circumstances, understood as connected with appropriate values that serve the interests of the dominant groups. There is no need to posit a persistent "black woman's identity." This does not mean that there is nothing where the posited identity was presumed to reside or that nobody is home. The would-be "subject" is in every case a particular individual with a name, a time of birth, and an eventual death. The subject is a real person who cannot be represented as such in social theory because she is unique and her existence is pretheoretical—and posttheoretical. Theorists have mistakenly tried to imagine women subjects in ways that would capture their concrete attributes as persons (e.g., white, black, Latina, etc.). Instead, what needs to be imagined are common situations. This is not difficult to do because for a very long time, human societies have been structured in ways that result in different kinds of problems for subsets of their female populations; and for every kind of social problem—our subject here is *social* theory—there is a kind of situation or set of circumstances. What feminists, especially intersectionalists, have been imagining as identities needs to be exchanged for descriptions of social circumstances. *Feminist social theorists need to view identities as external to real persons.*

Inclusive feminist social theorists need to understand how the interests of dominant groups constrain women in different ways through circumstances and situations. It is not necessary that theorists be restricted to discussions about their own conditions only. (In case anyone hasn't noticed, that restriction also makes it very difficult for women of color to create theories about white women.) I am proposing that feminist social theorists proceed as though women, all women, have no identities—either as things within them or dispositions to behave in specific ways—and that they be willing to undertake meticulous descriptions of the kinds of circumstances and situations that operate for the benefit of other people, in which women variably find themselves.

Distinctness from Psychology

Feminist social theory should be understood as distinct from feminist psychological theory, for several reasons. The development of sex identity and gender in individuals is a different kind of process, about different kinds of entities than societies, institutions, and the practices and traditions attached to them. Causal links between individual psychology on one side and society and institutions on the other are weak, without hypotheses of psychological determinism, which would still not be sufficient to account for what goes on in societies and institutions. Needed also would be a *methodological individualism* to reduce societies and institutions to individuals, either ontologically or epistemologically. The ontological reduction would proceed from a claim that only individuals exist and that societies and institutions are "nothing but" individuals. The epistemological claim would translate knowledge about societies and institutions into knowledge about the psychologies of individuals. I am not going to offer an analysis of the problems with such reductions here, except to recognize a consensus among liberatory theorists regarding them: they are too literal to capture human experience at this time; they easily lend themselves to conservative attitudes about social and political change; they make it impossible to talk about specifically social problems. While it is true that only individuals act and make choices, it is also true that individuals experience their lives in societies and institutions as though those entities make decisions, act, do things to them, and withhold things from them.

The social institutions and practices that disadvantage women compared to men and reproduce those disadvantages are imagined but real things that affect the real experiences and psychologies of individual women, of persons. In whatever ways women learn how to exist in these institutions and comply with their practices, their individual characters, personalities, and dispositions to believe in appropriate ways are not sufficient to account for the realities of the institutions. The individual woman is always within, and to varying degrees at odds with, any given institution that affects her directly or mediates her relations with others. (The same can be said about the relation of men to institutions, even though they may dominate the institutions and, through the mechanisms of the institutions, dominate women.)

Iris Young has provided a detailed, lucid critique of Nancy Chodorow's thesis that the formation of male gender in nuclear families with aloof fathers is also an account of male domination in society. Young is concerned to distinguish between theories of male gender formation and theories of male domination, so as to clear a space and state the requirements for feminist social change.[23] Of course, it could be countered that dominance, specifically dominance over women, is an integral component of male gender. If that claim were true (which it isn't because not all men dominate women), it would still fail to account for social institutions that were oppressive to women. While the most dominant men may be the most successful participants in the most important institutions in a culture (e.g., big corporations, government, the military, the academy, the church, the legal system, and, in the "private" sphere, marriage), men who are not typically dominant as a gender trait also benefit from such institutions.

Important social institutions have an inertial momentum that individuals experience as though the institutions themselves strove to perpetuate and reproduce themselves. Institutional authorities behave as though tradition were a value in itself. Institutions thus resist change that issues from individual psychologies, character, and dispositions. Institutions do change according to internal customs and rules, and they can be changed drastically through external intervention such as legislation, revolution, or war. They can also wither away or become more powerful. History is replete with all these kinds of institutional change, but there are no historical examples of an abrupt demise or radical change in institutions as a result of changes in individual psychologies alone. If space and time permitted, I would argue that it is easier to change institutions through organized political activity, resulting in new laws or the repeal of old ones, than it is to change individual psychologies. But even if a feminist psychological theory effortlessly resulted in changes in individual gender psychologies, feminists would still need to organize politically to change the institutions that relied on the psychologies disadvantageous to women.

The work of feminist psychological theory is therefore not a viable substitute for the work of political change. For that reason, feminist social theory, which has social change as its goal because it is a part of feminism as critical theory, needs to be undertaken as if psychologies of gender were irrelevant to the life worlds of individuals as mediated through institutions—even though they are highly relevant. Psychology is the immediate environment of individual awareness and the locus of individual happiness and misery. But social theory should ignore it because changing psychology will not change society and institutions. For example, during the last quarter of the twentieth century, gay and lesbian couples became visible and, to varying degrees, accepted as families within wider heterosexual communities. That represents important psychological change among homosexuals, as well as heterosexuals, and it has led to significant changes in private lifestyles, including raising children in families with same-sex parents. However, these psychological and social changes do not in themselves give homosexual couples access to the institutional benefits available to heterosexual couples because in most places, they cannot marry. Gay and lesbian marriage, as participation in the official institution of marriage, requires political organization and action toward legislation that specifically permits same-sex individuals to marry.[24]

NOTES

1. Susan R. Bordo, *The Flight to Objectivity: Essays on Cartesianism and Culture* (Albany: State University of New York Press, 1987); Pierre Bourdieu, *Masculine Domination*, trans. Richard Nice (Stanford, Calif.: Stanford University Press, 2001). As will become evident in this chapter and the next, cultural analyses of psychology are not that different from psychological analyses of culture.

2. Sandra Harding, "Why Has the Sex/Gender System Become Visible Only Now?" in *Discovering Reality: Feminist Perspectives on Epistemology, Metaphysics, Methodology, and Philosophy of Science*, ed. Sandra Harding and Merrill B. Hintikka, (Dordrecht, Holland: Reidel, 1983), 311.

3. Harding, "Why Has the Sex/Gender System Become Visible Only Now?" 320–21. Marx and Engels did not succeed in reducing gender to class by showing how removing class oppressions would solve the "woman question" (which is what the reduction would have amounted to in their terms). Rather, they treated the heterosexual man–woman relationship in marriage as a prehistorical given. For a convincing textual foundation for this claim, see Donna Haraway, "'Gender' for a Marxist Dictionary," in *Simians, Cyborgs, and Women: The Reinvention of Nature* (New York: Routledge, 1991), 127–48.

4. Knowledge of the relevant science is a cognitive condition, perhaps most important in intellectual communities. Broader social conditions in the United States enabled the discovery of what Harding calls the "sex/gender system," about which one could speculate as follows. The civil rights legislation included sex as an impermissible ground for discrimination. The drop in purchasing power of the U.S. dollar, accompanied by decreases in the growth of manufacturing and industrial productivity, made it necessary for wives in nuclear families to work outside their homes to sustain their families economically, and the rise of the service sector of the economy provided millions of new jobs for them. At the same time, nuclear family units became the primary consumers of an increasingly consumer-driven economy, now dependent for growth on new housing starts, new cars, and the purchase of big-ticket appliances. During the same period, white women began attending colleges and professional schools in increasing numbers. The control over reproduction afforded by the birth control pill, and the relaxation of puritanical sexual mores during the late 1960s, further contributed to greater mobility and autonomy for American women. Thus Harding's question can be viewed as the historical question of what made full-blown second wave women's liberation a social force, as well as an academic one (in the form of feminist scholarship). And although second wave academic feminists deserve great credit and gratitude for their achievements, it is likely that the viability of

second wave feminism in the academy was an effect, rather than a cause, of the economic, political, and social changes outside of the academy. The aversion and hostility of the American public toward academic feminists and their ideas makes it improbable that feminists caused the social changes.

5. Many earlier advocates for women (e.g., Mary Wollstonecraft and John Stuart Mill) thought that the way women were treated in society, particularly their exclusion from educational institutions, was morally wrong. But these writers emphasized the importance of educating women so that they could better fulfill the obligations of their traditional roles as wives and mothers. Mary Wollstonecraft's *A Vindication of the Rights of Women* and John Stuart Mill's *The Subjection of Women,* as well as other classic texts of the first wave, are often neglected by second wave feminists, as well as third wave, but they remain important for an understanding of the intellectual history of feminism.

6. In contrast to Harding's posit and my own, there is Gayle Rubin's definition of a "sex/gender system" that I quoted in chapter 2. Rubin defines the system as "the set of arrangements by which a society transforms biological sexuality into products of human activity and in which these transformed sexual needs are satisfied." See Gayle Rubin, "The Traffic in Women: Notes on the 'Political Economy' of Sex," in *Toward an Anthropology of Women,* ed. Rayna R. Reither (New York: Monthly Review Press, 1975); reprinted in *The Second Wave: A Reader in Feminist Theory,* ed. Linda Nicholson, (New York: Routledge, 1975), 28. The biological foundation assumed by Rubin is problematic, as I keep indicating in general terms, and I am not sure what sexual needs are or how they can be transformed and then satisfied in their transformed condition. These are objections I raise on a general theoretical level and they are partly why I am not considering Rubin's definition in the discussion above. Nonetheless, her introduction of the concept of a sex-gender system is an invaluable contribution to feminist theory, as is her attendant anthropological work on the use of women as commodities in kinship systems ("Traffic in Women").

7. Some feminist should write "The Terrible Things Women Have Done to Other Women and Why They Should Be Held Responsible for Them." While feminists have paid attention to competition among women as an effect of patriarchy and have emphasized the value of solidarity and sisterhood among women, they have not yet focused on the ways in which women have and do harm one another, in contexts where they are relatively free of domination by men. Such neglect idealizes and infantilizes women, to the detriment of individual practical empowerment. In this regard, Toril Moi's account of how Hélène Cixous dominated and perhaps humiliated Simone de Beauvoir is refreshing to read. Cixous managed to publish her celebration of generosity toward other women's texts, "The Laugh of the Medusa," in which neither de Beauvoir nor her writings are mentioned at all, as part of a 1975 issue of *L'Arc* that was devoted to de Beauvoir and had her picture on its cover (Toril Moi, *What Is a Woman?* [New York: Oxford University Press, 1999], 297–99). There is also Susan Ostrov Weisser and Jennifer Fleischner's edited anthology *Feminist Nightmares: Women at Odds* (New York: New York University Press, 1994), but the articles are mainly about literary and historical conflicts or general cases comfortably removed from the lived experience of feminists. Needed in this area is some healthy discomfort that could spur self-examination.

8. Indeed, the theoretical tendency of biologists to treat genes as the primary subject of evolution both erases and reinscribes a biological foundation for human

male–male dominance on a cultural level. Maxine Sheets-Johnstone's current work emphasizes the importance of relating biological theories of behavior to whole human beings and not just their genes. I refer here to "Real Male-Male Competition" (keynote address at Pacific Society of Women in Philosophy meeting, University of Oregon, November 2003). See also Sheets-Johnstone, *The Roots of Power: Animate Form and Gendered Bodies* (LaSalle, Ill.: Open Court, 1994). Nonetheless, evolutionary biology explains neither culture nor psychology unless cultural conditions and psychological factors are first projected backward onto species history—something that always results in a circular explanation. For further discussion of the tendency to assume a biological or evolutionary foundation for male dominance generally, see the second section of the conclusion to this volume.

9. For ideas of Marxian critical theories deriving from the Frankfurt School, see Raymond Geuss, *The Idea of a Critical Theory* (New York: Cambridge University Press, 1981). For a feminist view of critical theory, see Iris Young, *Inclusion and Democracy* (Oxford: Oxford University Press, 2000), 10–11; Young, *Justice and the Politics of Difference* (Princeton, N.J.: Princeton University Press, 1990), 5–8.

10. Laurie Shrage, *Abortion and Social Responsibility: Depolarizing the Debate* (New York: Oxford University Press, 2003).

11. William Saletan, *Bearing Right: How Conservatives Won the Abortion War* (Berkeley: University of California Press, 2003).

12. Virginia Woolf, *Three Guineas* (New York: Harcourt, 1938), 17–18.

13. Pierre Bourdieu, *Masculine Domination*, trans. Richard Nice (Stanford, Calif.: Stanford University Press, 2001), 4.

14. Bourdieu, *Masculine Domination,* 5.

15. Freud also used this concept, as I will discuss in chapter 6. For more on this anthropological concept, see Bonnie Mann, *Women's Liberation and the Sublime: Kant, Feminism, Postmodernism, Environment* (forthcoming, Oxford University Press).

16. This arrogance is typical of her external class privilege—Virginia Woolf's race and class insularity are fair game for the critics of second wave feminism, as described in chapter 1, above. Woolf grew up with servants whom her husband, Leonard, later described as "inherited" within her family (see Leonard Woolf, *Beginning Again: An Autobiography of the Years 1911–1918* [New York: Harcourt Brace Jovanovich, 1964], 87). Throughout their married life, except during World War II, when they lived in the country, the Woolfs always had servants and sometimes as many as four nurses to attend to Virginia when she became "mad" and suicidal (Leonard Woolf, *Downhill All the Way: An Autobiography of the Years 1919–1939* [New York: Harcourt Brace Jovanovich], 1967).

Furthermore, when in support of the quoted passage, Woolf chronicles the poverty and squalor of the lives of the daughters of educated men, as compared to their sons, she may be acting out a myth of her external class which held that women, in desiring more luxury, betrayed class values. Men of the English upper-middle and upper classes traditionally prided themselves on their ability to rough it in daily life, which women were expected to find difficult. For the explicit origin of the tradition of Spartan living conditions among the British upper-middle class, which was a new class in the seventeenth century, see John Locke, *Some Thoughts Concerning Education,* where he prescribes (he was a physician) abstemious diets, trained bowels, hard beds, bare heads, and wet feet for the young sons of gentlemen: "As the Strength of the Body lies chiefly in being able to endure Hardships, so also does that of the Mind. And the great Principle and Foundation of all Virtue and Worth is placed in this, That a Man is able to *deny himself* his own Desires, cross his own Inclinations, and purely follow what Reason dicers as best, tho' the Appetite lean the other way." John Locke, *Some Thoughts Concerning Education*, in *The Educational Writings of John Locke*, ed. James A. Axtell (Cambridge: Cambridge University Press, 1968), 112–13.

See also my discussion of Locke's theory of education for the sons of his social class in Zack, *Bachelors of Science: Seventeenth-Century Identity, Then and Now* (Philadelphia: Temple University Press, 1996), 141–54. Consider, as well, the self-denial of Christopher Tietjens in Ford Madox Ford's four-novel sequence *Parade's End*, which chronicles the end of colonialist upper-class English privilege. Tietjen's self-indulgent wife, Sylvia, repeatedly betrays and abuses him by mocking and sub-verting his class-based virtues and values.

17. Susan R. Bordo, *Unbearable Weight: Feminism, Western Culture, and the Body* (Berkeley: University of California Press, 1993), 139–64.

18. In her report on contemporary men's fashion images, "Beauty (Re)Discovers the Male Body," Bordo exuberantly and with a certain "campiness" (which may or may not be parody, of either homosexual male lust or the lust of middle-aged het-erosexual men who ogle young women) celebrates the display of male beauty and sexuality in recent ads, particularly those for underpants. The pictures accompany-ing Bordo's text display young men in poses that objectify their muscular torsos, but-tocks, and genitals. Many feminist critics of female fashion images have protested the objectification of young women's breasts, buttocks, and crotches in analogous ads. Does Bordo think that young men are immune from the same "crystallization of culture" that she sees in women's self-destructive emulation and self-comparison in response to mass media presentations of beauty ideals for women? I am reluctant to conclude that she is unconcerned with the well-being of young men who see them-selves projected as sexual objects for mass consumption, but there are no reassur-ing clues in her text. Susan R. Bordo, "Beauty (Re)Discovers the Male Body," in *Beauty Matters*, ed. Peg Zeglin Brand (Bloomington: Indiana University Press, 2000), 112–54.

19. See my discussion of this theory, which peaked before the eighteenth century, in *Bachelors of Science*, 154–67.

20. Naomi Zack, "The American Sexualization of Race," in *RACE/SEX: Their Same-ness, Difference, and Interplay* (New York: Routledge, 1997), 145–56.

21. Zack, "American Sexualization of Race," 154–56.

22. This doesn't stop cultural pundits from judging poor black women according to the modern theory in the type of insult added to injury so typical of American racism. First, poor black women were circumstantially constructed as lacking in the psychic dimension of maternity, and then they were vilified for it, according to stan-dards and family structures that the construction precluded them from having.

23. Iris Marion Young, "Is Male Gender Identity the Cause of Male Domination?" in *Throwing Like a Girl and Other Essays in Feminist Philosophy and Social Theory* (Bloomington: Indiana University Press), 36–61.

24. Indeed, as I revise this chapter, the *New York Times* reports that the Supreme Court of Massachusetts has ruled in favor of gay plaintiffs claiming that the restric-tion of marriage to men and women is discriminatory. The Massachusetts court has

advised its state legislature that it has six months to produce legislation that will enable same-sex couples to marry in Massachusetts. If marriage becomes legal for same-sex couples in Massachusetts, additional legal action will be necessary to determine whether such marriage will be recognized in other states (Terence Neilan, "High Court in Massachusetts Rules Gays Have Right to Marry," *New York Times*, November 18, 2003, A1). I think that from a feminist perspective, the freedom of same-sex couples to marry is generally liberatory (although some feminists may wonder how same-sex couples would see the institution of marriage as in itself liberatory, even given its financial and legal benefits).

5

Inclusive Feminist Psychological Theory and Gender Development

If the sociological and anthropological studies of the twentieth century taught one uncontested lesson, and if the problems raised by intersectionality can be generalized, the result is a shared feminist understanding that women have led a vast variety of kinds of lives and struggled in multiplicities of circumstances. Cultures with different gender roles for women may require different theories of gender formation, so that any encompassing theory would have to be quite abstract. For instance, a theory of gender formation for a society where gender differences are not strongly emphasized needs to be different from one in which they are.[1] Nonetheless, third wave feminists can reasonably require that psychological theories of gender development neither accept stereotypes that devalue women nor posit determinisms of biology or culture in the development of female gender(s).

In chapters 3–4, I claimed that individuals become women in cultures that preexist them; in this chapter I will focus on that process of individual gender development in three ways. The first is a brief consideration of Freudian psychoanalytic theory and post-Freudian psychoanalytic theory as feminists have revised it. The second is a consideration of what contemporary empirical psychology can contribute to a feminist understanding of the development of female gender in individuals. The third is a cognitive approach to women's subjectivity. As before, I am proceeding on the basis of a definition of women as those who are assigned to or identify with the historical, socially constructed FMP category of female birth designees, biological mothers, or primary sexual choices of men.

FREUDIAN AND POST-FREUDIAN PSYCHOANALYTIC THEORY

Sigmund Freud made lasting gender-neutral contributions to thought about human nature but founded a theory that was relative to his immediate patriarchal bourgeois culture. Freud's theory was masculinist and essentialist, as well as impossible to confirm or disconfirm with empirical evidence.[2] Freud's most enduring contributions were that early childhood experience has a disproportionate lifelong effect on an individual's mind and her development, that people are consciously unaware of a good part of their own emotional lives, and that gender identity and sexual desire are important human motivations.

Freud's culturally relative theory was based on the premise that the primary object of the libido (biologically driven sexual desire) of all infants is their mother. Infants and very young children experience oral and anal stages of libidinal organization and gratification. On reaching the genital stage of development at about age five, boys become aware of their masculinity as centered in their penises, and they desire their mothers sexually. They are also aware of genital differences between males and females, and they believe that women and girls once had penises but were castrated. Boys therefore fear that their fathers will castrate them if they express their sexual desire for their mothers. To avoid castration, boys repress those desires and identify with their fathers in the hope that when they grow up, they will be able to express their sexual desire for women other than their mothers. This process of repression creates a superego with the ability to make abstract moral judgments.

Freud's theory was different for girls, who he assumed were physically inferior to boys in not having a penis and morally inferior in not developing a superego. On reaching the genital stage, girls are also aware of the genital differences among family members, and they blame their mothers for their own lack of penises because they think that their mothers created them as copies of themselves. Girls desire their fathers sexually but have no reason to repress that desire because they believe that they have already been castrated. The absence of repression entails that girls cannot develop a superego, and they develop a lifelong resentment of males known as penis envy. Freud had a second theory of sexual development, which posited both male and female libidinal drives in both boys and girls but he is believed not to have been able to resolve this idea of universal bisexuality, with the foregoing oedipal theory that became the theory typically ascribed to him.[3] There have been modifications of Freud's theory that are less masculinist in the depiction of women's development and nature. Helen Deutsch, Karen Horney, and Clara Thompson claimed that the penis is not intrinsically valued as a physical entity but as a phallus, or symbol of the greater power that men, compared to women, have in society. Erik Erikson, following Bruno Bettelheim, disputed the existence of penis envy and used the concept of womb envy to refer to the resentment and sense of lack that males experience as a result of their inability to create children. Erikson revised Freud's devaluation of women as passive, envious, and weak, toward an understanding that women have distinctive personality traits that are positive in their own right, and positive bodily images of their own "inner space" and ability to nurture.[4]

Nancy Chodorow's modification of psychoanalytic theory into an account of the *cultural* reproduction of male and female gender roles in the family has been important to feminists. (A role is a set of socially expected behaviors, while a trait is an attribute of a person. Mothering would be a role, nurturing a trait.) Chodorow noted that in all societies, women are mothers. She agreed with earlier psychoanalytic claims that mothers are primary love objects for both male and female infants. Her innovation was to claim that women and daughters identify with each other; to mature into a woman, the daughter need not change that primary identification with her mother as a nurturing and relational individual. By contrast, a boy is expected to develop traits of autonomy and independence that not only are different from his mother's traits but require emotional distance from his mother, if not destruction of his earlier bond with her. Breaking away from Mother and being different from her, or not-her, is a primary component of masculinity. By contrast, femininity consists in being like Mother, which results in a female identity based more on relating to and caring for others than in being autonomously individuated. When a girl becomes a woman, her heterosexual relationship with a man may not fulfill her emotional needs of attachment, but becoming a mother herself does fulfill those needs.[5]

Freud, Deutsch, Horney, and Thompson assumed that all boys and girls had the same reactions to having or not having a penis or a phallus (the symbolic representation of male power). Underlying that assumption was acceptance of a masculine social order in which men were not only more powerful than women but considered superior to them as human beings. Erikson attacked the notion of male superiority by positing distinctive and valuable female traits, but his close connection of the existence of such traits with biological difference is a strong version of biological determinism, especially when the gender-specific traits coincide with traditional male and female roles in societies. Chodorow, without appearing to rely on biological determinism, accounts for the development of traditional gender traits by showing how gender traits result from the interaction of sex-typed roles in the family.

However, Chodorow's theory does not account for the existence of gender-specific roles in the family, unless one assumes that the gender traits, as caused by parental gender roles, in turn inculcate the gender roles in successive generations. But if gender roles cause gender traits, which in turn cause gender roles when a child grows up, lost is the force of Chodorow's account of gender traits as arising from the dynamic interaction between gender roles. The child could learn gender traits through simple imitation of the same-sex parent. There is then no need for Chodorow's theory of gender trait development, which requires that individuals develop their gender traits by participating in the dynamics of preexisting gender roles in the family. But if gender traits are not sufficient to cause gender roles, then what is the origin of gender roles? They could result from imitation of the parent of the same sex as the child. Furthermore, although Chodorow focuses on gender roles (which are more dynamic than gender traits), she assumes that gender-specific traits in the family are always connected to gender-specific roles, and vice versa. Such a uniform lineup between roles and traits assumes a fixity to women's nature that allow little room for personal change.

All of the psychoanalytic theories work with models of traditional parent gender roles, in ways that leave little space for changing those roles insofar as they are oppressive to women. It is not the case that women mother in all families, that they do so in the same way, or that all women are primarily relational and nurturing and all men autonomous and well individuated from women. The problem with the psychoanalytic accounts is that in purporting to be theories of universal gender nature and development, they do not allow a conceptual space for criticizing aspects of gender nature and development which result from male dominance that is unjust and could be otherwise. In this sense, the psychoanalytic theories can work as an ideology of what Sandra Harding calls the sex/gender system that has male dominance built into it (see chapter 4). What prevents these theories from being the nonideological descriptions and explanations that they purport to be is their lack of empirical support as universal descriptions, as well as the fact that they present gender roles and traits as an inexorable system (which it would be futile for individuals to resist or change in their own enactments of it).

As I indicated in chapter 1, the collapse of foundations in white feminism during the 1980s did not cause a downturn in the business of academic feminism. Au contraire. Part of the subsequent boom was fueled by the discovery and interpretation of so-called French feminism, particularly the works of Hélène Cixous, Luce Irigaray, and Julia Kristeva. Christine Delphy energetically criticized this trend in her *Yale French Studies* article, "The Invention of French Feminism: An Essential Move," in 1995. Delphy pointed out that both Cixous and Irigaray have insisted at various times that they are not feminists, and she described Kristeva's deliberate repudiation of women's activism as "prefeminist." Delphy also accused American feminists of appropriating the ideas of "French feminists" in order to return to biologically determinist notions of a universal women's nature, without having to take responsibility on their own for such ahistorical and fundamentally masculinist constructions of women.[6]

Delphy's claim that so-called French feminism is not considered feminism in France has apparently not been without influence. Toril Moi's 1985 *Sexual/*

Textual Politics was a widely read introduction of Cixous, Irigaray, and Kristeva to Anglo-American readers. But in her 1999 preface to *What Is a Woman?* Moi repudiates, as a failure of "voice" in her younger self, her apparent agreement with Cixous and Irigaray's claim that every integrated whole must be phallic.[7] Perhaps in a more direct response to Delphy's criticism, Kelly Oliver describes her 2000 *French Feminism Reader* as "a representative sample of French feminism in an Anglo-American context."[8]

Given the foregoing caveats (which should be partly understood as intrafeminist politics), it is important to consider whether the psychological theories of Cixous, Irigaray, and Kristeva can contribute to feminist psychological theory in ways that neither accept stereotypes that devalue women nor posit determinisms of biology or culture. As with the more traditional Freudians and Chodorow, I will proceed here with schematics of the main ideas.

Many commentators believe that Cixous, Irigaray, and Kristeva write about women's psyche on the basis of Jacques Lacan's interpretation of Freud. Lacan reconfigured Freud's theory of infantile sexuality on the basis of Ferdinand de Saussure's theory of meaning. According to de Saussure, human existence takes place in a linguistic symbolic order in which symbols or signs signify only other symbols or signs. Within this order, to be (exist) is to be a signifier, but no signifier has intrinsic meaning because every signifier's meaning is determined by its relation to other signs which it is not.[9] Lacan located the human entry into the symbolic order at the point in development when a child's father separates the child from its initial harmonious unity with its mother. The child is presumed to be male, and in entering language it becomes a signifier and a phallus that is constituted by its memory of *the imaginary*, which is the maternal unity that it now lacks. The desire for this unity is repressed and that repression creates the unconscious: "The unconscious is constituted by the effects of speech on the subject, it is the dimension in which the subject is determined in the development of the effects of speech, consequently the unconscious is structured like a language."[10]

Not only is the unconscious an effect of language for Lacan, but so is sexual difference as such:

> What I am saying, following Freud, who provides abundant evidence of it, is that this function [i.e., the biological function of reproduction] is not represented as such in the psyche. In the psyche, there is nothing by which the subject may situate himself as a male or female being. . . . In his psyche, the subject situates only equivalents of the function of reproduction—activity and passivity, which by no means represent it in an exhaustive way. . . . The polarity of the male and the female being is represented only by the polarity of activity, which is manifested through the *Triebe*, and of passivity, which is passivity only in relation to the exterior, *gegen die ausseren Reize.*[11]

Although Lacan appears to overlook Freud's very modernist and biologist realism about sexual differences in individuals (i.e., that men have penises and women do not), Freud claimed in "The Transformations of Puberty" that only activity and passivity counted in a psychoanalytic sense: "One uses masculine and feminine at times in the sense of *activity* and *passivity*, again in the *biological* sense, and then also in the *sociological* sense. The first of these three meanings is the most essential and the only one utilizable in psychoanalysis."[12]

Lacan can be understood as claiming that as a subject of psychoanalysis, the sexual human being is male only in the attribute of being active as a social and even biological subject; this active/male being is constituted by language. Thus for all practical purposes, gender, as we normally understand it, is an effect of language, whereas the roots of gender are perhaps not linguistic, except for the ways in which language affects the unconscious that is the subject of psychoanalysis. One would not think that Lacan's Saussurian reconstitution of Freud were promising for feminist psychological theory because it not only privileges masculine experience but severs existence from physical reality by having everything important about sex and gender take place in language. There is also the further question of whether feminist thought that proceeds on this basis can contribute to inclusive feminism.

Cixous takes up Lacan's claim that the symbolic order is composed of sexual binaries of male and female.[13] But she goes a step beyond mere taxonomy in claiming that the feminine side of the binaries is always vanquished and killed by the masculine side. Relying on Jacques Derrida's thesis that, in relations between signs that produce meaning, written language is more unstable than spoken language because of the factor of "presence" in speech, Cixous's strategy for the liberation of the female part of the Lacanian binary is twofold. First, women must write about their distinctive female existence, physicality, and experience. And second, women must redefine themselves out of the traditional binary system of male-female by identifying themselves as the sex that is multiple because women are inherently bisexual. Through the *jouissance* of this bisexual writing (which can be done by men as well as women), the old binaries may be overthrown.[14] Cixous's best-known works as translated into English, "The Laugh of the Medusa" and "Castration or Decapitation?" are deliberately written in a mix of narrative styles that combines poetry and prose in ways that enact the pleasure and liberation she advocates.[15]

Irigaray's *Speculum of the Other Woman*[16] was her second doctoral thesis in philosophy and psychoanalysis, and it eventually alienated her from her Lacanian colleagues.[17] Irigaray connected the notion of binary opposites to de Beauvoir's idea that man is the universal subject and woman the negative Other, and she applied that insight to parts of the canon in philosophy and psychoanalysis. Irigaray uses her trope of a speculum or mirror to argue that traditional philosophers and psychoanalysts mirror and privilege themselves as male subjects in their theories about human nature and the world. Irigaray's speculum metaphorically reflects the distorted and degraded representations of women in traditional texts. Her positive thesis is that the distinctive qualities of women need to be respected and honored as differences that exist beyond and instead of "envelopes" to be used by men. In *I Love to You,* Irigaray builds on her Marxist analysis of women as commodities in culture to argue for the representation of female difference as such in the legal code.[18]

Kristeva's core psychoanalytic concepts are presented in *Powers of Horror* and in the section "From This Side" in *About Chinese Women.*[19] To the traditional Freudian fear of castration, she adds a positive motive for the individuation of persons by claiming that the child experiences the mother as *abject,* a disgusting threat to its own boundaries. After the early desires for the mother and the connection with her are repressed, they return incestuously. For men, the repressed material emerges in projects of artistic creation, and for women, in childbirth and mothering. Insofar as both repression and the return of what is repressed occur in a symbolic framework, the reality of the abject expresses itself through the tones and rhythms of language, while the syntactic (grammatical) and semantic (cognitively meaningful) parts of language occur within the turn away from the abject. According to Kristeva, women do not exist as such, apart from their marginalization. Upon entering into language, the female child has the choice of identifying with either the abject body of the mother (the semiotic) or with her father (the symbolic):

> Women. We have the luck to be able to take advantage of a biological peculiarity to give a name to that which, in monotheistic capitalism, remains on this side of the threshold of repression, voice stilled, body mute, always foreign to the social order. . . . *Woman as such* does not exist. Either the term dissolves into as many individual cases . . . or, the problems of women have no interest except inasmuch they bring to an impasse the most serious problems of our type of society: how to live not only without God, but without man?[20]

Kristeva apparently means here that being a woman is first of all a factual contingency—one happens to be a woman rather than a man. Her emphasis on this contingency could be based on an assumption that there is an underlying human identity for both men and women. In the second part of the passage she seems to require an impossible universal definition that captures particulars. If whether a person is a woman or a man is a factual contingency and Kristeva thinks that women are too varied to define universally, then how would it be possible for Kristeva to say what the underlying human essence is, since generic human beings, even more than women, exhibit great variety? If Kristeva means to evoke the problems with any definition, then she has not shown why this is a special problem for defining women (see chapter 2, above).

The meaning of Kristeva's claim that women do not exist could lie in her Lacanian emphasis of Freud's view that maleness and femaleness are not in the unconscious as such. Since maleness is activity in the unconscious and femaleness is passivity, femaleness does not exist in contrast to maleness. But to extend that claim from its psychoanalytic theoretical context to human gender ontology within language is to reify psychoanalytic theory in a way that even Freud probably did not intend. The extension also reads what Lacan says about the symbolic, linguistic order back into the unconscious. Lacan would have no reason to do this, since it would blur the very distinction he wants to make between language and the nonlinguistic. In Kristeva's defense, it could be claimed that her entire project is to break down the division between the linguistic and prelinguistic, the expressed and repressed. But it is puzzling that she would first do it at the expense of women and then try to use that as a basis for valorizing women's contribution to the symbolic order.

Cixous and Kristeva both rely on language and the symbolic order as the foundation of both male and female gender. Irigaray also begins with the linguistic sex-gender system, but she tries to change the Freudian mythology of this system with a new myth that recenters women. Whether gender is differentiated only with the acquisition of language would seem to be a straightforward empirical matter, but the accounts in question should probably be understood less as descriptions of individual development and more as accounts of the entire Western psychic system, which is lived out *as though* gender were acquired with language. This reliance on language to either account for gender differences or, in Irigaray's case reconfigure them, is clearly not a form of biological determinism on its surface, although it would seem to be a kind of cultural determinism. The child learns a language and through that process acquires the gender that the linguistic system assigns to her. Once within the symbolic order, extraordinary liberatory efforts are required to resist stereotypes of gender—one would have to change the local language system, at least for oneself. From a psychological perspective, such resistance is necessarily personal, so one should not fault Cixous, for instance, for placing the burden of liberation on an individual woman's ability to write. Irigaray's resistance to the gender system is also a linguistic practice, that of reinterpreting the canon of Western letters and psychoanalysis and changing the old myths for new ones that can be deliberately lived. However, as Cynthia Willett points out, Irigaray seems to be uninterested in the material conditions that accompany the present male-centered system or in the conditions that would be necessary to sustain the new system she envisions.[21]

Of the three writers, Kristeva offers the most deeply psychoanalytic and original account of female gender. The choice she postulates when a female child begins to enter the linguistic realm is a radical innovation in psychoanalytic theory because of its focus on female development, as well as the possibility it opens to imagine early autonomy on a theoretical level. Still, the problem with this oedipal moment, even theoretically, is that it is not accessible to adult introspection, and it is not likely to work as a definitive moment for female gender in all cultural circumstances. Placed within the highly fraught, still-Freudian drama of the nuclear family, Kristeva's first choice could easily foreclose subsequent choices or minimize their importance.

Cixous, Irigaray, and Kristeva all encapsulate women's experience in symbolic orders, and they write as though changes in myth or language, in what theorists believe to be true about women, is the whole of what affects women's lives or is important about them. Writing oneself, finding oneself against masculinist myths and texts, or identifying oneself as having made a choice that one cannot remember making are not universal conditions or even possibilities for the psyches of all women. The conditions and possibilities do not hold for those whose lives are overwhelmed by the exigencies of biological existence, and even those who are only sometimes so overwhelmed. Surely, feminist psychological theory should not exclude conditions of material oppression as a starting point for liberatory change and self-empowerment. Complete encapsulation of gender within language and myth suffocates any real and meaningful existence outside of the purview of theory.

EMPIRICAL ACCOUNTS OF THE DEVELOPMENT OF GENDER AND PSYCHOLOGY

Feminist psychological theory need not capture everything important about the entire person as a concrete individual. It is sufficient if it can account for the acquisition of gender by individuals. In contrast to psychoanalytic theory, cognitive accounts of gender development, such as those now found in empirical psychology, allow for the possibility of individual change in oppressive aspects of gender. Of course, empirical psychology is no bed of roses either. Feminists now working within the field have good reason to view masculine gender bias as both a professional problem and an ongoing methodological program which structures many studies toward finding data that confirm notions of biologically determined psychological and cultural differences between human males and females, and supports beliefs that male traits and interests are superior to female ones.[22] However, feminist theorists outside of the field are at liberty to focus on psychological data and conclusions that they have antecedent reason to believe are relatively free of such bias. (That is, feminist philosophers are not obligated to critique and reform the profession or methodologies of empirical psychologists, nor could they expect any greater success than feminist psychologists who attempted to correct masculinist biases in philosophy.) There are now sufficient empirical psychological studies of gender identity, roles, and development that appear to be neither biologically deterministic, nor masculinist, and such studies support the theoretical presumption that any child develops in a preformed gender system. These empirical accounts all apply learning theory to gender development and this is why they are of great importance to feminist psychological theory across disciplines.

As discussed in chapter 4, female gender is not determined by biological female sex in a way unmediated by culture. The learning of gender by individuals can be understood as an active cognitive process, provided that behaviorist explanations of it have been exhausted and rejected.[23] In this section I will focus on cognitive accounts of gender learning, as well as the gaps in such accounts, that allow for individual agency. In the next section, I will consider how those gaps are important to women's subjectivity, both within the context of feminist psychological theory and outside of it.

Any specific gender system determines the child's gender identity, traits, and roles, given one assumption: the subsequently female child is assigned female gender status at birth. In the majority of cases, this assignment lines up with female chromosomes (XX), genitalia and gonads (vagina, uterus, and ovaries), and hormones ("normal" amounts of androgens and nonandrogenic progesterone). Although psychologists broadly accept this paradigm case of biological femaleness, studies indicate that chromosomes are not necessary for female gender development. Female hormones and genitalia do appear to be necessary, but the child's social environment and how others regard her have great influence on her gender development, regardless of the presence or absence of chromosomes, genitalia, and hormones considered female.[24]

There are no studies of unambiguous biological male infants raised as females. Given the significance of the penis as a phallus, or symbol of masculine power, it would probably be impossible for caregivers to raise an unambiguous biological male as a female. But given a nonessentialist view of female gender, the belief of some male-to-female transsexuals that they are inherently women might be a case of female gender development by individuals who are unambiguous biological males. The existence of male-to-female transsexuals who were raised as males suggests that there is more to gender development than biology and culture, even when culture is understood to include parental or caregiver attitudes. (The same could be said about female-to-male transsexuals who were raised as female.) And if we consider the complaints of violation by intersexed individuals who received female assignment surgery and hormones and were socialized as females it is further evident that genitalia, hormones, and socialization are not sufficient for the development of female gender. Barring an obscure and unconfirmed metaphysical gender substance, one obvious thing that could account for the dissatisfactions of both assigned-female intersexuals and pretransition male-to-female transsexuals is the absence in these individuals of active choice of and compliance with their assigned gender. Such cooperation with gender assignment might not be visible when the child's own gender identity preferences coincide with expectations of others about his or her gender.

There is substantial positive evidence of the presence of active choice and compliance when biologically paradigm female children develop into women, or biologically paradigm male children develop into men. Psychologists implicitly allow for active choice and compliance in much contemporary gender development theory by their widespread recognition of individual variation in gender development. Despite the prevalence and acceptance of gender stereotypes in society, individuals show great variety in traits they have and interests they pursue that are typical of their gender type. Writers who are not biological determinists about gender development note that some children are more attuned to gender differences and are themselves more gender stereotyped. For those children (and later adults), gender is believed to be more central to their "self-concept."[25]

During the 1970s, researchers realized that measures of typical masculine or feminine gender roles did not line up with sex identity as male or female. This led to measurements of androgyny, in which masculinity and femininity were treated as separate dimensions, so that a person could score high on tests as both masculine and feminine. Early conclusions that individuals with a high androgyny score were better adjusted were revised when it became evident that it was a high score in masculinity alone that was socially beneficial. By the 1990s, studies of interests, abilities, and social relationships, instead of studies of personality traits, were used to measure gender.[26] According to social gender stereotypes, males are believed to be agentive or instrumental, while females are believed to be relational and concerned with social interactions and emotions. In general, male stereotypes are more rigid than female stereotypes, and throughout all stages of development, males apply gender stereotypes more rigidly than do females. According to social learning theory, children acquire their gender identity due to positive and negative reinforcement (reward and punishment) and by modeling or identification with others who exhibit gender-appropriate behavior; they also require opportunities for practice.[27]

Social learning theories depart from Freudian accounts in claiming that gender learning is a lifelong practice, so that early childhood experience may not have a disproportionate influence over time.[28] Social learning theorists also share a belief that the individual child plays an active role in acquiring gender. Susan Cross and Hazel Markus state this perspective as follows: "Gender signifies one's membership in a group and confers a group identity. To this point virtually all research on gender identities had focused on women and women differ in how central their group identity is to their overall sense of self."[29]

Cognitive developmental theories hold that gender is developed through the child's ability to take in information and draw logical inferences from it. Thus, gender identities and roles are learned as the child is cognitively able to understand and process information at different stages of more general cognitive development. Lawrence Kohlberg's notion of *gender concept* had three successive developmental components: gender labeling, the understanding that a person's gender is stable over time, and the understanding of gender constancy over different situations. But Kohlberg's model was inconsistent with the fact that children display understandings of gender before they have been able to cognitively develop a gender concept.

Gender schema theory combines social learning and cognitive development perspectives to describe the development and organization of gender knowledge of sex-type appropriate behavior, roles, occupation, and traits. A schema is an organized body of knowledge that can be an individual's internal combination of social stereotypes. Researchers believe that gender schemas are highly meaningful and broadly applied mental systems that allow individuals to spontaneously divide their social world into the primary categories of male and female. Individuals are more likely to retain information that is consistent with the stereotypic content of their gender schemas, and to ignore or forget information that falsifies stereotypes. By the age of six, children exhibit knowledge of their own gender and by the age of eight, knowledge of the other gender, although girls know more about gender than boys do, and they know more about boys' gender than boys know about girls' gender.[30]

Contemporary gender development theory can be useful to inclusive feminist theory because the basic assumption is that the theorist is obligated to explain, in terms that do not rely primarily on prior biological or cultural determinations, precisely how a child acquires gender identity and learns the gender behavior typical of its sex designation. Whether the psychological account is social, cognitive, or based on a gender schema model, its burden is to show how the male or female gender of individuals comes into existence, when it did not exist before. This theoretical work is based on an assumption that gender differences can be changed, as well as a broad methodological commitment to show how described gender differences can be explained by differences in factors other than gender (e.g., social status).[31] The empirical psychological data and analyses do not have the narrative drama and rich language of psychoanalytic theories. However, the commitment to describing plausible processes of gender acquisition—whatever such processes may be—is exactly the kind of account necessary for feminist change, both the kind of change that is eventually political or directed toward social practices and institutions, and the kind of change that constitutes individual psychological therapy or small group consciousness raising.

WOMEN'S SUBJECTIVITY

Women's subjectivity can be theoretically posited as the spectacle of all of the factors that constitute a person's inner life, with the understanding that she has no choice concerning them. However, the existence of individual variation in gender development supports an element of individual choice. The element of individual choice is further confirmed by first-person experience among individuals who accept their gender assignment and, more dramatically, among those who reject or resist it. The theoretical alternative to allowing for individual choice is to insist on a completely deterministic model, whereby it is claimed that if all relevant external causes could be described, there would be no need to posit individual agency. The phenomena that need to be explained as the effects of either choice or external causes are individual variations in gender development and identity: children develop gender understanding and identities at different ages; some women have more stereotypically feminine or masculine traits and interests than others; some individuals reject their gender socialization completely at maturity. Given the uniqueness of human individuals, if all of the external causes of this variation could be described, all individuals, or a large number of types, would require distinctive causal accounts of their gender development and identity. Such determinism is probably not theoretically impossible, but the probability of its articulation within the next hundred years is very small. It is therefore more useful, as well as more respectful of human dignity, to assume that there is a degree of individual choice and agency in matters of gender development.

Women who retain the traits and enact the roles expected of them during childhood socialization now have the liberty to change such traits and roles. Because so many women who were born before the second wave of women's liberation did change their gender roles and traits in maturity, there is excellent reason to believe that women have the subjective freedom to choose or change their gender. Regardless of the long history of scant external liberty for women, feminism as critical theory now needs to find psychological theories that are not deterministic. In local cultures where women have external liberties, they are to some degree responsible for their gender roles and traits. That is a moral conclusion following from the two enabling conditions of external liberty and subjective freedom.

Not only might a concept of subjective freedom assist in understanding individual variation within a gender, but pathologies of female gender may be treated more effectively with such a concept. For instance, cognitive therapeutic techniques have been more successful than psychoanalytic and behavioristic ones in treating bulimia nervosa. Kelly Vitousek, in a review of recent research on bulimia nervosa and anorexia nervosa, claims that cognitive models of both diseases are supported by evidence that bulimic and anorectic individuals have "beliefs in the domains of weight, shape, and food, and are particularly prone to reasoning errors in these content domains."[32] Vitousek reports that cognitive therapy has been more successful in treating bulimics than anorectics. (Bulimia nervosa is an eating disorder that involves binging and purging, whereas anorexia nervosa involves extreme dieting toward self-starvation.) This is because anorectics are more adverse to treatment than bulimics. Anorectics also have beliefs about weight and body shape that are more closely connected to their individual needs for simplification and organization, whereas bulimics are more responsive to social expectations about weight and size.[33]

The majority of bulimics and anorectics are women. Feminists have understandably focused on cultural beauty ideals of thinness, which are accepted as personal goals by women with these eating disorders. However, this focus can make it seem as though media images have a direct and unmediated effect on women's life projects, without considering how individuals apply those ideals to their own lives, and how the practice of eating disorders is related to other individual psychological traits and needs. But just as social theories are not sufficient to explain individual psychology, so are psychological theories about some women insufficient to conclude that cultural constraints have the same effects on all women. For example, since both bulimia nervosa and anorexia nervosa occur primarily in affluent Western countries, it could be that an abundance of available food is important for the formation of these disorders, in addition to the connection between individual psychology and beauty ideals of thinness. But public beauty ideals and overabundance of available food are not sufficient to explain how the strength of the ideals and the threat to them by overabundance is meaningful on an individual basis. Psychology in the sense under discussion is about individuals, and this requires models of how cultural conditions are understood and conceptualized, as well as knowledge about the specific beliefs associated with the cultural concepts.

From a liberatory feminist perspective, what is interesting about the cognitive therapeutic approach to bulimia and anorexia nervosa is that it typically begins with a discussion between therapist and client about the pros and cons of the client's eating habits.[34] Such an approach appeals to self-interest and assumes that women who have self-destructive habits can still be motivated by self-interest. That approach and assumption expresses a fundamental feminist principle that well-being is an attainable goal for individual women. Perhaps it is time for feminists to seriously consider how women can be appealed to in their self-interest, not only as a social activist principle, but as a strategy for individual psychological change and healing. Perhaps it is time for a more general turn in feminism, away from psychoanalytic obsessions with the sexual identities of the sons and daughters of privileged families, and toward a more universal kind of attention to specific kinds of problems that can be understood on models that momentarily detach individuals from their problems in order to find solutions for them as concrete persons. That such attention begins with clinical information about the psychology of privileged women does not foreclose its theoretical and practical application to those disadvantaged. The shift I am suggesting would require a complete theoretical liberation from ideas that a few primary emotions or original conditions inexorably define the lives of women, and also from ideas of women, even very unhappy, disturbed, and severely disadvantaged women, as incapable of reasoning in their own self-interest.

It is not just women's problems that could be responsive to a cognitive psychological approach but gender development and change, as lifelong processes. Thus subjectivity from a feminist psychological perspective would no longer be the nebulous nonentity that Simone de Beauvoir's analysis of woman as Other suggested it was. Woman has already become a subject, intellectually as well as politically, among privileged groups in affluent Western countries and, as we shall see in chapter 8, among women in the Third World as well. In feminist writing, much of the development of woman as subject has focused on social imaginaries as the causes of pathologies of the privileged. The method is transcendental in a Kantian way: the theorist describes a malign set of beliefs and myths, not directly observed, but nonetheless posited by her as a background source of the deleterious things that are directly observed. Such often literary projects of transcendental speculation have proceeded from pessimistic and morbid examination of what in global terms are the peas disturbing the sleep of a few princesses, each tossing and turning atop her own twenty mattresses (not that she doesn't suffer). There is little application of such theoretical work to women globally.

In the West, particularly in the United States, optimistic approaches toward individual psychological change are often relegated to the self-help section of bookstore supermarkets as shallow strategies for the unlettered. Staff at women's shelters, health clinics, and crisis centers are left to deal one-on-one with clients who cannot be helped without some attention to their beliefs about gender, to their schemas and self-concepts, in ways that address those beliefs as not only possible but necessary, to change.

The intellectual aesthetics of academic feminists, who purport to plumb the psyches of women in general as objects and victims of patriarchal exclusion, serve to protect and leave unexamined their own privilege. Most academic feminists are materially privileged in having the leisure to pursue such studies, and they are psychologically privileged in not needing practical therapeutic assistance in order to fulfill the functions of their daily lives. If a young woman's parents cannot afford to send her to college, she will have to rely on often politically naive self-help books or bootstrap counselors when the problems of her life become overwhelming. If the college woman or her ("French") feminist professor find the problems in their lives overwhelming to the point where they also seek professional help, they are likely to be surprised by how ineffective their general theoretical knowledge is for solving their specific difficulties. If they have recourse to a "talking cure," instead of psychiatric medication, they will discover that as oppressive and wrong as the patriarchy may be, more specific events, conditions, and decisions must be addressed in order to solve their problems. Needed is an unapologetic feminist bridge between the tools of sophisticated cultural and psychoanalytic analysis and the best-seller level of practical advice. It is the task of third wave feminists to craft a psychology of self-help for individual women that is both personally empowering and politically aware. There should also be some theoretical connection between that level of unavoidably sophisticated self-help and the pamphlets about breast-feeding, contraception, and kitchen gardens distributed in some relatively stable parts of the Third World.[35]

If this apparent support of self-help and the foregoing endorsement of cognitive approaches to women's problems sound superficial, they are. But the depths of the psyche, as revealed through the projection of vaguely universal psychoanalytic cultural myths onto a hypothetical subject, are visible only to those who are indulged by a now fashionable form of "higher" education that bribes and corrupts female intellectuals who have gained entry to special parts of the academy now maintained just for them. Is there any better way to neutralize those who begin intellectual life with a passion to change the world? An ill-written book on codependence and "women who love too much" may go more directly to the problems recognized as their own by lower-middle-class and poor women in even the First World, problems rejected as unworthy of consideration by those who have been carelessly taught to gaze at evil imaginaries. (No one should be surprised when the crumbs of such pie in the sky, inevitably dropping to lower levels, become fuel for the "fire in the belly" of a very real backlash against feminism.)

Still, there remains heuristic value in the leisure activity of sophisticated and stylish understanding. In *About Chinese Women*, Kristeva explains how foot binding in China arose as a deliberate practice of women's suffering, which followed the replacement of an original matrilineal and matrilocal form of the family, with a patrilineal and patrilocal one. Kristeva also offers this impression from her 1974 trip to China:

> Only the moist, solitary eyes, a bit sad, made for looking inside rather than directly at you—only the eyes, with their soft, veiled irony, betray these women's suffering. In the evening, their sons and grandsons carry them on the backs of their bicycles like wounded Amazons. On the eve of May Day in Peking, when the lanterns are lit and everyone pours into the forbidden city, Tiananmen Square is full of Red Guards on their bicycles, ferrying their crippled grandmothers through the crowd.[36]

Why wasn't Kristeva ashamed to publish such a self-composed, poetic reflection about evidence of others' pain? After Kristeva says in the introduction to *About Chinese Women* that she owes her cheek bones to "some Asian ancestry," she confesses that she is molded by "(why not?) false colonial civility."[37] Kristeva and her readers would have benefited from self-examination of why she identified with Asianness, when she also permitted herself to express a legacy of superiority to it. Because there is no self-critical examination, Kristeva's readers may resort to speculation. Grandsons' practices of carrying their crippled grandmothers (instead of their girlfriends) on the backs of their bicycles at night suggests that there is something lovable about the disabled grandmothers, whose feet were bound in childhood—lovable precisely because of that particular disability. They are surely abject in the more usual meaning of "debased," but there is also a note of perversity insofar as the debility was deliberately inflicted and continues to be used as a basis for affection between men and women. Social practices in which people are injured and then use their injuries as a basis for what is considered to be normal affection may set up powerful ambivalences, but this does not excuse the theorist from criticizing the dynamic. The reader of such an uncritical theorist is left to speculate about the theorist's ambivalence between wanting not to be abject and wanting to be loved, about the conditions in her life that supported the suspension of resolution, and about her cowardice in not confronting her own ambivalence.

Still, *About Chinese Women* is an invaluable demonstration of how psychoanalysis is fundamentally a description of cultural drama. On Kristeva's account of Chinese history, the Western association of community with the symbolic order (the word) of patriarchy and the suppression of female *jouissance* has not been universal. And if it has not been universal, it need not be universal. This locates psychoanalysis as a description of cultural myth and suggests that deep psychology is not irrevocably located in the individual psyche but rather at the point of intersection between the individual psyche and society. Nonetheless, I am suggesting that feminists who are interested in inclusive psychological theory about individuals, which makes it possible for them to change and heal as an active, chosen process, had best remain superficial in the face of such theory. Consumption through uncritical reflection of the intersection between the individual and society is a luxury activity, tentative as a theoretical project and (so far) ineffective as a therapeutic one. Taken deeply, such reflection threatens to erase the concrete individual by overinscribing an imagined drama onto her. In writing herself into such a general imaginary, the individual may forget who she is, what she wants, and how she feels.

NOTES

1. Carol Nagy Jacklin and Chandra Reynolds, "Gender and Childhood Socialization," in *The Psychology of Gender*, ed. Anne E. Beall and Robert J. Sternberg (New

York: Guilford, 1993), 197–214; reprinted in *The Second Wave: A Reader in Feminist Theory,* ed. Linda J. Nicholson (New York: Routledge, 1997), 181–97.

2. Karl Popper, *Conjectures and Refutations: The Growth of Scientific Knowledge* (1965), secs. 1–2, 4–5, 9–10; reprinted as "Science: Conjectures and Refutations," in *Scientific Knowledge,* ed. Janet A. Kourney (Belmont, Calif.: Wadsworth, 1998).

3. Freud appears to resolve the apparent contradiction in a footnote in "The Transformations of Puberty," where he claims that the biological sense of masculinity and femininity is different from the psychoanalytic sense, which depends on the masculine designation of the libido as always active. Thus according to Freud, bisexuality is evident on a biological level. "Every individual person shows a mixture of its own biological sex characteristics with the biological traits of the other sex and a union of activity and passivity; this is the case whether these psychological characteristic features depend on biological elements or whether they are independent of them." See Freud, "The Transformations of Puberty," in *Three Contributions to the Theory of Sex,* in *The Basic Writings of Sigmund Freud,* trans. and ed. A. A. Brill (New York: Modern Library, 1995), 581 n. 5.

4. For recent reviews of Freudian treatments of gender, see Susan Golombok and Robyn Fivush, *Gender Development* (Cambridge: Cambridge University Press, 1994), 55–74; and Irene Fast, "Aspects of Early Gender Development: A Psychoanalytic Perspective," in *The Psychology of Gender,* ed. Anne E. Beall and Robert J. Sternberg, (New York: Guilford, 1993), 173–96. Freud's account is in "Infantile Sexuality," in *Three Contributions to the Theory of Sex,* 548–71.

5. Karen Horney wrote about motherhood as a form of psychic fulfillment for women, in mitigation of Freud's postulation of penis envy. Horney disagreed with Freud's claim that maternal desires and their fulfillment were only compensations for penis envy and she revised the Freudian concept of women's penis envy into a pathological condition. This made it possible to posit motherhood as an independent and positive part of woman's psyche. Karen Horney, "The Flight from Womanhood: The Masculinity Complex As Viewed by Men and by Women," in *Feminine Psychology,* ed. Harold Kelman (New York: Norton, 1967), 37–70. For Chodorow, motherhood seems to be a primary role and set of traits of women. That is, Chodorow adds a social interactive dimension to Horney's account. See Nancy Chodorow, "Oedipal Asymmetries and Heterosexual Knots," *Social Problems* 23, no. 4 (1976): 454–58; and Chodorow, "The Psychodynamics of Mothering," in *The Reproduction of Mothering: Psychoanalysis and the Sociology of Gender* (Berkeley: University of California Press, 1978).

6. Christine Delphy, "The Invention of French Feminism: An Essential Move," *Yale French Studies* 87 (1995): 166–97. Delphy is a Marxist–feminist sociologist who was a founding member, along with Simone de Beauvoir, of *Questions Feministes,* from 1977 to 1980, and she also participated in a National Center for Scientific Research project that funded eighty research projects in women's studies from 1985 to 1989. Delphy's strong social theory (or sociological) orientation raises the question of whether it is possible for her to accept a version of feminism that is primarily psychological. On this see Doris Rita Alphonso, introduction to "Sex and Gender/ Christine Delphy," in *French Feminism Reader,* ed. Kelly Oliver, (Lanham, Md.: Rowman & Littlefield, 2000), 59.

7. Toril Moi, *What Is a Woman?* (New York: Oxford University Press, 1999), xi.

8. Oliver, *French Feminism Reader*, viii.

9. Ferdinand de Saussure, *Course in General Linguistics* (New York: McGraw-Hill, 1966).

10. Jacques Lacan, *The Four Fundamental Concepts of Psycho-Analysis*, ed. Jacques-Alain Miller, trans. Alan Sheridan (New York: Norton, 1978), 149.

11. Lacan, *Four Fundamental Concepts*, 204.

12. Freud, "Transformations of Puberty," 572–600.

13. Lacan explores the binary signs of sexuality in complex ways that are connected with Chinese thought, as well as science. See "Sexuality in the Defiles of the Signifier," in Lacan, *Four Fundamental Concepts*, 129–60.

14. Hélène Cixous, "The Laugh of Medusa," *Signs* 1, no. 4 (1976): 875–99; trans. Keith Cohen and Paula Cohen, from "Le Rire de la Meduse," *L'Arc* 61 (1975): 39–54; Hélène Cixous, "Castration or Decapitation?" *Signs* 7, no. 1 (1981): 41–55; trans. Annette Kuhn, from "Le sexe ou la tete?" *Les Cahiers du GRIF* 23 (1976): 5–15.

15. Cixous, "Laugh of Medusa."

16. Luce Irigaray, *Speculum of the Other Woman*, trans. Gillian C. Gill (Ithaca, N.Y.: Cornell University Press, 1985).

17. Jennifer Hanson, introduction to "There Are Two Sexes, Not One/Luce Irigaray," in Oliver, *French Feminism Reader*, 201–6.

18. Luce Irigaray, *I Love to You*, trans. A. Martin (New York: Routledge, 1994).

19. Julia Kristeva, *Powers of Horror*, trans. Leon Roudiez (New York: Columbia University Press, 1982); Julia Kristeva, *About Chinese Women*, trans. Anita Barrows (New York: Marion Boyars, 1977), 11–44.

20. Kristeva, *About Chinese Women*, 14, 16.

21. Cynthia Willett, *The Soul of Justice: Social Bonds and Racial Hubris* (Ithaca, N.Y.: Cornell University Press, 2001), 150–51.

22. Sue Wilkinson, "Still Seeking Transformation: Feminist Challenges to Psychology," in *The Gender of Science*, ed. Janet A. Kourany, (Upper Saddle River, N.J.: Prentice Hall, 2002), 218–27; Anne E. Beall, "A Social Constructionist View of Gender," in Beall and Sternberg, *Psychology of Gender*, 140–44.

23. Cognitive approaches should be understood to include "knowing how" as well as "knowing what," or skills and performance, as well as knowledge that can be explained in terms of what an individual explicitly believes. Still, the question of whether these are distinctive forms of knowledge or whether "knowing how" reduces to "knowing what," or even the other way around in some cases, does not have to be answered in order to identify the cognitive dimension of gender learning. For discussion of the different kinds of knowledge, see Myrna Estop, *A Theory of Immediate Awareness* (Dordrecht, Netherlands: Kluwer, 2003).

24. Susan Golombok and Robyn Fivush, *Gender Development* (Cambridge: Cambridge University Press, 1994), 48–54.

25. Golombok and Fivush, *Gender Development*, 109; Susaan E. Cross and Hazel Rose Marcus, "Gender in Thought, Belief, and Action: A Cognitive Approach," in Beall and Sternberg, *Psychology of Gender*, 77.

26. Golombok and Fivush, *Gender Development*, 5–12.

27. Golombok and Fivush, *Gender Development*, 75–89.

28. Bernice Lott and Diane Maluso, "The Social Learning of Gender," in Beall and Sternberg, *Psychology of Gender*, 99–126.

29. Cross and Marcus, "Gender in Thought, Belief, and Action," in Beall and Sternberg, *Psychology of Gender*, 77–78.

30. Golombok and Fivush, *Gender Development*, 90–111; Cross and Marcus, "Gender in Thought, Belief, and Action," 55–98.

31. Mahhzarin R. Banaji, "The Psychology of Gender: A Perspective on Perspectives," in Beall and Sternberg, *Psychology of Gender,* 255.

32. Kelly M. Vitousek, "The Current Status of Cognitive-Behavioral Models of Anorexia Nervosa and Bulimia Nervosa," in *Frontiers of Cognitive Therapy*, ed. Paul M. Salkovskis, (New York: Guilford, 1996), 386.

33. Vitousek, "Current Status," 407.

34. Vitousek, "Current Status," 398.

35. See Zack, *Lacanian Feminism, Cognitive Psychology, and Self-Help* (forthcoming).

36. Kristeva, *About Chinese Women*, 85.

37. Kristeva, *About Chinese Women*, 12–13.

6

Inclusive Feminist Connections between Psychological Theory and Social Theory

Suppose that the acquisition of male or female gender is an individual cognitive learning process. That general model does not preclude the existence of strong emotions associated with gender difference, cultural and individual variation in what is learned, or the dependence of what is learned on preexisting gender power differences in culture. Neither does acceptance of the general cognitive model preclude specific narratives about the content of what a child learns. On the cognitive model, learning that takes place before the child can articulate her beliefs can be described as though she had certain beliefs.

Psychoanalytic theory provides a distinctive narrative of gender learning. Even Freud, despite his apparent view that gender complexes were externally determined in the child's life and his belief that there is a "sexual instinct" in childhood, nonetheless thought that what was in effect learning was more important than heredity in the acquisition of gender. He wrote:

> It is quite remarkable that those writers who endeavor to explain the qualities and reaction of the adult individual have given so much more attention to the ancestral period than to the period of the individual's own existence—that is, they have attributed more influence to heredity than to childhood. As a matter of fact, it might well be supposed that the influence of the latter period would be easier to understand, and that it would be entitled to more consideration than heredity.[1]

Feminist theorists who deploy psychoanalysis sometimes write as though individual men and women automatically instantiate and express culturally specific gender differences. That perspective evokes a notion of individuals as miniature versions of their cultures, a notion that rests on philosophical error and creates political confusion. The philosophical error goes back to Socrates, who in the beginning of *The Republic* told his interlocutors that society was simply the individual "writ large," and that it should therefore be easier to discern social virtues than individual ones.[2] Socrates' metaphorical perspective leaves out two obvious differences between individuals and societies: human individuals are integral biological beings, while whatever they may be, societies are not that; societies emerge from the interactions of individuals with traditions, values, rules, and patterns of material distribution, in ways that cannot be fully reduced to their components. The political confusion concerns neglect of the facts that changes in society do not affect all individuals in the same way, and that changes in individuals do not directly change society. Still, we know that there are important life-shaping connections between women and the societies in which they dwell. The task for third wave feminists as critical theorists is to develop a perspective on connections that enable certain changes in societies, which would fully empower women as the historical equals of men.

In chapter 5, I criticized the work of Cixous, Irigaray, and Kristeva on several counts. I argued that their debt to Lacan made it difficult to read them as addressing existing women, rather than women as factors in a discursive symbolic order. I also questioned the class and implied race bias in their approach to women's psychology. In general, I think that the main feminist problem with psychoanalytic theory is its lack of direct relevance to individual motivation and learning in a way that theoretically grounds either psychological or cultural change. Psychoanalytic theory also tends to posit unchanging universals, archetypes, and situations, which results in rigidity in the face of cultural change. This is a problem for feminism as critical theory because, as noted in chapter 4, critical theories need to be revisable in response to cultural change.

There are also problems with psychoanalysis as a clinical practice. The evidence has never been robust that psychoanalysts can effect cures based primarily on psychoanalytic theories. Moreover, psychoanalysis as clinical therapy has never been widely accessible. Before mass health insurance, its expense restricted it to economic elites. It has become less accessible even to them as a result of the insurance-financed structure of contemporary health care systems. Psychoanalysis has always been an independent subfield of the discipline of psychology, regarded skeptically by mainstream psychologists and isolated from their empirical findings. Problems of access, effectiveness, and scientific credibility render it curious that psychoanalytic interpretations of the masculine bias of culture have become so well received in the academic humanities, particularly among feminist philosophers.[3]

I noted at the end of my criticism of Kristeva's lack of self-reflection in *About Chinese Women* that psychoanalytic myth, understood as culturally relative, can be viewed as located at an intersection between an individual and her society. I suggested that because such myth does not present a successful drama for women, feminists as individuals with self-interests ought to maintain a personal distance from it. However, if psychoanalytic complexes of male or female gender occurred in all individuals within a culture in the same way, its content could not be easily dismissed and there might be little that an individual could do to change its relevance to her, even if she could recognize in herself the lasting effects of the inevitable childhood sexual trauma posited by the theory.

Despite the foregoing problems, classic psychoanalytic theory has been used by writers such as Irigaray, Kristeva, and Chodorow to suggest that myths different from Freud's could result in different outcomes for women. Their suggestions have been highly influential among feminists, possibly because they raise a hope that feminist revisions of Freudian psychoanalytic theory could be beneficial to women. In this chapter, I will first investigate the psychoanalytic connection between society or culture, on one side, and the psychology of individuals, on the other. Through interpretation of Freud's views about the connection and Gayle Rubin's revision of Freud, it will emerge that psychoanalytic theory, even if true, falls short of connecting women's psychology with aspects of culture that now ought to concern feminists. However, psychoanalytic theory can make a useful contribution to a feminist conception of women as a force in history. The second part of the chapter is a discussion of the necessity for women to become a historical force. The starting point for that process is difficult to imagine, so I invoke the title character of J. M. Coetzee's novel *Elizabeth Costello*.

PSYCHOANALYSIS AND SOCIETY

Psychoanalytic theory has appealed to feminist theorists because it focuses on sexuality and gender, topics not found in the other grand theories, which have generally ignored the concerns and life themes of women. Feminists have a greater affinity to Freud than Marx because Marx takes women for granted in the history of humanity and seems to have no compelling reason to consider them a historical force. Marx deals with history as dynamic series of public events, about the interests of men and under their control. Women are supporting, downstage characters in this drama, necessary for the reproduction of men and their labor.[4] Even when women are commodified as sexual objects, Marx's concern was not with that injustice but with how men corrupted each other in their use of women.[5] Freud, by contrast, paid attention to private events in the family, the area of life to which women were confined throughout modern Western history, and he posited sexuality, in both real sexual acts and childhood fantasy, as the motivational foundation and ultimate meaning of much of normal, as well as pathological, thought, emotion, and behavior. (Freud explicitly made this claim in *The History of the Psychoanalytic Movement*.)[6] Freud also used the importance of sexuality as a methodological guide, and he offered justification for that usage in *Psychopathology of Everyday Life* and *Wit and Its Relation to the Unconscious*. Second wave feminists since Simone de Beauvoir have recognized that human sexuality has a greater influence on the daily lives and destinies of women than men. Nonetheless, second wave feminists, and before them women psychoanalysts, have always been aware that Freud privileged men over women in his theory of human sexuality, which was built around the Oedipus myth. They have therefore sought to neutralize the Oedipus myth by explicating its specific cultural relativity, adding a greater role for women or turning to more egalitarian myths. Men in masculinist cultures have not widely accepted Freud's Oedipus myth theory that centers them, so there is an interesting question of what if anything women have to gain from intellectual struggles about how to revise Freudian psychoanalytic theory in favor of women. To answer that question about what is at stake, it is necessary to clarify how culture (society) connects with psychoanalytic sexual and gender dynamics.

This is not a question that has occupied feminist psychoanalytic theorists, in part because they seem to accept the premises of the psychoanalytic project, often without explicating them. So we have to go back to Freud himself for clarification about those methodological premises insofar as they are epistemological and ontological assumptions. In *The History of the Psychoanalytic Movement,* Freud's 1914 defense and explication of psychoanalysis for both external and internal critics, he answers Alfred Adler's charge that psychoanalysis is circular. Freud first quotes Adler as follows: "If you ask whence comes the repression, you are told: from culture. But if you ask whence comes the culture, the reply is: from the repression. So you see it is only a question of a play on words."[7]

Freud's answer is both insulting to Adler and anodyne about his own theory:

> A small fragment of the wisdom used by Adler to unmask the defensive tricks of his "nervous character" might have sufficed to show him the way out of this pettifogging argument. There is nothing mysterious about it, except that culture depends upon the acts of repression of former generations, and that each new generation is required to retain this culture by carrying out the same repression. I have heard of a child who considered himself fooled and began to cry because to the question "Where do eggs come from?", he received the answer "Eggs come from hens,"; and to the further question: "Where do the hens come from?", the information was: "From the eggs," and yet, this was not a play upon words. On the contrary, the child had been told the truth.[8]

So, according to Freud, the repression of individual sexuality (a chicken) makes it possible for a culture (an egg) to exist, and a culture in turn gives rise to the repression (another chicken) that will result in the persistence of the culture (another egg). This is quite straightforward if we understand that the chicken which hatches from a given egg is a different chicken from the one that produced the egg. But we should also understand what Freud is taking for granted here: culture requires repression; human beings always fulfill the requirement of perpetuating their culture. In order to universalize infant sexuality and the Oedipus myth, Freud also has to assume that the same kind of material is always repressed and that repression is a universal mediation between that material and culture.

Freud does not have to assume that all cultures as cultures are the same. In *Totem and Taboo,* he investigates ethnographic reports of "so-called savage and semi-savage races" in Australia, Africa, and other non-European cultures. Clearly, these cultures differed from one another and they all differed from the European cultures that existed when Freud wrote. But the repressed material is nonetheless universal according to Freud, first because he identifies in different cultures the same taboo against (primarily) son–mother and brother–sister incest and, second, because he understands the cultures of "so-called savage and semi-savage races" to be living examples of past stages of European history. Therefore Freud does assume that in the matter of repression of the oedipal material that interests him, all cultures—past, present, European, and non-European—are the same:

> There are people whom we still consider more closely related to primitive man than to ourselves, in whom we therefore recognize the direct descendants and representatives of earlier man. We can thus judge the so-called savage and semi-savage races; their psychic life assumes a peculiar interest for us, for we can recognize in their psychic life a well-preserved early stage of our own development.[9]

Returning to Freud's answer to Adler, one would expect to find in *Totem and Taboo* some examples of how repression causes culture in primitive societies. Instead, Freud presents a series of examples of gender relations, presumably typical of the non-European cultures he reads about, in which he interprets the incest taboo to be in effect. He uses the incest taboo to explain kinship rules and marriage prohibitions which concern familial relations that are not based on direct descent but on descent through a maternal or paternal line which preserves identification with a totem. Thus Freud uses the incest taboo to explain mating rules. However, this does not give us a full account of how repression of incestuous desires leads to the formation of culture in senses of culture that are not directly related to human mating. Freud may have thought that the nonmating aspects of culture were "sublimations" of sexual desire, particularly incestuous sexual desire.

However, the issue of sublimation was complicated for Freud in a way that renders his chicken-egg answer to Adler disingenuous. Citing the unanimity of all historians of civilization, he noted that "deflection of sexual motive powers from sexual aims to new aims, a process which merits the name of *sublimation*, has furnished powerful components for all cultural accomplishments."[10] But he also thought that the same process occurs in individual development in a way that is organically determined and "can occasionally be produced without the help of education."[11] Freud thought that childhood sexuality would inhibit itself due to organically determined "psychic forces of loathing, shame, and moral and aesthetic ideal demands."[12] Against what he said to Adler, culture is not the sole cause of repression, according to Freud. This notion of "natural" repression would of course be problematic for any feminist revision of Freud.

To return to the question of what parts of culture cause repression, Freud does not make clear how the nonsexual aspects of culture as sublimation, of which artistic creations were a prime example for him, would impose more repressions.[13] The point is that if circularity can be evaded (Freud tends to use the oedipal situation to describe or interpret cultural traditions while using it to explain the origins of those traditions) at best, all that Freud's perusal of the ethnographic literature in *Totem and Taboo* accomplishes is a fleshing out of his thesis that repressed incestuous desires cause certain kinds of heterosexual social rules, which in turn result in the repression of incestuous desires. In short, boys are prevented from having sex with their mothers and sisters and they grow up into men who prevent new generations of boys from having sex with their mothers and sisters. From a feminist perspective, the culture side of the promise of Freud's answer to Adler would be fulfilled only if it could be shown how something like Freud's theory of psychoanalysis accounts for the material conditions of women's oppression in parts of human life that are not directly related to either human sexuality or the social rules that regulate it. Fortunately, Gayle Rubin, in "The Traffic in Women: Notes on the 'Political Economy' of Sex," has provided the important outlines of exactly such a theory.[14]

In order to get her materialist psychoanalytic theory started, Rubin turns Freud on his head by reading his masculinist account of early sexual development as an accurate description of gender formation in a male-dominant sexist society. Rubin uses the same technique with Claude Lévi-Strauss's analysis of kinship, according to which women literally count as wealth in many non-Western cultures. They are circulated among men so that masculine power, or what Lacan called the phallus, is never exercised by women, although they are an object of and support for it. By putting Freud and Lévi-Strauss together, Rubin creates a theory of the link between psychology and social theory or between individual women and culture. This can in principle give us a full-bodied answer to Adler's objection to Freud's description of the connection between repression and culture. As objects of exchange in masculinist cultures, women are socialized from infancy to develop minds that enable them to fulfill that role. Moreover, and this is most important, the repression of women that occurs in Freud's description enables their future roles as objects of exchange between men in economic and status-related areas of a culture that go far beyond rules pertaining to heterosexual conduct and mating. As Rubin suggests, phenomena described by Lévi-Strauss as an exchange of women include exchanging women for wealth and status, as well as for other women; the repression of women toward their development into suitable objects of exchange is motivated by gains and advantages to men in areas of life that go beyond human sexuality and reproduction (and perhaps even gender). From this theoretical perspective, the repression of women now begins to resemble an *oppression of women*, which is precisely the necessary link between women's psychology and social theory that a feminist psychoanalytic theory would require to answer Adler's objection to Freud (among other things).

We now need to take a closer look at what a psychoanalytic account of women's sexual development looks like according to Freud, and/or revisionists such as Rubin, to determine whether such a theory can explain how female infants develop into girls who will become women in a way that is at least partly an effect of culture. We also need to determine whether this account allows for change in culture, as well as in how women develop. As Freud himself knew, and many of his critics have been quick to recognize, his theory of early sexuality is a dreary story for women. We are told in "Infantile Sexuality" that the boy suffers from a castration complex and at the same time finds it difficult to believe that girls and women do not have penises. But the girl immediately recognizes the existence of the penis and envies the boy for having one, to the point of wishing to be a boy.[15] In a footnote, Freud further insists:

> One has the right to speak also of a castration complex in women. Male and female children form the theory that originally the woman, too, had a penis, which has been lost through castration. The conviction finally won that the woman has no penis often produces in the male a lasting depreciation of the other sex.[16]

Before the oedipal period (ages three to five), Freud believed, girls have the same autoerotic activity of the erogenous zones, although they are quicker to develop sexual inhibitions than boys. The "object" of their pre-oedipal sexual desires is the same for male and female infants—the mother. The sexuality of the little girl is supposed to have a male character because according to Freud the libido is "regularly and lawfully of a masculine nature." It is object choice, not libido itself, that determines whether sexuality is male or female. The girl becomes female, first in turning away from her mother at the oedipal stage, and second in the repression of her libido at puberty. While puberty occasions an increase in libido for boys, for girls it represents a "new wave of repression." This is because the girl must deny the sexuality centered in the clitoris, which is analogous to the penis, and transfer sexual excitation and gratification to another "zone"—the vagina.[17]

Most striking in Freud's account is that the development of female infants into girls is marked by the disappointing realization of the absence of a penis and the transition from girls into women requires a radical change in sexuality. Thus for Freud, boys and men are the normal or typical sex—the libido in both sexes is masculine—and girls and women develop by accommodating themselves to human maleness (the existence of a penis) and masculine development (the surge in boys' libido at puberty). As development for girls, this process sounds more like a series of reactions than the unfolding or flourishing, albeit restrained and redirected, which characterizes the process by which male infants become men.

Rubin's evaluation of the Freudian account is that it is a description of obligatory heterosexuality, which has historically served the economic interests of men.[18] She suggests that insofar as Freud accurately described the process of creating a female psyche that was appropriate to the historical system of male domination, women should "unite to off the oedipal residue of culture." Toward that end, she claims that the girl would not be forced to give up her original love for her mother if men shared in early child care and could be primary object choices.[19] Rubin's social proposal is interesting because she is not arguing for greater respect for the bond between girls and their mothers, but for conditions that would not make such bonds the only possible libidinal bonds for girls. If girls could also form primary bonds with their fathers, heterosexuality would not be compulsory for women who had that experience, but voluntary. So Rubin's proposal does not contest heterosexuality per se.

Rubin also thinks that kinship, or the social form of family relationships, is no longer the main organizational mechanism of society:

> The organization of sex and gender once had functions other than itself—it organized society. Now it only organizes and reproduces itself. The kinds of relationships of sexuality established in the dim human past still dominate our sexual lives, our idea about men and women, and the ways we raise our children. But they lack the functional load they once carried. One of the most conspicuous features of kinship is that it has been systematically stripped of its functions—political, economic, educational and organizational. It has been reduced to its barest bones—sex and gender.[20]

This is a puzzling passage because it ignores the mechanics of male domination, through which sex and gender are used for social and economic purposes distinct from mating, among the "savage and semi-savage" races studied by Lévi-Strauss and Freud, and it further restricts the current problems raised by the male–female gender system to sexuality and mating. This makes it difficult to consider the question raised by Freud's response to Adler: Does the psychoanalytic situation of repression affect culture in ways that go beyond sexual relations? In a way, Rubin is caught in Freud's psychologistic trap. She believes that women have been the passive, libidinally deficient, resentful, and resigned sex and that liberating them requires social conditions that would result in a different psychosexual profile. However, we do not have good grounds to accept Rubin's premise that kinship, understood broadly to include its extension of gender difference to the economic organization of society, has now been reduced to sex and gender in a purely psychological sense, presumably restricted to the personal realm only.

Kinship systems are interesting to feminists for two reasons: first, they show how women are made by culture and, second, they illustrate how men benefit from the heterosexual sex-gender system. In a word, men rule in cultures with that system, but they do not rule only over women. Differences in male–female sex and gender still permeate our cultures in ways that greatly exceed sexual/psychological/personal gender differences, and that excess should motivate feminist social theory. Women have gained many liberties, including access to the male institutions of power from which men previously excluded them. But women who have gained access to such institutions are a long way from changing the destructive, predatory, and aggressive agendas and effects of those institutions. Even with women participating, the institutions of government, the military, business, religion, and education continue in the projects laid down for them in the days before women were admitted. Rubin seems to miss this because, thinking from a sexual (i.e., Freudian) perspective, she identifies the main problem of male dominance as "obligatory heterosexuality."

Strictly speaking, Freudian analysis doesn't support that characterization. If Freudian psychoanalysis is correct, when the female child is forced to change the object of her libido, it ejects her from what Rubin and others have seen as a primary lesbian situation in the female child's libidinous attachment to her mother. But, in fairness to Freud's description, there is no actual sexual "object choice" at that stage, as object choice is experienced by adults.[21] Leaving aside the Lacanian-inspired question (discussed in chapter 4) of whether Freud is always talking about the symbolic or linguistic order, Freud himself insists that childhood sexual activity which involves adults exists mainly in the fantasies of young children (unless they are "seduced," as Freud terms it).[22] The female child does not become heterosexual until after puberty and even then, the obligation is normative and not entirely (or effectively) obligatory. (Some women are lesbians and even Freud knew that.)

Furthermore, after her reproductive and active sexual years, the older woman may become celibate, and some women, who are neither older nor lesbians, may be celibate during their otherwise reproductive and sexually active years. What is effectively and universally obligatory in the Freudian description of women's development is assignment to the category of women in a general sense, an assignment that follows from female birth designation, without any actual heterosexual sexual acts being necessary.

In that sense of category assignment, together with an understanding of how, within cultures, the category of women is related to the category of men, Rubin's reading of Freud identifies an important link between feminist psychology and social theory: It explains how women become the sorts of people who can form partners with men for the sake of human reproduction, and once they have been trained for that purpose, for other purposes as well. But there is no reason to think that if fewer women became heterosexual adults or even if the deep psychologies of men and women became very similar, or the same, that men might not still oppress women as weaker versions of themselves or continue to draw them into the projects they designed in times of more explicitly masculine sexual dominance. At this time, for women to change the material conditions of their oppression and perhaps of the oppression of others, where men are the oppressors, it is necessary to distinguish between women's psychology and men's culture.

The distinction between women's and men's psychologies is not sufficient to be useful for addressing or changing men's culture. It is a big question whether individuals who are women, historically defined as the FMP category, can change men's culture. Only certain changes in men's culture would be comprehensive and deep enough to constitute the revolution in human relations that could in turn change the material benefit to men of the oedipal crisis or libidinous passivity of girls, assuming still that the Freudian description of how the different genders develop is roughly correct. I think we can say, less problematically, that Freud's assumptions that both libidinous development and its repression are to some extent instinctive or natural are false. Once Freudian psychoanalytic theory is taken to describe an unjust system that is not inevitable, the cognitive approach to beliefs about gender, discussed in chapter 5, becomes all the more important and relevant. The effects on girls of unjust and contingent aspects of the Freudian family drama can be understood as implicit or explicit beliefs that girls form about themselves, others, and human relations in their cultures. Such beliefs are in principle corrigible, either through cognitive relearning processes and/or deeper analyses of their accompanying affects.

Needed to complete the feminist psychoanalytic revision is a reexamination of concepts of the unconscious, repression, and sublimation. We do not know whether a just sex-gender system would still inculcate childhood traumata that would need to be repressed for successful or adequate social functioning. Neither do we know whether all human activities that appear to be nonsexual are forms of sublimation. Answers to these questions would be partly empirical and partly theoretical, perhaps even metaphysical. Fortunately, it is not necessary to have answers to them in order to discuss changes in the psychology of women or the rule of men. The Freudian psychoanalytic drama could probably be changed, and rather easily, if the nonsexual material purposes it supports were thwarted.

THE ENTRY OF WOMEN INTO HISTORY

The main social problem suggested by the feminist critique of psychoanalytic theory is not that women have been forced to become heterosexual, although that is a problem, but that the heterosexuality of women supports men in their unworthy nonsexual pursuits. The ease of human reproduction under heterosexual normativity has led to an unchecked expansion of *Homo sapiens sapiens*, the insatiably predatory species. Heterosexuality may be no more than an enabling aspect of that expansive predation. Feminist social and psychological theorists both need to remember that men's sexual relations with women do not consume the main part of their destructive energies, and that sterner stuff than a change in women's permitted libidinous objects is required to confront and redirect the nonsexual social problems of this time. I am restating the claim in chapter 4 that feminist social theory needs to be distinct from feminist psychological theory, but now for the reason that male domination is bigger than even a masculinist and unjust sex-gender system. However, resistance and aggression against this bigger system of male rule cannot be formulated as material and moral strategies until women have an understanding of themselves that allows them to think beyond their past identities or historical nonidentities as women. Feminist theorists need to think outside of the sex-gender system in ways that preserve women's relational identities and go beyond them, into the world, which is to say, for the first time, into history. Some version of psychoanalytic theory is useful for that goal, because it provides a narrative account of the development of women's minds, as they can be generally imagined, given the past of the sex-gender system and the exclusion of women from the culture of men. Although such a psychoanalytic account is no more than a starting point for the entry of women into history, it seems to distinguish them from men in an affective dimension that is more than mere participation in men's culture as lesser men. Future historians could recognize the time when the group known as women came to rule alongside of, or in place of, the group known as men. That historical goal is served by the psychoanalytic myth of how women in a general sense come to be psychically disadvantaged compared to men, together with an understanding that in reality what women are is no more and no less than those who have been assigned to, or identify with, the general category of female birth designees, biological mothers, or primary sexual choices of men (the FMP category).

It may seem strange that psychoanalytic theory, which was proposed as an account of individual development, is more useful as a social story for liberatory purposes. But psychoanalytic theory is a story about the inevitable psychic oppression of women. Not all women are psychically disadvantaged as the psychoanalytic myth describes, and those women who are cannot help themselves or be helped if helper and client believe that the psychic disadvantage is inevitable. Insofar as women as a category and imagined group of real individuals do not have the same power as men, feminism as critical theory is necessary, and psychoanalytic theory provides one compelling story of why feminism is necessary. As such, psychoanalytic theory is a heuristic or rhetorical device.

As critical theory, feminism, in addition to describing the condition of women socially and psychologically, must generate a politics capable of changing human history by balancing or overcoming the ruling power of men. Because it is not enough to create moral and political theories that can be enacted only within a broader life world in which men rule, women first need a historical identity, although not a standpoint, from which they can become a historical force. A standpoint is precluded because if women identify with their past conditions of oppression, they face the unnecessary danger of getting sucked back into them, and the only shared identity among women is a relational one whereby specific contents of gender are left blank for cultural and individual inscription. The psychoanalytic human female is one possible inscription, but as the oppressive content which it is, it is not something that can be productively identified with, and it is for that reason no more than an historical reference point for a new subject.

The modern European political and economic technologizing project, or history as we know it, continues as though its most influential participants are simply the heirs of their colonialist forebears. It is not known what it would take for women to become a historical force and it cannot be known whether women would succeed in redirecting men's trajectory if they became such a force. But women are the last hope for such redirection at this time. The Western U.S.-European corporate juggernaut has little difficulty in defeating or coopting men in other cultures, and it encounters no resistance from the natural environment, except for the slow morbidity that will eventually take all *Homo sapiens sapiens* with it.

The nineteenth and twentieth centuries saw a series of movements by labor, democratic liberals, ecologists, nonwhites, and women in all sectors of the technologizing project. None of the movements has been completely successful, but sufficient liberatory progress was secured so that a vision of the success of all of them in a new, pluralistic version of the capitalist world order can be entertained and upheld as an ideal. Nonetheless, that utopia is rapidly showing itself to be devoid of many of the human values of its constituent sectors. Perhaps war, other forms of unjust violence, famine, and disease could be eliminated and all of the modern and postmodern dreams realized. But the context and backdrop of such a utopia has not yet been reimagined in a way that corrects the historical rule of men as such. The structure of the human life world has been created by men as a fulfillment of their chosen values and constructed identities, even in its utopian form. It has not yet been possible to think about a life world with a background structure that at least included, if it were not supplanted by, the assigned values and constructed identities of women. If the world order so far has indeed been the phallic order, then the most that feminists have aimed for is a phallus of their own. In Freudian terms, feminists have not yet surpassed penis envy, with its attendant resentment and deficiency of libido.

We do not know if Freud was right about the importance and underlying pervasiveness of sexuality in all human endeavors. If we knew what sexuality is and we could be confident that it is a universal human something, its importance and pervasiveness in apparently nonsexual matters would be an empirical question that could be decided eventually by relevant scientists. But since we do not know what sexuality is, our understanding of its importance and pervasiveness depends on the fundamental terms with which we construct our anthropologies and psychologies.

We do not know what sexuality is, but we do know what heterosexuality has been—the sexual desire of human males for human females, and sometimes vice versa, which has the reproduction of the human species as its most general aim and central, generating value. The great overriding project of the human species so far in history has been its reproductive success as a biological species. However, this does not happen automatically, as it seems to in other species. Human beings require elaborate social systems and learned techniques of gender differentiation to bring them to the point of reproduction. Human reproduction, moreover, has two parts: first a new member of the species is created, and second that individual is encultured to contribute to its own acts of biological creation. For millennia in the West, the concept of reproduction has been held distinct from the concept of creation because only God was believed to be capable of creation, particularly the creation of human beings. That abrogation of responsibility has served to obscure several things: human children are not automatic replicas of their parents, either biologically or socially and culturally; the social reproduction of culture through deliberate, albeit traditional practices is a capability that could result in different cultures in the future. Human beings create human beings and they could create them in different ways, as well as create different kinds of human beings.

Nonetheless, it is difficult to offer a convincing theoretical description of the condition of women as beings now on the threshold of human history. I will therefore turn to a literary example, the title character Elizabeth Costello in the 2003 novel by J. M. Coetzee. Elizabeth Costello is a world-famous Australian novelist, sixty-six years old in 1995. She lives alone in Canberra, perhaps with a cat. Her son John, an academic physicist and astrologist, teaches in a college in Massachusetts, while her daughter lives in France. Elizabeth's sister, Blanche, is a Catholic nun who runs a hospital for AIDS patients in Zululand. Elizabeth's interactions with significant people in her life consist of visits and professional conferences and events, which require arduous travel to the United States and Europe. Such encounters are the substance of the novel.

All of the encounters are failures in human connection and communication, principally because Elizabeth expresses opinions that are at odds with basic assumptions of the others. Her son finds her embarrassing, irritating, and physically repellant, even though he is protective of her frailty and proud of her literary achievements. Her daughter-in-law, a philosopher, is intellectually contemptuous of her and infuriated by her moral advocacy of vegetarianism. Blanche, her sister, has an intransigent religiosity and thinks that Elizabeth's life and work is a human failure. A former lover, Emmanuel Egudu, whom she encounters while they both lecture on a luxury cruise, vaguely mocks her criticism of his theory that the African novel is an oral genre.

Elizabeth's varied audiences are disappointed, confused, and even angered by her talks. She talks about Kafka and realism on the occasion of collecting a $50,000 literary prize, when it was expected that she would discuss feminism and postcolonialism. She tells the audience on the cruise ship that the novel is always about the past of a particular nation . . . in a talk about the future of the novel. When expected to talk about her own work, she delivers an emotional diatribe against reason and philosophers, advocates for animal rights and vegetarianism, and compares the treatment of animals bred for food with the Nazi treatment of Jews. This comparison outrages a professor who accuses her of comparing animals to Jews and, presumably by implication, comparing Jews to animals because Jews were treated like animals. (The professor's logic is fuzzy here, and Coetzee doesn't help Elizabeth out with the rebuttal that she assumes at the outset that animals are entitled to the same treatment as humans.) In a conference on evil, she focuses on the evil of Paul West's fictional depiction of the execution of conspirators against Hitler. Elizabeth does not seem to enjoy any of her public talks and she is as uncomfortable or discomforted as those with whom she interacts. However, she never waivers and neither are they drawn to her or her views, beyond being impressed by her literary fame. The distance between Elizabeth and others in the novel remains constant, not so much in the mode of alienation but in the simple fact that no one changes or moves closer.

The conclusion of the novel is a protracted hallucination or reverie about a state of limbo in the afterlife. (It is not intended by the author to be an actual experience of the afterlife because Elizabeth Costello lives on in a subsequent short story by Coetzee, "As a Woman Grows Older," which is set six years later.)[23] Elizabeth alights from a bus to a border town with a large gate, past which she is not permitted entry. She is required to testify before a panel of judges who ask her to state her beliefs. She refuses to do this because, she says, her work as a novelist means that she is an observer who has no beliefs. After several failed appearances in court, she asks the gatekeeper,

"Do you see many people like me, people in my situation?"

"All the time," he says. "We see people like you all the time."[24]

We cannot conclude from any of this that Elizabeth is wholeheartedly altruistic, or even that she is someone with a good heart, who, as her son speculates, may not be "a thinker." Her novels are said not to be comforting and when her son thinks of her cruel insight "about sex, about passion and jealousy and envy," he concludes that there is something inhuman about her, like a cat: "One of those large cats that pause as they eviscerate their victim and, across the torn-open belly, give you a cold yellow stare."[25] When Elizabeth criticizes Blanche's simple attitude of compassion toward the afflicted, Blanche reproaches her for choosing "the wrong Greek," Apollo, instead of Orpheus.[26] A strange postscript to the novel consists of a letter to Francis Bacon from Elizabeth Chandos, who describes her husband's withdrawal from the world into apocalyptic visions and then implores Bacon to "save" him.

Elizabeth Costello is less a story than a description of a perplexing condition. If one considers Elizabeth Costello and her condition as universal of a type, a personification of contemporary feminist women who have repudiated their past identities as sexual objects, sexual females, wives, lovers, and so forth, several important insights result. Elizabeth may refuse to state what her beliefs are at the gate because as she says, she is a writer of fiction and as such merely observes. This can be taken to mean that as a writer of fiction she is not in a position to think about the world as it is. She makes things up.[27] But if we imagine Elizabeth to take the liberty of expressing real beliefs, I think she could say something like this:

> *I take it that in requesting my beliefs you are not asking for a list of all of the ordinary assumptions I walk around with, such as the fact that water freezes at a certain temperature, or that too much fatty food is bad for one's health. Rather, I take it that you want to know what my opinions are concerning subjects that are important.*
>
> *I do not think that all who die come to this gate, but only those who have made a kind of first cut, as in an employment interview. You see, I do not believe that there is effortless bliss on the other side of the gate, but rather more work to do, of a kind I have not had an opportunity to pursue so far. Nevertheless, I am supplicating you, as it were, because I would like to do this work. I envision it as the work of changing the world, for the better.*

The beliefs of mine that are relevant to this situation are those beliefs that are opposed to others of goodwill who also want to change the world for the better. My argument, if these beliefs taken together can be considered an argument, is this: fiction no longer has a future because the reader can no longer be trusted to be elevated by it. One has to appeal to too many readers to write fiction at this time, and taken together, en masse, the fiction-reading public wants to escape and be entertained. I have therefore concluded, first of all, that beliefs have to stated plainly in such a way that those who hear or read them, provided that they are not insane or otherwise deluded, will have no opportunity to misinterpret or evade them.

As I said, my beliefs are in opposition to others who can be considered of goodwill. I believe that humanity can save itself only if everyone returns to the most basic moral principle. Do no harm. We need to cultivate our imaginations so that we can empathize with all human beings and animals. You may wonder how the imagination is to be cultivated without fiction and my answer is Francis Bacon's answer. We must acquire more experience and apply reason to it.

In the normal course of a life, those of us who have been fortunate to have the enlarged experience of both our rulers and of members of groups who do not rule, such as women and Africans, and, yes, animals, but especially women, are in a privileged position to do the work of saving the world. All of the goodwilled people know that the world is now in a mess, but few directly state that men have created the mess. I am, of course, a woman, but as a result of my age, which has caused the normal functions of my gender to fade, I am able to suspend the subordinated and abused qualities of being a woman and plainly state my beliefs to men.

I have three more specific beliefs that might interest you. I do not think that educated people from cultures with oral traditions can afford not to write. I think that compassion requires reason as much as reason requires compassion. I believe that evil must be dismissed from the world and from our own hearts, without allowing ourselves to be fascinated by it.

That is all. Those are my beliefs, as a former woman who is not a man and a former fiction writer who is not a philosopher. To you they are Elizabeth Costello's beliefs, but to me, they are the truth.

If we read Elizabeth Costello as a feminist and the gate as the barrier between women and history, the statement of belief I have ascribed to her would constitute a moral demand for the entrance of women into history. It would be naive to think that such a demand alone would be effective to gain entry. Political strategy would be necessary and before that, a theory of history and individual freedom.

NOTES

1. Freud, "Infantile Sexuality," in *Three Contributions to the Theory of Sex*, in *The Basic Writings of Sigmund Freud*, trans. and ed. A. A. Brill (New York: Modern Library, 1995), 548.

2. "So, since we are not clever persons, I think we should employ the method of search that we should use if we, with not very keen vision, were bidden to read small letters from a distance, and then someone had observed that these same letters exist elsewhere larger and on a larger surface. . . . There is justice of one man, we say, and, I suppose, also of an entire city? . . . Is not the city larger than the man? . . . Then, perhaps, there would be more justice in the larger object and more easy to apprehend. If it please you, then, let us first look for its quality in states, and then only examine it also in the individual, looking for the likeness of the greater in the form of the less." Plato, *Republic*, in *The Collected Dialogues of Plato*, trans. Paul Shorey, ed. Edith Hamilton and Huntington Cairns (New York: Pantheon, 1961), 2.368.d,e.369a.615.

3. This is an intellectual curiosity now, but not an anomaly given the intellectual history of psychoanalysis. In *The History of the Psychoanalytic Movement* (1914), Freud was optimistic about the spread of psychoanalysis as a method of interpretation, through what he called "mental life" and the arts (in *Basic Writings of Sigmund Freud*, 918–24).

4. Heidi Hartmann, "The Unhappy Marriage of Marxism and Feminism: Toward a More Progressive Union," in *The Second Wave: A Reader in Feminist Theory*, ed. Linda J. Nicholson (New York: Routledge, 1997), 97–122.

5. For instance, when Marx and Engels address the issue of "free love" under communism, they justify it with the claim that because bourgeois marriage institutionalizes adultery, it is more immoral than a communist social-sexual system would be: "Bourgeois marriage is in reality a system of wives in common and thus, at the most, what the Communists might possibly be reproached with, is that they desire to introduce, in substitution for a hypocritically concealed, an openly legalized community of women." Karl Marx and Friedrich Engels, *The Communist Manifesto*, in *Karl Marx: Selected Writings*, ed. Lawrence H. Simon (Indianapolis: Hackett, 1994), 157–86, 173.

6. Freud, *History of the Psychoanalytic Movement*, in *Basic Writings of Sigmund Freud*, 992.

7. Freud, *History of the Psychoanalytic Movement*, 937.

8. Freud, *History of the Psychoanalytic Movement*, 937–38.

9. Freud, *Totem and Taboo*, in *Basic Writings of Sigmund Freud*, 775.

10. Freud, "Infantile Sexuality," in *Basic Writings of Sigmund Freud*, 552.

11. Freud, "Infantile Sexuality," 551.

12. Freud, "Infantile Sexuality," 551.

13. Freud, "The Transformations of Puberty," in *Basic Writings of Sigmund Freud*, 593.

14. Gayle Rubin, "The Traffic in Women: Notes on the 'Political Economy' of Sex," in *Toward an Anthropology of Women*, ed. Rayna R. Reither (New York: Monthly Review Press, 1975).

15. Freud, "Infantile Sexuality," 565.

16. Freud, "Infantile Sexuality," 565 n. 1.

17. Freud, "Infantile Sexuality," 581–82.

18. Rubin, "Traffic in Women," 48.

19. Rubin, "Traffic in Women," 151–52.

20. Rubin, "Traffic in Women," 151–52.

21. This is Freud's underlying assumption throughout "Infantile Sexuality," and at the beginning of "Transformations of Puberty," he makes it explicit: "With the beginning of

puberty, changes set in, which transform the infantile sexual life into its definite normal form. Hitherto, the sexual instinct has been preponderantly autoerotic; it now finds the sexual object" (572).

22. Sigmund Freud, *History of the Psychoanalytic Movement*, 908.

23. J. M. Coetzee, "As a Woman Grows Older," *New York Review of Books*, January 15, 2004, 11–15.

24. J. M. Coetzee, *Elizabeth Costello* (New York: Viking, 2003), 224–25.

25. Coetzee, *Elizabeth Costello*, 5.

26. Coetzee, *Elizabeth Costello*, 145.

27. Indeed, she makes a point of claiming that she does exactly that during a television interview. See Coetzee, *Elizabeth Costello*, 12.

7

A Feminist Theory of History

History as already written has been an account of past events, peoples, nations, individuals, institutions, and ideas. As a recognized discipline, history includes what is already presumed to be important in a specific regard. In regard to leadership and power among humans, which are already important to men, historians (who have mostly been men) have focused on men and their public and official achievements. This focus has yielded the history of all human beings—of women as well as men. Reclaiming the achievements of women from this public and official perspective does not change the fact that men have ruled. Women's actions, public as well as private, until very recently have been omitted from systematic studies of the past, underscoring the historical power and authority of men. From a feminist perspective, it is not sufficient to include women in history. Rather, they need to be relocated as the equals of men in those public and official achievements that women as well as men recognize to be world shaping for women as well as men. No rewriting of the past can accomplish this. For that reason, a feminist history at this time must include the future. Indeed, in contexts among women where there is shared information about the past, history might be entirely about the future.

And why not? History generally is an understanding of times different from our own, and one of its purposes is to improve our understanding of the present. But if feminists are to do more than speculate about the future, it is necessary to have a theory of history that explicitly includes the future in addition to, or even in place of, the past. Feminist history of the future requires a well-grounded understanding of what can and should happen, given shared world-shaping objectives that will better the lives of women. Such objectives would need to include those aspects of the world that indirectly influence the lives of women and, beyond that, visions of a better world for men and women, and the natural environment also. One way to surpass mere speculation and get beyond crystal ball–type wish lists is to have a link between the past and the present, and a link between the present and the future.

The link between the past and the present has already been constructed by second wave feminists in critical work about male dominance in the present, together with genealogical work about its ideological and material antecedents in the past. That historical project explains how and why women have been omitted from history, not only in being excluded from the record but in being prevented from doing the kinds of things that have been recorded. The feminist historical project about the link between the past and the present is robust across many scholarly disciplines, and its paradigm continues to yield knowledge that is relevant, interesting, and instructive. But the feminist historical link between the present and the future has not yet been constructed. In this chapter, I want to sketch a model for that link by a heuristic use of Jean-Paul Sartre's heuristic use of Karl Marx's theory.[1] I will begin with a brief consideration of existing feminist historical accounts of male rule, that is, of one aspect of the feminist historical link between the past and the present. I will then discuss how women are different from a social class in Marxist terms. After that, I will show how parts of Sartre's theory of social change highlight issues that are pertinent to a feminist theory of history, and how other parts of it are no longer relevant to such a theory.

FEMINIST HISTORICAL ACCOUNTS OF MALE RULE

Perhaps, before history was recorded, there was a time of matriarchy or at least equality in power between the sexes. Paula Gunn Allen in *The Sacred Hoop* makes a case for the existence of American indigenist traditions of women's leadership and political power before patriarchy was imposed by European invaders.[2] Carolyn Merchant and Merry Weisner have argued that before the early modern period in Europe, women participated equally with men in family industries, agriculture, and the production of goods, to the extent that households were self-sufficient, exporting economic units. Women also dominated in the practice of midwifery and crafts such as brewing and tanning.[3] This economic effectiveness of women did not constitute economic equality with men, and it existed before the industrial revolution conclusively moved workplaces out of households and institutionalized the division between work life and family life. It is now widely agreed among feminists that the public/private division of human energy began to structure Western culture during the seventeenth century. Since then, all of the important world-shaping power has emanated from the pubic sphere as ruled by men.[4]

Because no existing societies are matriarchal, it is difficult to see how the unrecorded existence of matriarchy and political gender equality (or preindustrial economic equality in some cases) could be directly relevant to feminist political theory at this time. Too little is known about ancient matriarchies and politically egalitarian societies that may have existed, and women's participation with men in household-based economics was not full parity. The economic gains of contemporary women have largely accompanied the entry of women into the masculine public domain. Given the modern history of the public/private division and male hegemony in the more powerful public domain, there is no material link from either ancient matriarchy and equality (or premodern economic equality in some cases) to either matriarchy or equality in the future. However, ideas of matriarchy and both political and economic gender equality suggest ideals that could be implemented in the future. Such ideals offer a standard that enables critique of political theory which has historically been compatible with the exclusion of women from domains of human power.

Carole Pateman in *The Sexual Contract* explains how social contract theory, which rationalized equitable and fair public relations among modern owners and citizens, ignored questions of fairness and equity in relations between men and women. Early social contract theorists, reasoning from an imagined (or imaginary) "state of nature," imported women into civil society along with men, but without the same public autonomy men had. According to Pateman, women were not identified as principals of the social contract but were the subject about which the social contract was presumed to be fair and equitable: "Women are not party to the original contract through which men transform their natural freedom into the security of civil freedom. Women are the subject of the contract. The sexual contract is the vehicle through which men transform their natural right over women into the security of civil patriarchal right."[5]

Pateman's concept of the sexual contract explicates how only men rule in societies that purport to be democratic and even have universal suffrage. If Pateman is correct in claiming that the (modern Western) social contract always presupposes the sexual contract, this means that the political inclusion of women (e.g., via suffrage) in societies assumed to be governed by a social contract cannot in itself enable women to be the political equals of men.[6] If Pateman is incorrect and political inclusion is sufficient for political equality, we have to ask why women are not yet politically equal to men, after almost a century of suffrage and almost half a century of legal protection for women against discrimination in employment and education. As things now stand, women are not the equals of men in political power and we do not yet have a political theory or ideology that could support a practice of women's political empowerment which would result in their equality. Neither theories of the social construction of gender, nor theories of how the public rule of men has been rationalized by men in Western history, can fill in for such a direct theory of women's political empowerment and exercise of power. Those theories are not about the future—and women did not have political power in the past.

All of the social contract theorists ask what would make government just from a perspective before or outside of (i.e., without) government. This theoretical approach is strange to critical theorists who believe that the identities through which human beings know one another and interact, that is identities of gender and race, are socially constructed.[7] Thus there is no basis for a definition of women that does not rely on some social construction. Because the political empowerment of women makes sense only from a starting point *within* society, it is important not to fall back on a false concept of women as fictional natural or biological beings who inherently have something in each and every one of them that makes her a woman. The definition of women I have been working with in this book—human beings who are assigned to, or identify with the disjunctive category of female birth designees, biological mothers, or primary sexual choices of men—avoids that naturalistic illusion. It is as the socially constructed category FMP that women might become politically empowered subjects in the future.

Because category FMP distinguishes women from the category of men via roles that are antithetical to political power as we know it, rule by women allows for a radically different kind of rule than the aggression, violence, exploitation, and destruction that have attended rule by men. As women were naturalized in social contract theory, so has political power been naturalized, and in addition reified, by imbuing it with those attitudes of rage, greed, and disrespect from which individual men take care to disassociate their individual characters. All of the "following orders," "playing the game," and "being realistic" self-descriptions of individual political behavior are examples of this reification. This is not to deny that any particular individual man is probably powerless to oppose the ruthlessness of a political system. Nonetheless, feminists might view existing political power as the medium for that aspect or part of the construction of manhood, which individual men find it convenient to disavow in public, where "public" means not only "out of the house" but also "known by all."

The task of a mature feminist politics is for women to hold men accountable and responsible for the way they exercise political power, as a medium for the disavowed part of their construction of manhood. This could be done by other men, but historically men have been unable to resist either the domination or corruption of men more powerful than themselves. The task of accountability must be done for the good of all human beings and the preservation of the planetary life world. If undertaken by women, it probably must be done without violence and it is as close to being impossible as a possible task can be. But it is a task that can be undertaken only from within society by women as social beings. What preliminarily qualifies women for this task is not some peace-loving or altruistic or nurturing essence but two things more superficial, evident, and indisputable than that. First, because they are not men, women (understood as category FMP) are not stereotypically afflicted with the destructive aspects of masculine gender constructions. Second, where there are electorates, women now have suffrage on close to a worldwide basis, and they are more than half of all the voters.

For women to hold men morally accountable, they would have to rule politically or gendered rule would have to be equal. The question to be answered now is, What would it take for women to modify their social identities without losing them, so that they can undertake the task of ruling? The short answer is that they would have to become something like a social class.

WOMEN AS A SOCIAL CLASS

Iris Young, in a summary of the lesbian and nonwhite challenges to second wave feminism, suggests that feminists wanted a universal definition of women so that there could be a "counter theory to Marxism . . . a feminist theory that would conceive sex or gender as a category with as much theoretical weight as class."[8] The question of a universal definition of women is not the same as the question of whether women are a social class.[9] Chapters 1–2 justify a universal definition of women that is based on their shared relations of identifying with or being assigned to category FMP. But that it is possible to construct a universal definition of women does not automatically mean that women are a social class. Indeed, women understood as those assigned to, or identifying with, category FMP, are only vaguely analogous to a social class because social classes, as understood in Marxist theory, are defined by their relation to the dominant means of production in a society. Each class owns different kinds of things or furnishes different kinds of labor to the economy, which have a price in that same economy. Much of women's labor, such as reproductive work, domestic work, child care, family work, and so forth, has not been monetarized. In particular, units of women's reproductive labor are not uniformly priced or available in the marketplace in orderly ways, if we use other services as a comparison.[10] Without its being monetarized or priced, this work is not officially recognized as part of the economy. Therefore women cannot be an economic class in Marx's sense, unless there is a drastic change in the requirement that classes do or can participate in the economy in recognized ways or in our understanding of what classes are.

Thus far historical classes have been, as Pateman has pointed out, implicitly based on the work and ownership of men within them. Under capitalism, the ruling classes are those that own the most in a hierarchy of classes, as that ownership has been translated into political power and authority. Racial hierarchies intersect with class hierarchies, but whites dominate overall. Racial identities are not the same as class identities and cannot be fully reduced to them, owing to racisms that operate within each socioeconomic class. Furthermore, racially specific man–woman systems vary in gender roles and duties as a result of variations in material and political conditions. (For instance, because Africans American men have been denied economic opportunities in a patriarchal American past, African American women have a longer history of working outside the home than white women, and they have done different kinds of work than white women.) Nonetheless, disadvantaged racial groups have sex-gender systems that are similar to the sex-gender systems of advantaged racial groups, in the most general sense of distinguishing between men and women and dividing their labor.

Once specific taxonomies of race and class are understood, women are the ones who identify with or are assigned to the FMP category, within each race, class, class sector of a racial group, or racial sector of a class. Thus far, women have had the class status of the men in their race/class group because it is the men in such groups who have had their work priced, or owned property or capital. Because so much of women's work enters the economic system indirectly, their work does not qualify them to be leading participants in class systems or to constitute a distinct class, insofar as class systems have been economically understood. Given the historical identity of women as females, mothers, men's sexual choices (i.e., given a historical understanding of what women are in society), the inclusion of women in professions and other officially monetarized sections of Western economies, over the last thirty-odd years, does not so much represent economic inclusion or gains for women, which could eventually be translated into political power for women, as it represents a growing androgyny in the workplace. Such androgyny allows women to perform and be paid for work formally restricted to men, without in any way undermining the power and authority of men. In contexts such as the home of a heterosexual couple, to which women who benefit from androgyny in the workplace cannot extend that androgyny (or construct new forms of it), they are not relieved of their nonmonetarized women's work but are still expected to perform it in a "second shift."

The construction of women as a class in a Marxist sense would therefore require a major revision of the principles of social structure. Ideas of economic values would have to change. That could occur through a wide scale and official monetarization of women's work. But before considering what such monetarization might look like, we need to remember that our ultimate interest here is not economics but politics, which I am assuming is driven by economics. That is, if the Marxist view that economics drives politics is correct, then political power has to be preceded by economic power in order for a class to exist and then become able to rule. Perhaps I should say more about the Marxist framework that I am using in this regard.

According to Marx (roughly speaking), because human beings have to produce the materials to sustain their existence, they are motivated to acquire and possess those things. In modern capitalistic society, material goods are economic goods that are represented by money. Those who have large amounts of money or the apparatus to accumulate money and spend it to acquire more money have capital—they are capitalists. Capitalists as an economic class require large numbers of individuals who do not have capital to repetitively sell them their labor in exchange for wages that enable their physical and social survival. The wages allow the workers to "reproduce" their labor so that they can continue to work. The prices that capitalists sell their goods for, minus the cost of producing them, which includes the cost of labor, is their profit. Capitalists compete with each other for markets. Because capitalism is a competitive system, in order to keep going it must continually expand by renewing the material resources of production, keeping the cost of labor cheap, and finding more markets.[11] The ideological, or normative political, implication of the Marxist analysis is that the profits of owners should belong to the workers, or that the workers should be owners.

The feminist critique of the Marxist analysis has been that women have furnished domestic, social, and biological reproductive work to both male capitalists and workers, without being paid wages. Many women were paid in kind when it was possible for a male wage earner to support a wife and children. It became necessary for middle-class wives and mothers to work outside the home to help support their households, beginning with U.S. inflation in the 1970s (which was, coincidentally, when the second wave feminist critique of the standard Marxist analysis got going). Before then, throughout history, when poor women worked outside the home, they, as middle-class women after the 1970s, performed unpaid "women's work" in addition to wage work. Whether women are supported to perform only "women's work" or they work outside the home to, in effect, support their own women's work, women's work represents a boon to capitalists because it reproduces the workers capitalists employ, both creatively in the biological sense, and supportively in taking care of them at home so that they can report to work the next day. This is a gift to capitalists that results from instances of the sex-gender system in which women are obligated to do women's work for men, without pay.[12] The normative, but not yet political, implication of the feminist critique of the Marxist analysis is that women should be paid for their domestic, social, and biological work.

Assume that all women were paid for their women's work when wage earners other than they benefited from it.[13] They would still not be able to acquire wealth or become capitalists as a basis for political power because women's work per se does not result in products that can be exchanged for stored capitalist wealth. Family social work, gestation, and child care are interactions between particular, existent individuals, from which workers cannot be alienated without defeating the goals of such work. A woman who performed such work for high pay could not employ other women to perform the work for her, without radically changing the nature of the work. Women's work, except for repetitive drudgery, is personal work. It is not only personal in the sense of "private" but personal in being attached to the histories, personalities, and goals of specific individuals.

Like other wage earners, women who were paid for their personal women's work would be able to unite on the basis of their economic interests. Many women would be better off economically if all women were paid for their labor at standard rates. However, they would be only relatively better off, since such a system would require a radical redistribution of wealth. There might be more money in circulation chasing the same amount of material goods, which would mean that all material goods would become more expensive and less accessible to those on the low end of the wage scale. Because simply paying women for what they are already doing would not result in more production within the present economic system, the transfer of wealth would probably be accomplished through fiat inflation, simply by creating more money or credit. Paying women for their currently unpaid labor could destroy the current economic system, especially if women who work for low wages in the Third World were paid. As prices of goods and services rose, people would buy less of them, business would contract, there would be massive unemployment, and all of the other factors of a major economic depression would ensue. One result of the depression might be that women might go back to doing their women's work without pay because there would be no money to pay them and the work itself is necessary for human survival and the support of other work. But all of this is unlikely to happen because the capitalists who politically control the present system through the translation of existing wealth into political power would never consent to pay for women's work to begin with. Still, women might organize and force such consent by going on strike and refusing to perform their women's work.

What is interesting about a women's strike scenario is it posits women as a social class that has no defined relationship to existing means of production, because as women they are not currently paid for their work. To take that scenario seriously is to begin to see the limitations of any Marxist analysis that defines social classes in terms of their officially recognized relationship to the means of production. Marxism defines production narrowly as the economic products of human society as it has been ruled by men. There is thus a circularity based on gender that is necessary to get a Marxist analysis going and keep it going. Only things produced by men, and women working as men work, have economic value; and the dynamics of economic value are sufficient to account for everything that is important in human history, which is also defined by men. (It should be remembered that at this time, men are as much a socially constructed category as women and that some workplaces are androgynous in reality, despite their historically masculine methods and products.)

One does not have to be a feminist to make a distinction and defend a difference between material things that result from human labor and the kinds of "intangibles" that are associated with women's work (as historically assigned). Government-sponsored welfare programs for a while provided some monetary acknowledgment of the value of women's work, as do maternity and paternity leave and perhaps some forms of alimony that accompany child support. But generally, in the United States at least, society values women's work as a necessity that can and should be taken for granted. In the Western tradition, women's work is supposed to be accompanied by commitments and emotional attitudes that have what Kant called "dignities" rather than "prices." Women are supposed to perform their women's work out of love or something that "no amount of money can buy." From that perspective, which many feminists, particularly ethicists of care, might partly share, it would be morally wrong to put prices on women's work, or on some core of it, such as the love of mothers for their children. More radical Marxist feminist critics might argue that all women's work, insofar as it is unpaid and controlled by men, is a form of gender slavery, but other feminists would object that motherhood, at least, is not only chosen by many women but is also greatly fulfilling to them as autonomous beings.

There is another view of the exclusion of women's work from the realm of what can be priced, namely, that it does not merit entry into modern or postmodern economic systems. Some consumers might believe that women's traditional material products and services are not as good as commercial commodities and services because they are irregular, homemade, hand-made, amateurish, and not competitive with mass-produced products and standardized services. Unsentimental futurists might hold that women's traditional psychic and biological services would be more justly and efficiently performed by trained professionals: teachers, counselors, mediators, and in the biological realm, sex workers, egg donors, and tenders of artificial wombs.

Whether one takes the position that women's work ought to be priced, should not be priced, or cannot be priced compared to manufactured commodities or professional services, the result is the same. The basis on which women could be a social class, with economic interests transferable into political power, would not likely be their work as women. Indeed, to consider human rule on an axis of gender rather than material production requires thinking beyond a standard Marxist analysis of history and social class. It requires thinking beyond economics, beyond what people do to contribute to a material system. Since the essential definition of women I have been working with does not posit any special female substance, nature, psychology, or development, there is nothing intrinsic to women, individually or en masse, that requires them to be a distinctive social class in a Marxist economic sense. Rather, if they are to be a distinctive social class, it will need to be based on their external identification as human beings assigned to a category FMP, and the striking fact that they are over half of the human population. The contingency of the FMP identification, together with the population fact, could be sufficient to catapult women into human history, given a theoretical link between the present and the future mentioned earlier and a specific political program. I now turn to Sartre for that present-future link, although somewhat guardedly.

SARTRE'S HEURISTIC USE OF MARX

In the *Critique of Dialectical Reason* and *Search for a Method*, Sartre connected his theory of individual human freedom and responsibility, as developed in *Being and Nothingness*, to Marxism.[14] In *Search for a Method*, he first proclaimed Marxism to be the dominant philosophy of his age—in a very broad conception of philosophy:

> If philosophy is to be simultaneously a totalization of knowledge, a method, a regulative Idea, an offensive weapon, and a community of language, if this "vision of the world" is also an instrument which ferments rotten societies, if this particular conception of a man or a group of men becomes the culture and sometimes the nature of a whole class—then it is clear that the periods of philosophical creation are rare. Between the seventeenth century and the twentieth, I see three such periods, which I would designate by the names of the men who dominated them: there is the "moment" of Descartes and Locke, that of Kant and Hegel, finally that of Marx.[15]

Thus Sartre conceives the philosophy of Marx or Marxism as normative and descriptive, theoretical and practical, a discourse and a practice, something in the world as well as in the mind, perhaps what we would call a paradigm or a "research program," real politics, as well as a critical theory. In short, philosophy for Sartre is all-encompassing. I don't know if feminism, in the comparatively minimal form of critical theory that it has seemed daring to claim for it in this book, could in the same way qualify as a total and even totalitarian structure of both those aspects of psychic and material human life that are pernicious and those that are benign. I think that for some feminists, feminism is such a totality of thought and reality, while for others it applies only to limited aspects of human life. But, and this is an important insight for any general or universal theory, including feminism (as the second wave was obliged to accept), insofar as such theories are "philosophy" in Sartre's sense—and feminism is at least in part such a theory, or part of one—they must be continually contextualized, as description and prescription for human experience. Sartre himself emphasized that philosophy cannot be created in a way that is insulated from experience, and it cannot be applied to experience without further consultation with experience.

> What is necessary is simply to reject apriorism. The unprejudiced examination of the historical object will be able by itself to determine in each case whether the action or the work reflects the superstructural motives of groups or of individuals formed by certain basic conditionings, or whether one can explain them only by referring immediately to economic contradictions and to conflicts of material interests.[16]

For Sartre, these "economic contradictions" and "conflicts of material interests" constitute the immediate social situations in which human beings live. The interaction of individuals with them are what in earlier writings motivated Sartre's philosophy of existentialism. Human beings were abandoned in the world in a way that revealed them to themselves as well as it revealed the world. Consciousness became aware of itself in a concrete situation and in that awareness was a freedom that could not be escaped. The individual was always forced to make choices (which revealed values) and animated and gave sense to value systems. Because of this freedom, regardless of external constraints or the lack of liberty, individual existence was the starting point for Sartre's philosophy. Moreover, the individual was responsible for the entire world because it was the individual who made the world meaningful as such, and because in choosing for oneself, a choice was made for everyone.[17] Sartre himself summed up this philosophy in "Existentialism Is a Humanism":

> Man is nothing but what he makes of himself. Such is the first principle of existentialism. It is also what is called subjectivity, the name we are labeled with when charges are brought against us. But what do we mean by this, if not that man has a greater dignity than a stone or a table? For we mean that man first exists, that is that man first of all is the being who hurls himself toward a future and who is conscious of imagining himself as being in the future. Man is at the start a plan which is aware of itself, rather than a patch of moss, a piece of garbage, or a cauliflower; nothing exists prior to this plan; there is nothing in heaven; man will be what he will have planned to be. . . . When we say that man chooses his own self, we mean that every one of us does likewise; but we also mean by that that in making this choice he also chooses all men. In fact, in creating the man that we want to be, there is not a single one of our acts which does not at the same time create an image of man as we think he ought to be.[18]

Throughout "Existentialism Is a Humanism," Sartre emphasizes the fundamental component of individual choice in human life: "Man is nothing else than his plan; he exists only to the extent that he fulfills himself; he is therefore nothing else than the ensemble of his acts, nothing else than his life."[19] Awareness of this inescapable choice is the basis of anguish:

> The existentialists say at once that man is anguish. What that means is this: the man who involves himself and who realizes that he is not only the person he chooses to be, but also a lawmaker who is, at the same time, choosing all mankind as well as himself, can not help escape the feeling of his total and deep responsibility.[20]

In his engagement with Marxism, in strong contrast to earlier formulations, Sartre locates existentialism as an "ideology, . . . a parasitical system living on the margin of Knowledge, which at first it opposed but into which today it seeks to be integrated."[21] Existentialism, which began with individual, first-person human experience as the starting point for philosophy, is, for the later Sartre, no more than a factor or a term or a real component of events in human society, most generally understood.

However, if Sartre seriously intended to demonstrate how existentialism is no more than a local ideology of Marxism (i.e., of what he considers philosophy), I do not think that he would have devoted as much of *Search for Method*, as he does, in criticizing the a priori theorizing of Marxists (which he repeatedly calls idealism) and grappling with the contradiction between the determinism of historical forces in what he calls the *pratico-inerte*, and the necessity of individual action for history to occur, not to mention the power of individual action to redirect those forces. (This emphasis on self-chosen individual action as the foundation for consciousness, self-consciousness, and change recurs throughout his biographical work on Flaubert, Genet, Baudelaire, and Freud.) Indeed, little in the content of Sartre's earlier existentialism changes when he connects existentialism with Marxism, and despite his enigmatic claim that existentialism is a local ideology of Marxism, the tail clearly wags the dog in *Search for a Method*: "As soon as there will exist for everyone a margin of real freedom beyond the production of life, Marxism will have lived out its span; a philosophy of freedom will take its place."[22]

I suggest that Sartre's overall intention is to emphasize existentialist choice as a way of realizing the utopian egalitarian dreams of Marxism. Once that has been accomplished, the distinction between the freedom of consciousness and the liberty of individuals in an oppressive society will no longer be a contradiction. The conditions of inequality and injustice that Marxism brings to light become the matter or situation on which free consciousness works. On this interpretation, Sartre's Marxism is already embedded in his early existentialism. In *War Diaries* (Notebook 14), in addressing the question of whether poverty is a revolutionary or paralyzing force, he writes,

> The truth is that for poverty to become a revolutionary force, it must be taken up and adopted by the pauper as *his* poverty. And not only that, but it must be

taken up as a situation that *must change*: in other words, must be replaced by the pauper in the midst of a human world in which it would be strictly intolerable. But poverty on its own is never intolerable: it is strictly *nothing*. The workers of 1835 had a standard of living infinitely below that which the worst off today would deem unacceptable. And yet they endured it, since they hadn't grasped it as a contingent situation not inherent to their essence.[23]

What is new in Sartre's later Marxism is a powerful "ideology" of the ability of individuals to act as groups that can change their common pratico-inerte—the material state of society in which they find themselves. This pratico-inerte is understood by Sartre to include residues from childhood socialization because the child develops a personality in a context in which her elders live out their social class constraints and impose them on the child. In a more standard Marxist sense, the pratico-inerte consists of the unintended collective consequences of the actions of many individuals, such as the social effects of the alienated products of labor (e.g., in our day, environmental pollution).[24] There are aspects of the empowerment Sartre envisions from group organization, which are useful for a feminist theory of history, and there are constraints in Sartre's now-Marxist existentialism, which might be self-defeating in such a theory. I will consider them in turn.

Several feminist theorists who are resigned to the impossibility of a universal definition of women (i.e., a universal women's identity) to facilitate conceiving of women as a social class have turned to Sartre's notion of the *group-in-fusion*, which arises from a series of anonymous individuals.[25] As noted earlier, the issue of whether women can be defined as a group is different from the issue of whether they are or could be a social class in Marxist terms. Marx, even with the help of Sartre, does not offer a basis on which women can be a class because Marxism has no conceptual tools for recognizing their distinctive work. But I propose that women, as category FMP, are already a group. All women everywhere recognize that they have been assigned to the category containing human beings, who have been designated female from birth, or are biological mothers, or are the primary sexual choices of men. This is more a matter that feminists need to acknowledge than it is some special liberatory insight that feminists ought to impart to the mass of women. Even formally uneducated women probably know more about their shared relational identity as women than do many academic feminists. However, feminists can create, develop, and impart to other women a future vision of women *as a historical ruling group*. Marxism, as reworked by Sartre, can offer feminists the opportunity to directly address and struggle for political power, not on the basis of an economic social class identity— which has been constructed by men to directly exploit, and indirectly support, the entire sex-gender system in which men generally dominate women—but on the basis of the fact that women constitute more than half of the voting public in present democracies. It is not necessary that women find an identity on which they can unite because they already have it, and they are furthermore also broadly aware of the superiority of their numbers. All that women need from feminists now is a spark to ignite awareness of themselves as a historical group.

Sartre does not conceive of specifically historical groups any more than Marx does because he assumes, along with Marx, that all human groups are given in an ontology of serial collectives, groups-in-fusion, and economic classes. The historical nature of these entities goes without saying for both Marx and Sartre. That such collectives, groups, and classes are ruled by men allows for the "dialectical" possibility of opposing and dislocating the entire Marxist system. Just as Freudian theory can be useful to feminists as a description of a status quo that should be changed, so can Marxist theory. The Marxist system (i.e., the structure of the male-dominated material social world as Marx more or less correctly described it) could be opposed by women through their broad awareness that they are a historical group. This self-awareness of themselves, by women, is only possible after their realization that women have been excluded from history. One cannot have a taxonomy of historical groups unless there are at least two. When there was just one, that group, the group of men, were simply the subjects of history.

Once opposed by women who are aware of themselves as historical subjects, the reigning group of men could be dislocated by the possibility of substituting a nonpriced system of values for parts of the priced one. However, as stated earlier on in this chapter, to speak of history in this sense is to evoke the future, and this is where Sartre, in both of his incarnations, is of the greatest use to feminists: Sartre (in a more accessible way than Heidegger) situates the future as a necessity for action in the present. Human life is an interlocking succession of interlocking plans, and plans require a distance from the present, against which a future situation, in some way different from the present one, is imagined. The imagined situation in the future then both motivates and at the same time serves as intention or goal for present action. We are given this formulation for individual action in *Being and Nothingness*:

> Situation and motivation are really one. The for-itself [i.e., individual consciousness that chooses] discovers itself as engaged in being, hemmed in by being, threatened by being; it discovers the state of things which surrounds it as the cause for a reaction of defense or attack. But it can make this discovery only because it freely posits the end in relation to which the state of things is threatening or favorable.[26]

And in the *Critique of Dialectical Reason*, there is a parallel formulation for the cooperative action of what Sartre calls a group-in-fusion but which feminists could view as the historical (or historicized) group of women:

A group will constitute itself only on the basis of specific circumstances, directly or indirectly connected with the life and death of organisms. But the practical movement of organization, in so far as it transcends its conditions toward its objectives, actualizes an external determination, which the gathering has already interiorised as a fantom possibility of producing itself in the field of freedom.[27]

The process of group organization is analogous to individually chosen action. As action reveals both situation and motive, the process of group organization creates a situation in which external constraints make freedom possible. The interesting difference between the freedom of individuals and groups is that the freedom of individuals is given, while the freedom of groups may emerge only against external determinations, or obstacles. This suggests that a future political organization of women might be liberating in direct proportion to the force of their historical oppression.

There are several ways in which Sartre's notion of historical autonomy would constrain a feminist theory of history. First and most obviously, his subject is unrelentingly male. Throughout both *Search for a Method* and the *Critique of Dialectical Reason*, his examples are projects of conflict and revolt that are the acts of either individual men or groups led by them: boxers, worker rebellions, men's creative projects. Sartre seems not to think that women could be agents. In *Search for a Method*, he repeatedly draws on an anthropological example in which he describes a ratio of 100 women to 250 men in an island culture as a condition of "material scarcity."[28] Such theoretical sexism is rather easily dealt with. Women are as fully subjects as men and it would be in bad faith for them to regard themselves as part of the pratico-inerte. The foregoing conception of women as an historical group bypasses and overcomes this sexism.

More serious problems with Sartre's account in the *Critique of Dialectical Reason* concern his notions of need and scarcity. They appear to have been wholeheartedly taken over from Marxist materialism, which not only describes human motivations but ends up positing all human values as reducible to the acquisition, possession, and increase of material objects: "Everything is to be explained through *need (le besoin)*; need is the first totalising relation between the material being, man, and the material ensemble of which he is part."[29]

For Sartre, human needs cannot all be satisfied, which results in struggle. "The origin of struggle always lies, in fact, in some concrete antagonism whose material condition is *scarcity (la rareté)*, in a particular form; and the real aim is objective conquest or even creation, in relation to which the destruction of the adversary is only the means."[30] The struggle among humans to satisfy material need is the result of scarcity insofar as "the whole of human development, at least up to now, has been a bitter struggle against *scarcity*."[31] While Sartre recognizes that scarcity is a historical contingency that varies due to "over-population or under-development," he insists that there are causes of the variation, such as climate or the richness of subsoil that "condition History through social structures without being conditioned by it."[32] He concludes that despite its contingency, "scarcity is a very basic human relation, both to Nature and to men."[33]

In postindustrial consumer societies, material objects have symbolic as well as direct utilitarian value and they become signifiers of status according to race, class, gender, age, occupation, and myriad other social machines that maintain unjust human hierarchies and distribute power. As a result, it is difficult, based on what *appears* to be scarce, to define what people need and what is in reality scarce on a global scale, because the myriad economic machines of capitalist technology do not present resource materials without profit-motivated intervention; the capitalist system of production operates as a middle man between many natural goods and human consumers. Needs appear to be preemptive over desires, but the desires of some appear to determine what others need. For example, is state-of-the-art medical care a need or are conditions of life that would render much of it unnecessary a need? Is animal protein a human need, or do human beings just need protein in a general sense, which could be provided by organisms grown lower down on the food chain than the great populations of chickens, cattle, pigs, and other "products" of agricultural factories? And how much of the world should we consider in identifying scarcity? Does the fact that some populations experience famine establish that there is a scarcity of food, or is the real problem a failure to distribute available food equitably, or a First and Second World practice of disrupting self-sufficient Third World economies in order to draw them into the global system of manufacture and trade, prosperity, and depression?

If needs and scarcity are relative to specific contexts, then which contexts ought to be considered primary in defining basic human needs and determining what is scarce? Neither standard Marxism nor Sartre's version of it provide grounds for judging what human needs are and identifying which needs cannot be fulfilled for everyone, owing to a final or absolute scarcity. Suppose, for instance, that all human beings need to consume on a regular basis a certain amount of water that is free of industrial impurities. Suppose also that present trends continue and a point is reached when only the affluent can afford such water. We could say either that there is a scarcity of water, as an absolute material fact of the kind to which Sartre thought he was referring, or we could say that the economic system has depleted natural stores of unpolluted water and that something is wrong with that system, the correction of which is a need. In our consideration of human needs and scarcity, human action and policy should be subjects, as much or even more than material objects.

If there is to be a significant alternative to rule by men as they have been historically constructed, and if women are the only group that could provide this alternative (because there are sufficient numbers of women and they are not men), then the alternative would have to be envisioned, if not implemented, before such judgments about need and scarcity could be made. Perhaps the notions of need and scarcity, which have been taken so seriously in liberal and even radical (left) political thought, depend on believing that human beings are inevitably motivated by material acquisition and possession. Suppose that such materialist motivation and struggle is a contingency and that affective, creative, and aesthetic motivations and struggles are (or could be) equally or more important in human life. In that case, Marxism should be viewed as descriptive of past and present human economies but not accepted as prescriptive or normative, since the most it could offer is an equitable satisfaction of human needs as understood against the scarcities that those contingent economies have recognized or created. If women are able to organize as an historical group, with a vision of a future radically better than the human past and present, there is no reason for them to limit their vision to the needs, desires, and lacks of *Homo economicus* as understood by Marx and recreated by those who call themselves Marxists, including Sartre.

NOTES

1. Further to my critical remarks in chapter 5 about feminist "appropriations" of patriarchal texts, I think the main problems with Sartre's text in this context are not the sexist ones but his failure to carry through with a thorough critique of Marx, in keeping with the existential principles he brings to Marxism. Sartre's existentialism can be used by feminists, without accepting his assumption in both *Search for a Method* and *Critique of Dialectical Reason* that his subject is masculine, not to mention his well-criticized association of women with objectified immanence and the *en soi* (in itself) in early works such as *Nausea* or *Being and Nothingness*. All one needs to do in such cases is remember that women are conscious beings, capable of the same personal, if not yet social, autonomies as men. For that kind of philosophical appropriation, Sartre's latent intentions and neuroses are irrelevant, although Sartre himself apparently underwent a transformation of the masculinist bias of his human worldview, toward what Guillermine de Lacoste has called a "feminine economy," in parts of *Notebooks for an Ethics* and later interviews such as those recorded in *Hope Now* by Benny Levy or the appendix of Simone de Beauvoir, *Adieu: A Farewell to Sartre*. For an informative discussion of this transformation, see de Lacoste, "The Beauvoir and Levy Interviews: Toward a Feminine Economy," in *Feminist Interpretations of Jean-Paul Sartre,* ed. Julien Murphy (University Park: Pennsylvania State University Press, 1999), 272–79.

2. Paula Gunn Allen, *The Sacred Hoop: Recovering the Feminine in American Indian Traditions* (Boston: Beacon, 1986), 251–74.

3. Carolyn Merchant, *The Death of Nature: Women, Ecology, and the Scientific Revolution* (New York: Harper & Row, 1980); Merry E. Weisner, *Women and Gender in Early Modern Europe* (Cambridge: Cambridge University Press, 1993).

4. Linda J. Nicholson, *Gender and History* (New York: Columbia University Press, 1986).

5. Carole Pateman, *The Sexual Contract* (Stanford, Calif.: Stanford University Press, 1988), 6. Strictly speaking, it is a misnomer to call a presumption that women are subordinate to men a contract, insofar as a contract, as used in Western social contract theory and in Western societies for transactions between citizens, requires the consent of all parties. Charles Mills makes the same mistake in calling the subordination of nonwhites to white Europeans a "racial contract" in his book that is presented as analogous to Pateman's *The Racial Contract* (Ithaca, N.Y.: Cornell University Press, 1997). See my comments on this error in Zack, "The Racial Contract according to Charles Mills," in *Racial Liberalism and the Politics of Urban America,* ed. Curtis Stokes and Theresa Melendez (East Lansing: Michigan State University Press, 2003), 24–29. The important point that emerges from both Pateman's and Mills's books is that some people are conceptualized as intrinsically subordinate politically in the historical context of social contract theories that purport to eliminate subordination or oppression as a condition of government.

6. Pateman exempts Hobbes from the early contract theorists who denied power to women in the state of nature because Hobbes claimed that women had a natural power over their children as "lord mothers" (Pateman, *Sexual Contract,* 4–7). Locke should also be exempted because he grants women property rights and rights to the products of their labor after marriage in civil society. He claims that mothers have equal standing with fathers as parents in the state of nature, except for their dependence on men during pregnancy and early child rearing and the necessity for leadership in the marriage relationship; he reasons that insofar as child rearing, or parenting in its most important sense, is temporary, fathers and mothers can separate once children are grown (John Locke, Second Treatise, in *Two Treatises of Government,* ed. Peter Laslett [Cambridge: Cambridge University Press, 1991], bk. 2, chaps. 6–7. Throughout the *Second Treatise*, there is no indication that by "property" (the protection of which was the purpose of government as Locke conceived it) he meant women, in addition to "life, liberty and estate." Locke also takes pains, in the First Treatise and throughout the *Second Treatise*, to distinguish political from patriarchal power (see bk. 2, chap. 15). Although Locke's feminism here should probably be read as a rhetorical device in his arguments against patriarchal views of government which held that rulers were like fathers, the rights he accords to women do undermine a sexual contract in Pateman's sense. See also Naomi Zack, *Bachelors of Science: Seventeenth-Century Identity, Then and Now* (Philadelphia: Temple University Press, 1996), chap. 11.

7. The question from the absence of government is also posed by John Rawls who, in *A Theory of Justice* (Cambridge: Harvard University Press, 1971), instead of a state of nature as the starting point from which government is then justified, begins with a thought experiment in which the framers of a government do not know those social facts about themselves, which could result in their benefiting from some social structures and rules rather than others. As Susan Moller Okin notes, Rawls intended to include gender among those social facts—the framers would not know whether they were male or female. See "John Rawls: Justice as Fairness—For Whom?" in *Feminist Interpretations and Political Theory,* ed. Mary Lyndon Shanley and Carole Pateman (University Park: Pennsylvania State University Press, 1991), 183, in reference to

Rawls, "Fairness to Goodness," *Philosophical Review* 84 (1975): 537. The important question raised by Okin and others has been whether women, as culturally constructed subordinate beings, can be imagined as full participants in that starting point before government, which is close to the question of whether women can be full participants in liberal democratic civil society.

8. Iris Marion Young, "Gender as Seriality: Thinking about Women as a Social Collective," in Murphy, *Feminist Interpretations of Jean-Paul Sartre*, 205.

9. Young goes on to "appropriate" Sartre's notion of *seriality* as a basis for a theoretically restricted but nonetheless universal definition of women. According to Young's interpretation of Sartre from volume 2 of *Critique of Dialectical Reason*, a *series* is a collective based on common social experiences, but without initial solidarity or recognition among members; series have the potential to organize into groups (and eventually classes). Young, and in a parallel way (published in the same anthology), Sonia Kruks, draw on these ideas to refer to (what I would call) the denotation of "women," from whom (they both hope) feminists emerge: women are a series, but feminists are a group that might become, through coalitions, a class. (Iris Marion Young, "Gender as Seriality: Thinking about Women as a Social Collective," in Murphy, *Feminist Interpretations of Jean-Paul Sartre*, 211–26; Sonia Kruks, "Identity Politics and Dialectical Reason: Beyond an Epistemology of Provenance," in Murphy, *Feminist Interpretations of Jean-Paul Sartre*, 256–61.) Aside from the conflation between a definition of women and the political goals of feminism (distinguished above in the text), which I think render Young's and Kruks' "appropriation" undeveloped, Sartre's notion of seriality is not necessary here, if it is possible to begin feminist political theory with a universal definition of women. More about this later in the text.

10. To be sure, there are housecleaners, social secretaries, babysitters, sex workers, nannies, surrogate mothers, and egg donors, not to mention people who are paid to prepare and serve food and clean clothing. But this work, even when performed according to legal contracts, is not considered an important part of contemporary postindustrial First World economies, and in many cases it is routinely purchased by the affluent only.

11. Karl Marx and Friedrich Engels, *The Communist Manifesto,* in *Karl Marx: Selected Writings*, ed. Lawrence H. Simon (Indianapolis: Hackett, 1994). Karl Marx, *Capital*, trans. Ben Fowkes (London: Penguin, 1990), vol. 1.

12. Christine Di Stephano, "Masculine Marx," in Shanley and Pateman, *Feminist Interpretations and Political Theory*, 146–63; Heidi Hartmann, "The Unhappy Marriage of Marxism and Feminism: Toward a More Progressive Union," in *The Second Wave: A Reader in Feminist Theory*, ed. Linda J. Nicholson (New York: Routledge, 1997), 97–122; Michele Barrett, "Capitalism and Women's Liberation," in Nicholson, *Second Wave*, 123–30.

13. This leaves open the question whether women (or men) ought to be paid for doing their own women's work. A positive answer would raise the issue of what a "living wage" was in any given society, so that all who worked for wages would have the choice of doing their own women's work or paying someone else to do it. The question of whether those who do not earn wages and are poor should be paid for their women's work is the question of whether welfare programs are desirable.

14. It is not clear which of these works comes first. Hazel Barnes explains that Sartre published both works together but he thought *Search for a Method* was a theoretical

conclusion to the *Critique*. Still he did not want to have *Search* printed after the *Critique*, partly because he thought it would then seem that "the mountain had brought forth a mouse," and partly because he had written *Search* first. See Barnes, introduction to Jean-Paul Sartre, *Search for a Method*, trans. Hazel E. Barnes (New York: Vintage, 1968), ix. In addition, Sartre's unfinished volume 2 of the *Critique* was yet to appear posthumously when Barnes wrote. Jean-Paul Sartre, *Critique of Dialectical Reason: The Intelligibility of History*, vol. 2, ed. Arlette Elkaim-Sartre, trans. Quintin Hoare (New York: Verso, 1991).

15. Sartre, *Search for a Method*, 9.

16. Sartre, *Search for a Method*, 42.

17. Jean-Paul Sartre, *Being and Nothingness*, trans. Hazel Barnes (New York: Philosophical Library, 1952).

18. Jean-Paul Sartre, "Existentialism Is a Humanism," trans. Bernard Frechtman, reprinted in *Existentialist Philosophy: An Introduction*, ed. L. Nathan Oaklander (Upper Saddle River, N.J.: Prentice Hall, 1996), 311.

19. Sartre, "Existentialism Is a Humanism," 316.

20. Sartre, "Existentialism Is a Humanism," 312.

21. Sartre, *Search for a Method*, 8.

22. Sartre, *Search for a Method*, 34.

23. Jean-Paul Sartre, Notebook 14, in *War Diaries: Notebooks from a Phoney War, 1939–40*, trans. Quintin Hoare (New York: Verso, 1999), 297.

24. Sartre, *Search for a Method*, 35–84.

25. See Iris Marion Young, "Gender as Seriality: Thinking about Women as a Social Collective, in Murphy, *Feminist Interpretations of Jean-Paul Sartre*, 200–228; Sonia Kruks, "Identity Politics and Dialectical Reason: Beyond an Epistemology of Provenance," in Murphy, *Feminist Interpretations of Jean-Paul Sartre*, 229–52; and also Peter Diers, "Friendship and Feminist Praxis: Insights from Sartre's *Critique of Dialectical Reason*," in Murphy, *Feminist Interpretations of Jean-Paul Sartre*, 253–71.

26. Sartre, *Being and Nothingness*, 627.

27. Sartre, *Critique of Dialectical Reason: Theory of Practical Ensembles*, trans. Alan Sheridan-Smith (New York: Verso, 1976), 1:263

28. Sartre, *Search for a Method*, 73–74, 91.

29. Sartre, *Critique of Dialectical Reason: Theory of Practical Ensembles*, 1:80.

30. Sartre, *Critique of Dialectical Reason: Theory of Practical Ensembles*, 1:113.

31. Sartre, *Critique of Dialectical Reason: Theory of Practical Ensembles*, 1:123.

32. Sartre, *Critique of Dialectical Reason: Theory of Practical Ensembles*, 1:123

33. Sartre, *Critique of Dialectical Reason: Theory of Practical Ensembles*, 1:123

8

World Paths toward Women's Political Equality

Women's commonality is directly relevant to feminist political goals and activism throughout the world. The theoretical insights developed in earlier chapters of this book can ground a perspective from which to answer a primary question raised by postcolonial and difference feminisms: Is it possible for women to speak with one another without oppressing each other and ending up with the same First World feminists in positions of theoretical dominance?

Feminists generally, and I think justifiably, have concluded that it is not possible for First World feminists to speak for those in the Third World, for rich women to speak for poor, or white for nonwhite. Each distinct group or intersection of women who are advocating for themselves need to speak for themselves. Groups that have not yet found a voice or made their way to an effective forum are in principle included by the formal, relational definition of women I have proposed—there are already places for them at the table, which will continue to be set until they show up.

A less obvious issue than who may and can speak is whether it is possible for feminists to listen to one another and on that basis provide assistance. Needed is not some impossible common tongue but a common ear. A universal definition of women allows for that very modality because it is the common ground on which discourse among women across their myriad differences can occur. Women can listen to one another, not only by beginning with what they have in common, in theory, but by continuing to recognize that commonality across their differences as a basis for their ongoing solidarity. Such recognized commonality and solidarity does not in itself resolve issues of cultural relativism raised by differences. Nonetheless, it supports fully contextualized understandings of different women's values and circumstances. When values appear to be incommensurable, there is now no reason to believe that this is the result of different women's identities, as things or substances or even performances, which are inherently part of women. Incommensurable differences in women's values can be understood to result from different cultural coercions and commitments, as well as from differences in individual and group choices and interpretations. Differences in circumstances should be understood to be external to women's common identity. This is in keeping with the suggestion made in chapter 4 that feminist social theory be reductive vis-à-vis differences in what appear to be women's identities. Thus any woman in the distinctive circumstances of another, which are different from her own, would experience or suffer what the other does, given one major proviso: what have been called the identities of race, class, sexual preference, ability, age, or anything else, are understood to be part of the distinctive circumstances. In other words, identities other than the shared relation of identifying with or being assigned to the whole category of female birth designees, biological mothers, or heterosexual choices of men (category FMP), are reduced to circumstances external to being a woman. As noted in chapters 1–2, this is a form of essentialism but is not substantialism. What women share is not a thing that makes an individual a woman but the same relations of identifying with, or being assigned to, the whole disjunction of human birth females, biological mothers, or men's sexual choices, all of which are historically constructed, interpreted, understood, and enacted.

The acknowledged capability among women of experiencing or suffering what other women experience or suffer adds the possibility of empathy to solidarity. As Amy Coplan describes it, empathy is the imagined position of the self in the circumstances of another.[1] When one cannot imagine oneself in the circumstances of another, which include different life conditions as well as relevant social identities, commonality may fall short of empathy but still enable sympathy. Successful empathy requires an accurate assessment of whether one knows enough or has experience enough to be accurate in one's imagined displacement into the circumstances of another. One must be able to know if one has got it right. Successful empathy thus requires the ability to evaluate one's own competence to accurately imagine oneself in the circumstances of another, as she experiences them. This dimension of self-reflection, necessary for successful empathy, is in itself a practical feminist virtue.

Within their respective societies, in comparison with men, First World women in the west and north are, in general, more liberated than Third World women. However, as noted in chapter 7, this kind of women's liberation has not yet gone beyond inclusion in political structures that remain governed by men. The reason inclusion has fallen short of shared political power in the West is theoretically expressed within, and in practice based on, the history of Western political theory. Beginning with Aristotle, women and their work were located, both theoretically and literally, in private homes.

Men and their work, particularly men of the ruling class and work that shaped society in the most fundamental ways, were located in public positions and offices. Women were private and outside of history, men public and officially constitutive of history. Furthermore, the public work of men also shaped and reinforced the unrecognized and officially unrewarded private reproductive work of women and, importantly, the social reproduction of this gendered division of labor. Second wave feminists have offered comprehensive and definitive accounts of these structures and dynamics.[2]

Sometimes neglected is a further analysis of how, even in the north and west, despite almost a century of women's liberation, society and individuals continue to value, assign, and live out the private social and biological reproductive roles assigned to women, and to accept their containment in a private sphere that remains outside of the spheres governed by formal equality. Part of the neglect may be due to the fact that women's control over their own biological reproduction has been granted on a legal basis that recognizes private rights and rights to privacy. But there is a big difference between the legal umbrella of privacy that protects individual liberty as a negative right not to be prevented from action that does not violate the negative rights of others, and the social, moral, and legal umbrella of privacy that allows gender inequalities to persist in ways that would not be permitted in the public sphere. The private traditional roles of women, and their accompanying goals, duties, satisfactions, sacrifices, and pains, continue to harness major amounts of human energy. Often there is inequality in comparison to men that goes along with these roles, although they also continue to be chosen by the majority of women; this factor of choice is probably what keeps principles and practices of formal gender equality outside the private sphere of gender. Be that as it may, the principles of gender equality that have been successful in securing public roles for women can also be applied to the *configuration* of public and private roles, in actual women's lives. We can ask whether women's public and private roles support each other and are supported together as two sets of roles belonging to the same persons. Where such support is lacking, feminists can address how it could be created (assuming that both sets of roles are valuable).

Women are not yet equal partners with men in First World politics. Part of this inequality is related to the division of gender roles that persists in private. For women to be full participants in public political power structures that are now dominated by men through their socially constructed roles of masculinity, one of three changes would have to occur in "high politics": men as well as women would perform the women's roles; women's roles would no longer exist as such, and the official political goals of society would change to reflect the goals of women in women's roles. If men and women alike performed women's roles, that in itself would not change the official value or undervaluation of such roles or their location in the private sphere.[3] If women's roles were replaced by biotechnologies and professional services, we would arrive in a future state of affairs thus far imagined only in science fiction. Not only might this state of affairs turn out to be a dystopia, but as most human beings now live and express themselves, there is little reason to think that they would welcome it as a goal. The third change would be a revaluation of values so that the actions performed in women's roles (women's work), which largely remain unpriced, as discussed in chapter 7, would have a new value equal or greater to that of the kinds of work that are now priced. I submit that this revaluation of values is our only prospect for checking the destructive and cruel technologizing project that Western men have for their own benefit imposed on all other living beings through their invented system of prices, or monetarization, which is the "mind" or score-keeping mechanism of the project.

In the eighteenth and nineteenth centuries, northern and western political systems were constructed to achieve the goals posited by masculinist society, according to those desires of men that were so accurately described by Marx and Freud. In the beginning of the twenty-first century, the goals of northern and western men have crystallized into "global maximization," or the spread of First World democratic forms, consumer culture, and capitalist production.[4] These structures of capitalist production are a deeper invasion of the south and east because they go beyond colonialist appropriation and exploitation of resources to reconfigure the basic institutions of their source societies. The theme of such reconfiguration is that the structure of the source societies should duplicate First World democratic politics, consumer culture, and capitalist production. (For example, while the first U.S. war against Iraq was about the control of oil produced by Kuwait, the second U.S. war against Iraq concerned a reconfiguration of Iraq's fundamental social, political, and economic structures as an oil-producing nation friendly to the United States.)

It should be noted that the discussion of north–south divisions, prevalent in much postcolonial feminist scholarship, can obscure the fact that women of color and poor women in the north do not participate in the gender egalitarianism of affluent groups in the workplace. Moreover, as Lorraine Code remarks, white feminists from northern countries that are not First World powers do not enjoy the same privileges or bear the same responsibilities for global maximization as their counterparts in the United States.[5] One result of these First and Second World differences is that it may be easier for Second World women to achieve political parity with men because the men of their ruling groups, having less international power, are less invested in the aggressive, exploitative constructions of their gender.

The purpose of this chapter is to examine some of the theoretical and real-life factors that are pertinent to the revaluation of values necessary for rule by women. The main content of the chapter is a comparative discussion of

First, Second, and Third World feminist political inclusion. Before beginning this discussion, however, some consideration of First World androgynization and the ecological concept of sustainability is in order.

ANDROGYNIZATION AND SUSTAINABILITY

To the extent that it has occurred, political inclusion of women in First World culture is parallel to an androgynization of women in the work life of the culture. Women participate in the same way that men participate, and not as human beings who can be understood as identifying with or having been assigned to socially constructed categories of female birth designees, biological mothers, or primary sexual choices of men (category FMP). Therefore, given the different values that could be realized through rule by women, as women are understood in the way that has made feminism necessary, feminists should reexamine the gender dynamics of situations in which women are merely included in men's power structures. In traditionally male contexts, women's androgynization may be necessary for efficient and dignified functioning, as well as women's ability to compete with men; women may create their own androgynization for those reasons. However, such androgynization of included women conceals the reality that the same power structures which androgynize them as a condition of their professional inclusion continue to reproduce them as human females, mothers, or men's heterosexual choices in their "second shifts" and in the private domain overall.

Less privileged women who become androgynized through work or political inclusion may suffer even more than the stress and life role compression of their higher-status counterparts. Consider, for example, the circumstances of Nicole Goodwin, a twenty-three-year-old African American woman who enlisted in the army in 2001 and became pregnant in 2002 as a result of a relationship with another soldier. She returned to the United States to give birth in 2003, and four months later she served four months in Iraq and completed her tour of duty in Germany. After her honorable discharge, Goodwin returned to the United States to reclaim her baby, who had been taken care of by friends in California. Back home in New York City, she and her one-year-old daughter, Shylah, were homeless in April 2004. The New York City Department of Homeless Services determined that she should live with her mother, who lived with two other women and a child in a two-bedroom apartment. Relations between Goodman and her mother were not good. So she walked the streets from agency to agency in the Bronx, pushing a stroller crammed with clothes and diapers, carrying her child to her chest in a Snugli, and wearing a heavy backpack over her shoulders. Dan Barry wrote in the *New York Times,* "Ms. Goodwin has perfect posture and a steady gaze, and she keeps in mind the Army leadership acronym: L is for loyalty; D is for duty;

R is for respect; S for selfless service; H for honor; P for personal courage. 'And I is my favorite,' she says. 'It's integrity.'"[6]

Nicole Goodman's androgyny as a soldier (perhaps less the result of gender equality in the military than of its reliance on the proof as volunteers) is but one example of how contemporary women's andogyny is imaginary, context specific, and largely conditional. The androgyny is imaginary because women as such continue to exist and socially reproduce themselves by their own choice, as well as in compliance with the preferences of others. There is no evidence that many women would choose an androgynous gender identity or that the culture which has granted women formal equality has thereby created a space for such an identity. Professional standards and practices make it easier and more efficient if women in new work roles suspend or minimize their traditional gender traits, but no one thinks that women do not or ought not live out those traits in what remain their private lives. That the demands of androgynized work for women—but not men—conflict with their private roles to the detriment of performance at both sets of roles tends to be taken for granted as a price of women's formal equality. No widespread political attention has yet focused on the conflict between values underlying both sets of roles, as a social problem rather than an issue for personal choice.

Contemporary women's androgyny is context specific because each work context has its own requirements for successful gender comportment on the part of women. The androgynization is conditional, given glass ceilings for successful women and the greater ease that men still have in functioning in the new contexts with androgynized women as participants. (Goodwin's relationship with her baby's father ended when she became pregnant, although whether he succeeded or even survived, thus unencumbered by parenthood, was not part of Goodman's story as reported.)[7]

The facts of women's uneven equality in dominant nations and their androgynization in privileged and not-so-privileged work circumstances, undermine simple generalizations about women's advantages in such cultures. Nevertheless, many feminists in the United States seem content to intellectually preside over the imaginary demise of women, which their androgynization seems to represent, or at least over the demise of those women who become androgynized through success in prestigious work (or as a result of their relations to powerful men).[8] By contrast, many Third World feminists have expressed unease with the prospect of such erasure of women through formal equality with men, partly because their cultures do not permit it and partly because they remain explicitly committed to identities as female birth designees, mothers, or men's sexual choices. Their political efforts have been directed toward greater entitlements as mothers and wives. If such Third World feminists are called "traditional women," this should not blur their difference from First World traditional women who largely accept their women's roles as assigned in their male-dominated social economic and political societies, nor from politically conservative traditional women in their own cultures.[9]

What may Third World feminists who theorize and seek to actualize greater power for women as historically constructed contribute to the kind of rule by women envisioned in chapter 7? This might not be the best way to formulate the question because it could suggest that the efforts of Third World feminists should be viewed instrumentally by First World feminists. My intention in posing the question this way is to encourage western and northern feminists to keep an open mind about historical directions for feminist activism and politics that at first sight may appear to be conservative and reactionary. In its instrumental form the question can motivate informative comparisons between the political inclusion of First and Second World, and First and Third World, women in their respective social contexts.

The concept of sustainability is relevant to the kind of revaluation of values that would choose or rank dignity over price. Sustainability exists whenever a flourishing living system or relations between flourishing living beings can perpetuate themselves without complete reliance on an external monetarizing-technologizing (MT) system. Perpetuation is a relative notion because in the long run, after our sun cools down, there will be no living systems and beings as we know them. Still, we can coherently imagine sustainability in the relevant sense, over about one hundred years, which is probably the extent to which the most far-sighted self-actualizers can extend their concerns in concrete ways.[10] There are two ways in which sustainability can occur in present historical circumstances. First, it may already exist and require only noninterference for its perpetuation. Natural bodies of water before pollution would be an example of this. Second, sustainability may require partial intervention from an MT system. An example of this would be natural bodies of water that have been restored or cleaned up after pollution (either once or on a continual basis). Unsustainable systems require complete intervention from the MT system, for example, a human-made body of water that was continually circulated, filtered, and replenished by external means (e.g., a swimming pool).

The environmental or ecological goal of sustainability does not in itself undermine the existing MT system, although it can limit further incursions by that system. If sustainability in this sense is applied to women in their traditional roles through transfer payments or welfare, it materially supports those roles. If the transfer payments are a grudging form of charity, the dignity of those roles remains unrecognized and may be further devalued. Moreover, sustainability alone is not sufficient to undermine the pricing axis in MT systems. Funds transferred in welfare programs, for example, are completely spent on goods from economic sectors of the same system that dispenses them. Necessary to undermine or shift the MT axis are transfers of

funds that do not make their way back into the system, transfers that inter-
rupt or short-circuit the circulation of money. Again, environmental practices
offer a lesson in very broad terms.

When coffee is grown on clear-cut land, songbirds lose their habitat.
When coffee is grown in the shade, natural environments can be sustained.
Consumers pay more for shade-grown coffee, but the higher price does not
enrich the coffee growers because their expenses are greater. The extra
money spent on shade-grown coffee enriches (so to speak) the songbirds
and other living beings in their ecosystems, and that extra money and what
it represents leaves the MT system. Similarly, when American indigenists
claim that they do not want money but land on which they can continue their
cultural traditions and from which they can directly obtain a livelihood,
their goal is a form of sustainability that undermines an MT system. Among
the Third World poor, microloans, which are often made to women, enable
families to buy livestock and tools at affordable rates of interest. But the extreme poor may lack the skills to utilize and repay such loans. The
Bangladesh Rural Action Committee is presently experimenting with direct
grants of domestic animals for women to raise.[11] If the recipients improve the
health and nutrition of their families with these calves, goats, and chickens,
their material lives after they receive that assistance become sustainable (or
more sustainable).

Both the indigenist aims and the transfers in kind to Third World poor
women are forms of sustainability that enable human flourishing outside local, and perhaps global, MT systems. Nothing about these options ensures or
even necessarily betters the lives of women per se. However, both examples
represent models of self-sufficiency that could be part of a revaluation of the
male gender-biased values that have thus far driven the global MT system.
Material self-sufficiency that coexists with the MT system is still, at best, a
means for avoiding that system. It would not constitute substantial change in
the history of rule by men unless everyone found ways to avoid the MT system. Rule by women in present political systems in the First and Second
Worlds and the influence of women in Third World politics hold the promise of change in MT systems. The rewards of the androgyny of northern and
western women in their liberated roles can function as means for sustaining
such women's traditional roles, if they need or choose to spend their money
in those ways. Single women who are heads of households need to do so,
and women with partners who contribute to household income are in fact
doing so, although their domestic economic understanding may not identify
their outside work as androgynous. There is no general cultural, or even
specifically feminist, ideal of a woman who suspends her traditional identity
to pursue economic activities for the express purpose of supporting the enactments of that identity. Many like to believe that working mothers and
wives are materially supported by their partners or other family members.

The imaginary economic unit of the household or family thus serves to mediate between women's earnings as androgenes and women's work as women. The cost of sentimental attachment to a model of domestic economy that no longer obtains may be the continued failure of women to demand and enact full political participation. Given that political power is based on economic and material power, women could now have political power equal to men's if the economic value of their androgynous work were combined with the monetary and nonmonetary values of their women's work (i.e., not all material values need be monetary ones).

POLITICAL INCLUSION OF WOMEN IN THE WEST: THE UNITED STATES AND NORWAY

Women have a long history of political activism and participation in the United States. While the events in that history are broadly known and have been examined by feminists and scholars of women's studies in several disciplines (e.g., history, political science, public policy studies, sociology, etc.) a brief, borrowed summary will be useful here. Janet Boles emphasizes that insofar as political parties have dominated American politics since 1789, the vast majority of women elected officials have been affiliated with parties. Thus American women have agreed with Elizabeth Cady Stanton's claim that women have to be involved with political parties "inasmuch as our demands are to be made and carried, like other political questions, by the aid of and affiliation with parties."[12] Women were party workers in the pre–women's suffrage era of the nineteenth century, although as noted in chapter 1, black women were excluded from white women's political efforts, not merely as an effect of external cultural conditions but as deliberate white supremacist policy.

Rule by women could be accomplished through the medium of women's political parties. The only viable U.S. women's party was the National Women's Political Party. Its president, Mrs. O. H. P. Belmont (née Alva Smith Vanderbilt), hoped that it would constitute a unified women's party, against which both the Republican and Democratic Parties would merge in opposition. What happened instead, of course, was that after women got the vote in 1920, they joined, or voted with, either the Democratic or Republican Parties. Still, both parties granted women formal equality early on. In 1920 the Democratic National Committee granted equal representation to women on national committees, and the Republican National Committee did the same in 1924. However, parties do not officially control nominations decided in primaries. Geraldine Ferraro, nominated as vice president in 1984, was the only woman on an adequately funded major party presidential ticket. There have been underfunded major party presidential campaigns by women, such as the Republican candidacy of Margaret Chase Smith in 1964 and the Democratic candidacy of Shirley Chisholm in 1972. Third parties, such as the Populist, Progressive, Prohibition, and Socialist Workers Parties, have led the major parties in support of suffrage, women's office holding, and equal-pay legislation. Such parties nominated at least twelve women of color between 1980 and 1992, and Winona LaDuke ran as vice president on Ralph Nader's Green Party ticket in 2000.

Directly relevant to an idea of rule by women as proposed, there have been other exclusively women's parties in addition to the pro-suffrage National Women's Political Party. The Equal Rights Party nominated Victoria Claflin Woodhull for president in 1872 and Belva Ann Bennett Lockwood for president in 1884 and 1888, both on platforms advocating equality across racial and national groups and, in 1884, full citizenship for Native Americans (about fifty years ahead of its official time). In 1989, the National Organization for Women formed a Commission for Responsive Democracy that announced the creation of the Twenty-First Century Party, the Nation's Equality Party, chaired by Dolores Huerta.[13]

Until the 1960s, men were more likely to vote than women, but since 1980 women have been more likely to vote, particularly among African Americans and Latinos. After the Republican Party withdrew its support of legal equality and abortion rights, conservative and new Christian women's groups gained control of the women's planks in that party. Since 1976, women's activist groups have mainly supported the Democratic Party. During the 1990s, over half of Democratic state party officials were African American women, and the interests of other women of color were voiced through the Democratic National Party's Latino Caucus and the National Democratic Council of Asian Pacific Americans. In 1972 the Republican National Commission declared that each state should try to have equal numbers of men and women delegates in national convention state delegates, and in 1979 the Democratic National Convention mandated a similar measure on a national level. Over half the African American, Latino, and Native American Democratic delegates have been female in recent decades.

Despite impressive gains in women's political participation over the twentieth century, there is a big difference between groups crafting political policy that satisfies their specific interests and simply choosing among political alternatives crafted by more powerful groups, which are more general than their specific interests or even opposed to them. When women's groups influence party platforms, it is understood by powerful party members that this is supposed to secure votes for white male candidates from larger groups of women and nonwhites. Whether those candidates win or keep their campaign promises is the other side of those contingencies.

Thus, when women participate in party-based political processes, as they have in the United States, there is no direct line to anything resembling rule by or for women. Participants in the process may identify by race or gender, but there is expectation that those who rule will be "neutral" (i.e., white and male in such identities) and that their raced and gendered subjects will have found their interests largely expressed by their participation in the process leading up to the victory of this or that white man. Regardless of their degree of participation, the American party system androgynizes all women and "deraces" women of color, by the time the votes are counted. Whether more women in office would change this is an open question, dependent on whether successful women's candidates focus on the gender-based concerns of their female constituents or on some combined male and androgynized female constituency.

The structure of women's political participation has taken a different direction in Norway since 1970, and its contrast with the U.S. structure is illuminating. In 2002, Hege Skjeie summarized the inclusion of women in the Norwegian parliamentary system as a credo that she described as "mirrored" in the 1995 Beijing Platform for Action. The Beijing Platform read:

> Women's Equal Participation in decision-making is not only a demand for simple justice in democracy but can also be seen as a necessary condition for women's interests to be taken into account. Achieving the goal of equal participation of women and men in decision-making will provide a balance that more accurately reflects the composition of society and is needed in order to strengthen democracy and promote its proper functioning.

Skjeie formulates Norway's political gender quota policies as a "credo on difference":

> Norway's policy on women's political participation rests on a widely shared political credo. The core of this credo can be summarized as follows: gender constitutes an important political category that needs to be fully represented; and women's political interests and orientation cannot, and should not, be viewed as merely equivalent to men's political interests and orientation.[14]

Although the Beijing Platform called for women's equal participation so that women's interests would be taken into account, Norway's credo stresses that women's interests and orientation are not "merely equivalent" to men's. In principle, the Beijing Platform could be implemented if women participated as fully as men in decision making in high politics but did not frame fundamental policies or what the subjects of decisions would be (i.e., what decisions were about). Norway's credo takes the further step toward women's participation in determining the subjects of decisions in high politics. Deliberate allowance for that kind of political empowerment of women would seem to require an assumption that women have different conceptions of the subjects of decisions in high politics. And indeed, based on two surveys conducted by Skjeie, that is exactly what the Norwegian perspective on politics and gender appears to be.

Since the mid-1980s, studies of Norway's political elite have shown a consensus among local politicians, party organizers, cabinet ministers, and members of parliament that gender makes a difference in politics. In an interview series with 146 out of 155 parliamentarians, conducted between 1988 and 1992, 74 percent of the men and 86 percent of the women stated that women's participation made a difference in party viewpoints; in a related survey the figures were 83 percent of the men and 93 percent of the women. According to the parliamentarians, women's interests included social and welfare policies, environmental protection, equality polities, disarmament policies, and educational policies. Men's interests were named as economic and industrial policies, energy issues, transportation, national security, and foreign affairs.[15]

Skjeie emphasizes the lack of overlap among perceptions of men's and women's interests, by both men and women in the political elite. She also reports the development of a politics of care that addresses state provision of opportunities for women to combine motherhood with economic independence. Norwegian care politics includes publicly sponsored child care, extensions of paid parental leave, more flexible work hours, and increased pensions for unpaid care work. Despite broad political consensus about the importance of care policies, women MPs voted differently to implement them, depending on their party affiliation, and few voted against their parties. Furthermore, in routine politics, older forms of bargaining prevail over gender differences.[16]

Women have been close to fully included in Norwegian politics. From the 1970s until the mid-1990s, the percentage of women in politics increased from 10 to 40. Major parties, except for the right-wing Progress Party, have stated policies on the inclusion of women. In 1993, three women party leaders presented the three competing government platforms.[17] This combination of high women's participation in ruling politics and the implementation of care politics presents a striking contrast with U.S. politics. Even greater contrasts exist in the Norwegian understanding of the political value of gender interests over individual rights. Skjeie writes: "Elaborated through the growth of a new feminist movement, arguments on the interest of the group based on the collective good, rather than on individual fairness, have become important in legitimizing new representation."[18]

The implication here is that the collective good in question is the good of men as well as women. Nonetheless, the stereotyping of gender interests among the Norwegian political elite indicates an absence of the kind of androgynization of included women discussed in the preceding section; and the concern about combining support for motherhood with the economic independence of mothers could be an example of the kind of sustainability I discussed earlier.

THIRD WORLD WOMEN'S ACTIVISM

The reader may wonder at this point if my use of sustainability as a feminist standard does not posit women's traditional roles and work as intrinsically valuable. Insofar as they have been instrumentally viewed in patriarchal traditions, this might not be a bad thing, but it could nonetheless result in women's regression instead of liberation. There are two ways to answer this concern. First, there is no reason to believe that women's traditional roles and work are inherently oppressive. Rather, it is the conditions under which women have lived and the value placed on their roles and work in configurations with men's roles and work that have constituted women's oppression. Second, insofar as men have ruled, politics is gendered; while a political revaluation of women's roles and work might not change the gendered nature of politics, it might change the genders of those wielding ultimate power. Of course, we do not know what the nature of women's power or the combined nature of men's and women's power would be if women ruled or shared rule with men. Perhaps we can get a glimpse of the kinds of changes possible through reports of women's movements and feminist concerns outside of the north and west. What is instructive about such reports for western and northern feminists, particularly in the United States, is that they begin with women as they have been historically understood and proceed with liberation on that basis.

Cynthia Enloe suggests that toward the end of the Cold War, protests by soldiers' mothers through family groups not sanctioned by the Soviet government sped demilitarization processes. In 1990, a grassroots organization, Materninskoe Serdise (The Mother's Heart), demanded information on sons reported missing in action. Gorbachev authorized an investigation which revealed that out of 8,000 Soviet soldiers who died annually, 50 percent committed suicide, 20 percent died from beatings and other inflicted injuries within the military, and 10 percent died from accidents, which left only 20 percent who had been killed through military duties. Such figures further undermined the willingness of Soviet women to support their Cold War government.[19] Enloe argues that this situation, as well as the realization of Brazilian women in the 1970s and 1980s that domestic violence was of a piece with their government's militarized anticommunism, shows how women's gender work is a major contribution to war regimes. Even American 1950s-style nuclear family consumerism can support such regimes. Enloe refers to Vaclav Havel's letters from prison to his wife, in which he explains how an agreeable mass domesticity was encouraged by the Czechoslovakian regime after 1968, so that the country's participation in the Warsaw Pact would not be challenged by its citizens.[20]

Enloe's insights go beyond the critical view that women's work, as an unpaid contribution to the reproduction of soldiers and workers, is a gift to

government and business. Women's roles are coerced as an active component of the most problematic enactments of male gender. This suggests that
rule by women would require a complex unraveling of the ways in women
have cooperated and complied in the problematic aspects of rule by men.
For instance, women in all countries have sent their young sons off to war
because they could not refuse, their sons wanted to go, others wanted them
to go, and so forth, through all of the reasons hinging on women's lack of
power. But women have also sent their sons to war and accepted their
deaths with pride because they believed it was right and glorious to do, necessary for national defense and survival, and a fulfillment of their own roles
as the protected ones.

Some non-Western feminists have challenged their culture's gender contracts more directly. Azizah Yahia al-Hibri argues that while Muslim women
are committed to their religion, which is based on the Qur'an, they have both
civic and personal freedom in their choice of politics and specific cultural
traditions. As a legal scholar, al-Hibri has tried to show how the Qur'an itself
posits fundamental equalities between men and women. The oppressive nature of women's lives in many Islamic countries is due to differences in how
the Qur'an has been locally interpreted, given patriarchal traditions that often preexisted Islamic conversion.[21] In addition to illumination about the
religious position of women in Islam, al-Hibri provides an important intellectual example of how a feminist scholar can justify liberatory projects by a
text or principles to which men as well as women in a culture are already
committed. This kind of inclusiveness is likely to have greater success than
justifications applying to women only, in contexts (the world) in which men
still rule, and, strategically, it holds men accountable for inequalities that violate accepted doctrines.

Parallel to the text-based strategy implied in al-Hibri's interpretations of
the Qur'an is the way some Third World women have relied on secular con-
stitutions to further objectives of greater gender equality. Shirin Rai argues
that Western feminists have often neglected to consider the importance of
even "weak" Third World states in supporting women's struggles against social and economic inequalities. Rai notes that since the 1980s, radical judges
on the Indian Supreme Court have upheld constitutional interpretation as a
form of social intervention against existing statutory interpretations:

In a landmark case *People's Union for Democratic Rights v Union of India* the
Supreme court allowed the petitioners to charge the Government of India for
failing to uphold the fundamental rights of its citizens. The judgments, in favour
of the petitioners who had argued that the Indian Government had failed to en-
force Article 23 of the constitution which prohibits "traffic in human beings and
forced labour," established a precedent of interpreting the fundamental rights of
Indian citizens in a more flexible way.[22]

Generalizing about effective political strategies for women's liberation in developing countries is difficult. Throughout her discussion, Rai emphasizes that most Third World governments lack funds for welfare or educational projects for poor women, and most women in the Third World have little positive contact with their government.[23] Donna Pankhurst and Jenny Pearce observe that when women gain democratic rights (e.g., suffrage) in developing countries, only those who are already privileged by ethnicity or class may be able to utilize them, particularly in societies that become democratic without a historical base of strong civil liberties.[24] (But even in societies that have such a historical base and decades of women's formal political equality, poor and nonwhite women remain disadvantaged on the basis of the conditions of their gender, compared to those of white middle-class women.)

Distinctions should be drawn between women's political mobilization in times of relative peace and women's politicization in reaction to conditions of widespread violence, terror, and civil disruption. Rohini Hensman documents striking examples of the second form of politicization, particularly in Latin America.[25] In the late 1970s, after a military coup in Argentina that resulted in the abduction and death of about 30,000 children and adults, the Madres of the Plaza de Mayo began a process of demonstration, which was the beginning of organized protest against the dictatorship. At the same time Mujeres por la Vida (Women for Life) became an umbrella group of grassroots women's organizations against the dictatorship in Chile. Under similar conditions, women's organizations sprang up in Brazil to protest human rights abuses and scarcity in daily life. In Nicaragua, the Association of Nicaraguan Women Confronting the Nation's Problems publicized atrocities committed by the National Guard and demanded release of political prisoners. During the civil war in Sri Lankra in the 1980s, a Mother's Front successfully led opposition to government policies that had resulted in a reign of terror against Tamil ethnic groups, in which 60,000 had been killed. In India, Pakistan, and Bangladesh during the late 1980s, women's groups struggled against religious fundamentalism to protect their own rights and temper militant policies.[26]

Such activism, in which women have apparently politicized their traditional roles, has led Hensman and other feminists to speculate that the state itself may be vulnerable to effective protest from women who are otherwise confined to the private sphere.[27] While states require compliance from women, there is thus far no historical evidence that mothers' protests have resulted in lasting and deep structural changes and dislocations in state power—anywhere. What the Third World mothers' protests may represent, however, is the power of women to enter directly into the gender contract between a state and its citizens, as principals. The gender contract underlying many states recognizes only men as principals and men in turn are supposed to be responsible for the well-being of women in their traditional roles. But when enough men are missing, suddenly killed, or disempowered, women must negotiate for their own well-being as mothers and wives in order to sustain their traditional roles. There is no evidence that this kind of women's activism has lasting effects on the liberation of women or that it is anything more than an emergency measure, acceptable to men who retain their rule, only in dire circumstances. However, it does demonstrate the power of women in their traditional roles to restore the patriarchal conditions that sustain those roles, when there is no other way in which the roles could be sustained in specific cultures. It demonstrates the latent power and necessary value of traditional women. There is no deep reevaluation of values evident in such activism, although there is inspiring affirmation of those women's values that western and northern women take for granted, and feminists in those cultures have often rushed to surpass.

In terms of the more general issue of women's political identities, in pursuing liberation, women can proceed from their traditional roles or in opposition to them. When women gain suffrage it is at first as women, traditionally understood and identified. After women are political citizens, they can use that power to support their traditional roles, as has been the case in the Second and Third Worlds, or to assume roles previously reserved for men, as women in northern and western countries have done. Clearly, both projects are important and valuable. However, a pursuit of equality with men in work and civil life will not fully liberate even privileged women in the United States, as long as they continue in their traditional roles when those roles remain unchanged except for their compression in second shifts.

Neglecting to support women's traditional roles while they have civil or formal equality, particularly in the United States, carries dangers. Some cultural observers have remarked on the resurgence of hypermasculine ideals in American society. The valorization of extreme masculine aggression, particularly during the present military action and domestic security policies of the post-9/11 "war on terror," has combined with a popular backlash against feminism that began after 1980.[28] One overlooked result of this revaluation of masculinity has been a more masculine climate overall, so that androgyny as gender neutrality is no longer an ideal for men. This removes the possibility of a gender middle ground for men and women in many work contexts. Of course, the problem is not with masculinity per se (whatever that may be) but with the ways in which masculinity is measured as a virtue: aggression leading to violence, exploitation leading to greed, overconsumption leading to addiction and gluttony. Drawing on Americans' investment in personal identity, from the goodness of masculinity the goodness of its preferred expressions follows—now for women also, to the extent that they are equal with men. This is another reason why full equality with men is not in itself a sufficiently liberatory feminist ideal, although the paradox is that it might appear to be a necessary strategy for achieving the ideal of a just society, which both affirms and respects all living beings. At this time the predicament of western and northern, particularly U.S., liberated women and feminists is that to get anything done in the public world of power, we have to give up the desire, credibility, and perhaps ability to act from our shared identities as human beings who identify with or have been assigned to a certain category. We may have lost our foundation of a distinctive gender as a means for making the world better. The arrogant question posed earlier in this chapter about what we can learn from women activists in the Third World now becomes the plaintive question, What would we do if their dire circumstances became our own?

NOTES

1. Amy Coplan, in "Empathy and Self Other Differentiation," a paper she read at the May 2004 Pacific SWIP (Society for Women in Philosophy) meeting at UCLA, correctly identifies empathy as an imaginative process. Although not sharing my reduction of social identities to circumstances, Coplan agreed with me in the discussion following her presentation that empathy requires a second-order assessment of one's qualifications for accurately understanding what I call the circumstances of another but some might still call race, sexual preference, or any one of many social identities.

More immediate than empathy, and also more general, is compassion, a disposition toward others that exceeds imagination because it is a direct emotional sensitivity or reaction to the goals of others as living beings. I have not discussed compassion in this context of feminist politics because compassion is an optional individual emotional attitude and does not constitute a political or public virtue. Still, I would expect that compassionate individuals are already predisposed to be empathetic, especially women toward other women. I am not sure that compassion can be specified as compassion for one type of human or even sentient being, or that compassion lends itself to accurate self-assessment of whether one has succeeded in a particular case, based on one's past experience. The best treatments of compassion come from Eastern traditions. See, for instance, Jeffrey Hopkins, *Cultivating Compassion: A Buddhist Perspective* (New York: Broadway/Random House, 2001).

2. For a summary of this feminist scholarship, which is also a basis for contrasting First and Third World feminist concerns, see Georgia Waylen, "Analyzing Women in the Politics of the Third World," in *Women and Politics in the Third world*, ed. Haleh Afshar (London: Routledge, 1996), 7–24.

3. The term "high politics" is apt for referring to the most powerful government offices and activities. I'm borrowing it from Waylen, "Analyzing Women."

4. On the term "global maximization" and its underlying concept, see Lorraine Code, "How to Think Globally: Stretching the Limits of Imagination," in *Decentering the Center: Philosophy for a Multicultural, Postcolonial, and Feminist World*, ed. Uma Narayan and Sandra Harding (Bloomington: Indiana University Press, 2000), 67–79.

5. Code, "How to Think Globally," 67–79.

6. Dan Barry, "Home from Iraq and Homeless," *New York Times*, April 24, 2004, A1.

7. Barry, "Home from Iraq and Homeless," A12.

8. The leadership ability of women of the most privileged classes, particularly royalty, is a historical fact, extending across many cultures.

9. In both Latin America and South Asia, progressive movements by mothers have opposed military dictatorships. Such movements have met opposition from women who, because of political connections and economic privilege, have not suffered in the same way from the same governments. See Rohini Hensman, "The Role of Women in Resistance to Political Authoritarianism in Latin America and South Asia," in Afshar, *Women and Politics in the Third World*, 60–64.

10. On self-actualization, see a classic text, Abraham H. Maslow, *Toward a Psychology of Being* (New York: Van Nostrand, 1968).

11. Celia W. Dugger, "Debate Stirs over Tiny Loans for World's Poorest," *New York Times*, April 29, 2004, A1.

12. Janet K. Boles, "Political Parties," in *Reader's Companion to U.S. Women's History*, ed. Wilma Mankiller, Gwendolyn Mink, Marysa Navarro, Barbara Smith, and Gloria Steinem (Boston: Houghton Mifflin, 1998), 456–59. I rely on Boles's article for historical facts about women's political party participation in the discussion that follows in this section. Boles's sources are Barbara C. Burrell, "Party Decline, Party Transformation, and Gender Politics: The USA," in *Gender and Party Politics* (London: Sage, 1993); Anne N. Costain, "After Reagan: New Party Attitudes toward Gender," *Annals*, May 1991, 114–25; and Jo Freeman, "Feminism vs. Family Values: Women at the 1992 Democratic and Republican Conventions," *PS: Political Science and Politics*, March 1993, 21–28.

13. Boles writes that it is "unclear whether this group would operate as a political party by contesting elections or act as a social movement/interest group" ("Political Parties," 457). As of this writing (June 2004) I have been unable to determine whether the Nation's Equality Party currently exists as a viable political entity.

14. Both Norway's credo, as Skjeie formulates it, and the Beijing Platform are in Hege Skjeie, "Credo on Difference: Women in Parliament in Norway," www.idea.int (accessed May 2004). The web posting is an updated version of the case study, originally published in the International IDEA, *Handbook: Women in Parliament: Beyond Numbers* (Stockholm: International IDEA, 1998).

15. *Handbook: Women in Parliament*.

16. *Handbook: Women in Parliament*.

17. *Handbook: Women in Parliament*.

18. *Handbook: Women in Parliament*.

19. Cynthia Enloe, *The Morning After: Sexual Politics at the End of the Cold War* (Berkeley: University of California Press, 1993), 12–13.

20. Enloe, *The Morning After*, 16–17.

21. See Azizah Yahia al-Hibri, "Muslim Women's Rights in the Global Village: Challenges and Opportunities," in *Critical Race Feminism: A Reader*, 2d ed. (New York: New York University Press, 2002), 375–84; and al-Hibri, "Deconstructing Patriarchal Jurisprudence in Islamic Law: A Faithful Approach," in *Global Critical Race Feminism: An International Approach*, ed. Adrien Katherine Wing (New York: New York University Press, 2000), 221–33.

22. Shirin Rai, "Women and the State in the Third World," in *Women and Politics in the Third World,* ed. Helen Afshar (London: Routledge, 1996), 25–39.

23. Shirin Rai, "Women and the State in the Third World," 25–39.

24. Donna Pankhurst and Jenny Pearce, "Feminist Perspectives on Democratisation in the South: Engendering or Adding Women In," in Afshar, *Women and Politics in the Third World,* 40–47.

25. Hensman, "Role of Women in Resistance," 48–72.

26. Hensman, "Role of Women in Resistance," 48–72.

27. Hensman, "Role of Women in Resistance," 48–72.

28. On this subject, thanks to Bonnie Mann for giving me copies of these sources: Richard Goldstein, "Neo-Macho Man," *The Nation,* July 24, 2003; Michael Schwalbe, "Lessons in Death, Born in the USA," *Raleigh News and Observer* (North Carolina), May 5, 2003.

Summary and Conclusion

There are limits to the amount of theory, critique, and analysis that even patient, gentle readers will abide. Examples on the way may not be sufficient to render the material digestible. A clear summary is now needed, then specific suggestions, and perhaps a last engagement with what no longer works, in theory as well as practice. That is the purpose and content of this conclusion.

SUMMARY OF CHAPTERS 1-8

During the late 1970s, second wave feminists abandoned hope and enthusiasm for a universal definition of women for two main reasons: a challenge that their work was biased by white race and middle class, and a rejection of biological determinism. The charge by black and poor women that establishment feminism was overly focused on the problems of white middle-class women led to the theory of intersectionality, whereby each intersection, as an identity formed by multiple oppressions, is entitled to speak for itself, and no other may speak for it. Biological determinism became untenable on empirical grounds because women found that their aptitudes and talents were limited mainly by patriarchal culture. The understanding of cultural differences in women's gender also supported difference feminism.

While feminism has flourished as an intellectual occupation after splintering into varied intersections, and higher education remains highly segregated racially. Women of color in the academy, the outside U.S. society, and throughout many local movements all over the world, are left largely to their own devices. The now-accepted inability of feminists to advocate for women in any universal way creates a political void, insofar as feminism could be a practical advocacy for women that improves life for all—women, children, men, and nonhuman natural beings.

The abandonment of a universal definition of women was premature, however. The expectation that such a definition, or a universal women's identity, could capture all important concrete differences in women's lives, ignored what women have in common. No definition of members of any group can capture how they differ from each other, but only what they share. All women share the nonsubstantive, relational essence of being assigned to or identifying with the historical, socially constructed, disjunctive category of female birth designees, biological mothers, or heterosexual choices of men—category FMP. Category FMP captures what women have in common as the imagined but real group that is the logical contrary of the group of men, in human male–female, man–woman gender systems.

Simone de Beauvoir's definition of women as Other can now be read as an overgeneralization of the situation of some women, who are so oppressed that they are not recognized as having attributes that can be compared to those of men. The idea that all women share a relation to category FMP makes it possible to account for women's differences on a common basis. Women thus understood are not radically different, and their commonality is an important foundation for social and political action, as well as feminist theory.

The new understanding of women as sharing a relation calls for a theory of gender development that recognizes a component of individual choice and cooperation. Gender identity is culturally imposed, not only in terms of approved social roles but also to the extent that sorting of human infants as either male or female expresses a social dichotomy that is imposed on a continuum of biological sexual difference.

From the child's perspective, her gender development is a negotiation between what she believes about herself and what others expect of her. In being designated female, she is expected to create a system of beliefs and practices that are appropriate to the body she lives in. The external imposition of others' beliefs requires cooperation from the gendered subject for her to become her assigned gender. That cooperation is obscured by acceptance of gender assignment in the vast majority of cases. In terms of power dynamics, women's autonomy may also be obscured when they use it to develop skills that objectify or subordinate themselves; however, such skills can be redirected toward greater liberation. One example of this is the late-twentieth-century shift in beauty ideals from that of passive, sedentary object to active, athletic subject.

The study of gender in individuals is addressed by the discipline of psychology, while sociology and anthropology are the study of gender in society. Feminism as critical theory is normative, and so is feminist social theory.

Changes in individual psychology or revisions of deep psychoanalytic theories do not automatically result in changes in society. Social institutions need to be addressed directly and politically for such change to occur. In addition to its normativity, inclusive feminist social theory needs to be factual, comprehensive, and capable of explaining women's oppression. Inclusive feminist psychological theory needs to focus on beliefs and intentions that become motivational for individual women; for that reason, cognitive clinical psychology provides more empowering models than does psychoanalysis. However, Freudian theory is a useful way of describing female gender formation in oppressive masculinist sex-gender systems. In the same way, Marxist theory should be understood as a description of economies dominated by men as they have been traditionally constructed.

While women as traditionally understood are not a social class because their work is not monetarized, women could become a historical group based on a vision of their rule in the future. Such rule by women would be facilitated by the fact that women are not men and they compose over half the voting population in existing democracies. But, if political power is ultimately based on economic power, rule by women would require a revaluation of the kinds of work that have not yet been monetarized and perhaps a revaluation of monetarization itself. The revaluation of the kinds of things that are monetarized, in comparison with the kinds of things that have unpriced and unpriceable values, is needed to correct the destructive and exploitative aspects of historical rule by men and to assess prior models of absolute scarcity. First World feminists have not yet undertaken such revaluation in political terms, partly because their political inclusion, like their economic inclusion, has been conditioned by their androgynization. One cost of androgynization has been that women's traditional roles are no longer sustainable or sustained in many cases, despite formal political equality. At the same time, the systems that grant women formal equality continue to reproduce them in traditional ways, as female birth designees, biological mothers, and men's heterosexual choices.

Feminist political theory needs a global view to be inclusive, and also because First World liberated women may not be as liberated as they think. The inclusion of women in the Norwegian parliament has been accompanied by an idea of economic self-sufficiency for women in their traditional roles. Even though the Norwegian political elite continues to gender-stereotype the political interests of men and women, or perhaps because of this dichotomy, there is inclusion of women as such. In the late twentieth century, mothers groups in the Third World organized to lead political reforms under conditions of extreme civil instability, and their success represents the ability of traditional women to enter into the social contract as principals. Although these women have not succeeded in ruling in their respective countries and there is little indication that their progressive programs go beyond a restoration of patriarchal support for women in their traditional roles, their example raises the question of what U.S. women would be able to do as women if they experienced similar misfortunes.

The formal equality of women in the First and Second Worlds could enable them to take on the responsibility of correcting the disadvantages of rule by men by assuming rule themselves. While the idea of rule by women on the highest levels of power and government is now utopian, it may be the only hope for sustaining life in the face of the ongoing monetarizing-technologizing project.[1]

UTOPIAN FEMINIST POLITICAL THEORY

The ultimate questions for feminist political theory at this point are: Can women rule? and How can women come to rule? The written record of history attests to the normality and universality of rule by men. There have been evolutionary and biological explanations of why men have ruled, but they do not show that rule by men over both men and women is inevitable or necessary. Before revisiting the failure of such deterministic explanations of rule by men, it is useful to establish that it is possible for women to rule, since the crush of history can overwhelm hope of matriarchy. There is no contradiction in claiming that at some time in the future, say on December 21, 2028, the governments of all the major countries in the world will be controlled by women, and that these governments, as institutions that organize their societies and represent them in dealings with other societies, will have as much power then as they do now. But, as Hume showed, there is no contradiction in making any empirical prediction.

The logical possibility of rule by women could acquire a positive probability through the following scenario. Establishment feminists and women's advocates throughout the world form women's political parties. Women's parties put women on the ballots on every level of government, and a large number of women in the electorate, as well as some men, vote for their candidates. Women's parties have platforms with policies to implement common objectives of peace, environmental preservation, sustainability of women's work, social services for mothers and children, universal educational opportunities, and universal health care. There might be variation in both the forms of these objectives and in the endorsement of other objectives, such as gay marriage, higher minimum wage, abortion rights, racial integration and affirmative action, legalized prostitution, animal rights, and human population control. The two universal objectives of rule by women would be the end of violence and preservation of natural environments.

The main obstacles to such rule by women are the exploitative requirements of capitalism and the use of violence as a medium for resolving conflict, both of which are embedded in rule by men. Those obstacles are also the social mechanizations to which rule by women would develop in opposition. Given a gendered, Sartrean–Marxist dialectical view of this currently utopian political scenario (see chapter 7), it could be said that once women begin to organize politically on the basis of gender, it will become increasingly evident that their organization, as a group, opposes the political organizations of men. Looking back to Mrs. O. H. P. Belmont's expectation that the U.S. Republican and Democratic Parties would unite against the National Women's Political Party (see chapter 8), we can say that before women gain political strength as a reaction to their opposition, they will have to constitute themselves as an opposition.

To return to the utopian scenario, if women organized politically on the grounds of gender, their rule would acquire a certain probability because in democratic countries, the candidates of organized political parties have some chance, no matter how small, of winning elections. Even if women's political parties were not successful and all they accomplished was to split votes so that otherwise progressive male candidates lost elections, in time, they might reform the goals of men's progressive parties. But this last hope is the resigned and pessimistic view. The optimistic view is that women's political parties could radically change human history through the repeated victories of their candidates.

For women to change history by becoming an active part of history in its official political dimension, there would have to be women leaders who were intellectually and emotionally capable of inventing and playing a different game than the one men have invented and played. Furthermore, and this is what makes the utopia theoretically easy to envision and viable for implementation, it is not necessary that rule by women, insofar as it will be better than rule by men, be conceived to depend on pacific or nurturing temperaments that women have been stereotyped to have or that some women may have in reality. We are speaking of women here as no more (and no less) than category FMP.

No one doubts that there are women who are free of the need for men's approval and have the ability to rule independently of instructions from men in the political and economic game that men have invented. Both first and second wave feminism established the existence of intellectually and emotionally independent women. Recent history has also yielded examples of women rulers: Margaret Thatcher, Madeline Albright, and perhaps Hillary Rodham Clinton, and earlier, Golda Meir and Indira Gandhi. But so far, all women rulers have played the men's game. What history has not yet yielded are examples of independent women with political power who have opposed the violent, exploitative trajectory of men's history. And that is precisely the point of envisioning rule by women. That rule by women would be based on objectives of benefit to women, men, and natural environments, rather than on the presumed pacific or nurturing temperaments of women, is precisely what could make it defensible theoretically and viable politically. The externalization of the objectives of rule by women from any presumed temperament of women puts less pressure on women in their utopian political capacity. By the same token, this externalization, combined with the numbers of women in world populations, means that matriarchy need not require androgyny, or a neutralization or blurring of male–female sex-gender differences. Women would not have to change their traditional identities to become politically powerful, although some (more than have already done so) probably would change those identities. Furthermore, insofar as patriarchy, in the form of rule by fathers, has for a long time (theoretically, at least since John Locke's *Two Treatises of Civil Government*) been distinguished from civil government, the term "matriarchy" should not imply either rule by women who are mothers or rule that reproduces the authority, concerns, and skills of mothers. Women just contingently, due to their numbers, are the group that could legitimately overthrow rule by men as we have known it.

But what about the temperaments of men as a determinant of their historical rule, not to mention their reluctance to relinquish their rule? The twentieth century has yielded sufficient examples of nonviolent regime and policy change that liberated oppressed groups; these examples support optimism about a future success of women's political parties. Think of Mahatma Gandhi's successful efforts in expelling the British from India, Martin Luther King's success in securing civil rights for African Americans, and, of course, the nineteenth- and early-twentieth-century leaders of the struggle for women's suffrage. To be sure, the leaders of these nonviolent movements had dedicated followers, but their ability to attract and keep followers, while adhering to principles of nonviolence, was a large part of their success. If feminists build the theoretical context and activists build the political structures, the requisite leaders of women's political parties will develop and appear. However, the violent and domineering temperaments of men, which seem to have enabled their rule, have been an overwhelming force in human history. This raises the question of whether rule by human males is inevitable.

The deterministic arguments about rule by men basically assert that there is something about some men, owing to their body chemistry or the way human beings have evolved as a biological species, that makes male rule inevitable. I noted at the end of chapter 3 that human sex-gender, male–female, man–woman systems have dramatically increased the size of the human population, to the point where it now grows in multiples of itself every few decades. Evolutionary explanations of male rule connect male dominance to "reproductive success." In *Demonic Males* ("demonic" because they have large brains and violent temperaments) Richard Wrangham and Dale Peterson describe human beings as a species of primates who, in shared ancestry and present traits, have much in common with chimpanzees. Like chimpanzee societies, all known human societies have been characterized by male dominance through male violence against other males and females. Wrangham and Peterson point out that among bonobos, a second close evolutionary relative of *Homo sapiens sapiens*, and a species that evolved from common ancestors with present chimpanzees, males are neither dominant nor violent. They attribute the "nondemonic" quality of bonobo males to the existence of environments with food supplies adequate to support stable large-group social organization. (This food has been available for bonobos because they do not share their habitat with gorillas, who would otherwise eat it; chimpanzees, by contrast, have evolved in shared habitats with gorillas and need to forage more for food.) Bonobos live and travel in stable groups of 16.9, compared to groups of two to nine as the norm for chimpanzees. It is not necessary for individual bonobos to leave their groups in search of food, and the absence of solitary and vulnerable individuals eliminates an opportunity for male gangs to attack such individuals, as happens among chimpanzees. Within the bonobo groups, females form nonkinship alliances that enable them to protect both females and males against violent males. Bonobo males do not form alliances within the large groups.[2]

Wrangham and Peterson believe that violence in primate males has resulted in the reproductive success of those who are dominant, who in turn, through either genes or the example of their behavior, have offspring who are violent. But they do not believe that male dominance in either chimpanzees or human beings is inevitable, for two main reasons: (1) if environmental conditions support the formation of large social groups and female alliances within them, male violence can be checked by females and (2) human beings are capable of thinking and acting against both inherent temperament and biological and social history.[3]

Still, the application of primate gender differences and social patterns to human beings is not as simple as Wrangham and Peterson imply. Human beings have for a long time existed in groups much larger than the 16.9-member bonobo groups that enable alliances among female bonobos. But the resulting human female alliances, whether based on extended family connections, work, or other common interests, have not resulted in significant checks on male dominance through violence. Furthermore, human males seem to have formed alliances among themselves in all societies. Perhaps what is required is a kind of women's organization more directly connected to the type of power men have exercised historically—political power. Thus the question is open whether women's political parties would be sufficient to check male power based on violence.

Wrangham and Peterson imply that women, unlike men, are not inherently violent, in either groups or interactions among groups. The assumption is that groups or gangs of women, unlike groups or gangs of men, would not attack individuals or smaller groups with the aim of dominating or killing them. If women *were* routinely able to get away with such behavior (i.e., if there were not more powerful groups or gangs of men), we do not know whether women would be as peaceful as female bonobos. However, the entire question of inherent gender temperaments can be sidestepped if political conditions are understood in terms of avowed goals rather than traits of the gender that has power. The reason rule by women is worth taking seriously is not that women are more temperamentally suited to rule than are men (although many may think women are thus suited and some women may be), but that women are a large enough group to supplant men through democratic elections that would have at stake something like the goals of government. In principle, men could have powerful political parties with the objectives of peace and environmental preservation, or men and women could unite to form such parties. But such efforts have not met with significant success thus far.

WHAT NO LONGER WORKS THEORETICALLY

With the utopian scenario of rule by women and its implementation by women's political parties in mind, two things might be considered: (1) the ways in which feminist theory has not been sufficiently radical to enable direct contestation of rule by men and (2) problems and conditions in thought and reality that obstruct such a contestation. In other words, why haven't other feminists thought of the demographic political solution, and why might such a solution be difficult to implement? The currently utopian idea of rule by women in contemporary democracies is such an obvious third wave next step that there must be deep reasons for its not having been previously voiced (so far as I know). My broad question to other feminist political theorists is, therefore, What are you thinking about that renders such a currently utopian vision, utopian?

Clearly there is a rich density of interconnected matters that feminist political theorists have already thought well about. First, there was the issue of structural or formal political equality with men, symbolized and to a large degree implemented in the achievement of women's suffrage. Next there were and continue to be legal issues of women's equality to men, such as access to professional employment and higher education. And that has been followed by a return to formal and substantive political equality in the existence of women who hold political office on the basis of affiliation with political parties, albeit still run by men. Feminist political theorists have thought long and hard about the ways in which political systems that purport to be egalitarian have in fact privileged men. And they have thought about relations between women of different classes, castes, or races that have different locations in hierarchies of masculine political power. Nonetheless, feminist work on women's suffrage, social equality, political participation, and analyses of the bias toward men in political theory have all occurred in the framework of men's rule.

On the way toward liberation from that framework, feminists have considered the relation of women to the state, in abstract ways that could render the utopian description of rule by women through women's political parties, incomplete, if not merely glib. Judith Butler seems to directly address the relation of women to the state in *Antigone's Claim*. Butler begins by recounting Sophocles' play through its interpretations by Hegel, Lévi-Strauss, and Lacan. Butler is not explicitly concerned with the practical possibility of matriarchy—at least that is not her stated concern in this work. Rather, the interpretations she addresses, as well as her own, presuppose a force of the sex-gender system that fundamentally separates women from the state. Butler notes that for Antigone to bury her brother and then not deny that she has done so requires that she assume the authority of a law opposed to the state's law, and then use a language to describe her deed, which is the language of those she is opposing. To resist the state, which belongs to men, Antigone must become "manly":

> To publish one's act in language is in some sense the completion of the act, the moment as well that implicates her in the masculine excess called hubris. And so, as she begins to act in language, she also departs from herself. Her act is never fully her act, and though she uses language to claim her deed, to assert a "manly" and defiant autonomy, she can perform that act only through embodying the norms of the power she opposes.[4]

The chasm between what Antigone represents as a woman and the state is much deeper than a male–female difference within society. Antigone's otherness to the state, according to Butler, represents a gap between kinship, or the family, and the state. According to Hegel (and others) the family is necessary for the state as the source of sons who will be sent to war to defend any particular form of the state, and the state is necessary to support any particular form of the family.[5] Butler maintains that forms of the family and the state are always implied in one another, and she claims that structuralists and poststructuralists have universally defined members of the family in terms of the permissibility or impermissibility of their sexual relations with each other (e.g., a mother is someone with whom a son and daughter do not have sexual relations). Rules against incest determine positions in the family, which are the same as roles in the family. Moreover, the incest taboo is not only a universal cultural taboo but it is also, according to Lévi-Strauss, a taboo without which there cannot be culture or civilization as we have known them throughout human history. With Lacan's movement of this taboo into the symbolic order, as a condition of it, the incest taboo becomes a reified universal condition of language.[6]

Butler's interest in Antigone is based on the ways in which Antigone represents a crisis of kinship because she is not permitted to officially grieve the loss of her brother. Butler aims to use this crisis to reexamine both kinship and language, or the symbolic order, as understood by Lacan. While Butler intends to "refuse the conclusion that the incest taboo must be undone in order for love to freely flourish everywhere," she also wants to interrogate the repressive aspects of an absolute deference to the incest taboo:

> The point then, is not to unleash incest from its constraints but to ask what forms of normative kinship are understood to proceed as structural necessities from that taboo. . . . What new schemes of intelligibility make our loves legitimate and recognizable, our losses true losses? This question reopens the relation between kinship and reigning epistemes of cultural intelligibility, and both of these to the possibility of social transformation.[7]

In other words, according to Butler's readings, kinship and the incest taboo together make political power as we have known it, or the state, possible. Drawing on Luce Irigaray, as well as the sources already mentioned, Butler claims that for critical theorists Antigone has come to represent "kinship as the sphere that conditions the possibility of politics without ever entering into it."[8]

Insofar as the incest taboo defines positions within the family, after the existence of culture (i.e., it defines women in some sense), does this mean that for women to have real political power, the incest taboo would have to be dislodged? The question is on its face preposterous, but the fact that it is suggested by the implications of the canonical interpretations of *Antigone* consulted by Butler underscores the existence of forbidding factors against real political power for women. Most feminists are by now desensitized to the dangers of androgyny that could be posed by women's rule, but the overwhelming majority of both women and feminists would balk at undoing the incest taboo. But in specific reference to the present concern for the possibility of rule by women, what exactly does Butler think the incest taboo has to do with Antigone's claim?

Let's return to Butler's readings. Hegel generalizes Antigone's situation as the prepolitical condition of women in the family, who have no voice in public and political life in the state. Butler insists that Antigone represents an unwritten and unwriteable law in a sphere that enables the existence of the state in the way the unconscious enables the conscious: "This is a legality of what does not exist and of what is unconscious, not a law *of* the unconscious but some form of demand that the unconscious necessarily makes on law, that which marks the limit and condition of law's generality."[9]

According to Butler, for Lacan, the Oedipus complex is universal, not because it appears everywhere but because where it does appear, it appears as that which is everywhere. Antigone represents the laws prior to all codification and is therefore a symbolic limit that humans may not cross. She manifests a kind of death drive, something enigmatic and compelling that crops up in any pursuit of what is good. In leaving the symbolic order, Antigone leaves the conditions for a supportable life.[10] Butler interprets Lacan to claim that Antigone's absolute valuation of her brother as a particular human being locates Antigone on the nonhuman and humanly moribund side of the symbolic order. In contrast, Butler claims that Antigone's violation of the incest taboo in her love for her brother locates her outside the symbolic order, an order that is nonetheless "limited by its constitutive interdictions" (i.e., the incest taboo must be violated to remain in force as a taboo).[11] Butler concludes that because Antigone's claim is intelligible in the public sphere, it represents an appropriation and perversion of the mandates of this sphere. Thus Butler reads *Antigone* as "establishing the question of whether there might be new grounds for communicability and for life?"[12] Indeed, in the rest of this remarkable essay, Butler uses the aberrant forms of kinship in Antigone's family—her father, Oedipus, is also her brother, and her brother Polyneices is also her nephew, while at the same time her gender is changed to male by the words of her father—to explore the possibility of displacement of heterosexual exogamous normativity in the psychoanalytic family toward gay families, single-parent families, and blended families.[13]

Important as these considerations are, Butler's proposed reconfiguration of Lacanian psychoanalytic cultural history succeeds neither in showing how the incest taboo precludes political rule by women nor in envisioning rule by women. The "new grounds for communicability and for life" would at best liberate and restore to full human status those who do not instantiate the heterosexual exogamous family. This would be a huge social good in feminist terms, but there is nothing in Butler's own analysis to suggest that it would change the political gender of the world. However, Butler characterizes Lacan's location of Antigone outside the symbolic order as the problem of valuing a particular in a system that functions on abstractions and stipulates a fundamental interchangeability of particulars. And that insight suggests the level on which such a change would have to be conceptualized.

It is exactly the interchangeability of particulars resulting from abstraction that facilitates the kinds of violence and exploitation that would be eliminated as the aim of government if rule by men ended. We cannot say that all particulars ought to be valued as particulars in opposition to some aspect of the symbolic order that would value only their abstract properties. That would be too broad a restriction on order and even language, of any kind. Rather, the question is, Which particulars ought to be made exempt from systems of abstraction within symbolic orders, particularly economic ones? If it can be agreed, in some contextualized, existentialist, and non–a priori version of Marxism (as discussed in chapter 7), that the economic order drives the political order, then a major feminist project of revaluation needs to be undertaken. The project is to determine what can and what cannot be given an economic value, or price, that makes it interchangeable with others of its kind that are given the same price. Thus, in the present order, a young man who is not protected by a privileged family and is not committed to an educational institution that conditionally guarantees the price of his labor in the future may be sent off to war. The hourly or daily or yearly labor of a woman in a "developing" nation may be valued according to the prices of subsistence consumer goods in her nation, and priced accordingly. An area of wetland inhabited by waterfowl may be valued by its price as a site for suburban housing, and its value to waterfowl ignored.

It should go without saying: no matter how nonheterosexually normative and endogamous the psychoanalytic family may become on something like Butler's interpretation of Antigone's claim, that change will not in itself protect conscripts, exploited workers, or ecological niches. What is private and social is political in its dynamics and, in one way or another, eventually supported or condemned by the state. But to change the private and social is not to change or abolish the state as we know it; private or social change may at best lead to change in the laws within the state. It has been the aim of government to protect the monetary interests of those who have the power to monetarize the life, time, and place of others, without careful concern for the value of these beings as particulars, before they are inducted into the abstract monetary order. Hence, what is needed is a careful revaluation of kinds of particulars to determine which ones should be exempted from the monetary symbolic order.[14] This revaluation ought to be based on a deep understanding that such exemption confers a greater dignity and value on those particulars than the ones in the monetary symbolic order. That is what a revaluation of values would mean in this case.

NOTES

1. I write "utopian" to preserve credibility. I do not mean "utopian" in the fictional sense explored by Charlotte Perkins Gilman in *Herland,* Monique Wittig in *Les Guérillères,* or in recent works of science fiction, such as Jean Slonczewski, *A Door into Ocean.*

2. Richard Wrangham and Dale Peterson, *Demonic Males: Apes and the Origins of Human Violence* (New York: Houghton Mifflin, 1996), 108–26, 200–230.

3. Wrangham and Peterson, *Demonic Males,* 231–52.

4. Judith Butler, *Antigone's Claim* (New York: Columbia University Press, 2000), 10.

5. Butler, *Antigone's Claim,* 35–37.

6. Butler, *Antigone's Claim,* 10–24.

7. Butler, *Antigone's Claim,* 30 and 24, respectively.

8. Butler, *Antigone's Claim,* 2.

9. Butler, *Antigone's Claim,* 33.

10. Butler, *Antigone's Claim,* 44–52.

11. Butler, *Antigone's Claim,* 53.

12. Butler, *Antigone's Claim,* 55.

13. Butler, *Antigone's Claim,* 57–82.

14. Zack, *Women, Money, and the State* (forthcoming).

Select Bibliography

Afshar, Haleh, ed. *Women and Politics in the Third World*. London: Routledge, 1996.

Alcoff, Linda M. "Cultural Feminism versus Post-Structuralism: The Identity Crisis in Feminist Theory." In Micheline R. Malson, Jean F. O'Barr, Sarah Westphal-Wihl, and Mary Wyer, eds., *Feminist Theory in Practice and Process*, 295–326. Chicago: University of Chicago Press, 1989.

Al-Hibri, Azizah Yahia. "Deconstructing Patriarchal Jurisprudence in Islamic Law: A Faithful Approach." In Adrien Katherine Wing, ed., *Critical Race Feminism: A Reader*, 221–33. 2d ed. New York: New York University Press, 2002.

——. "Muslim Women's Rights in the Global Village: Challenges and Opportunities." In Adrien Katherine Wing, ed., *Critical Race Feminism: A Reader*, 375–84. 2d ed. New York: New York University Press, 2002.

Allen, Paula Gunn. *The Sacred Hoop: Recovering the Feminine in American Indian Traditions*. Boston: Beacon, 1986.

Alphonso, Doris Rita. Introduction to "Sex and Gender/Christine Delphy." In Kelly Oliver, ed., *French Feminism Reader*, 59–63. Lanham, Md.: Rowman & Littlefield, 2000.

Banaji, Mahhzarin R. "The Psychology of Gender: A Perspective on Perspectives." In Anne E. Beall and Robert J. Sternberg, eds., *The Psychology of Gender*, 251–74. New York: Guilford, 1993.

Barrett, Michele. "Capitalism and Women's Liberation." In Linda J. Nicholson, ed., *The Second Wave: A Reader in Feminist Theory*, 123–30. New York: Routledge, 1997.

Barry, Dan. "Home from Iraq and Homeless." *New York Times*, April 24, 2004, A1.

Bartky, Sandra Lee. *Femininity and Domination: Studies in the Phenomenology of Oppression*. New York: Routledge, 1990.

Beall, Anne E. "A Social Constructionist View of Gender." In Anne E. Beall and Robert J. Sternberg, eds., *The Psychology of Gender*, 127–47. New York: Guilford, 1993.

Beall, Anne E., and Robert J. Sternberg, eds. *The Psychology of Gender*. New York: Guilford, 1993.

Beauvoir, Simone de. *The Second Sex.* Translated by H. M. Parshley. New York: Knopf, 1952.

Best, Deborah L., and John E. Williams. "A Cross-Cultural Viewpoint." In Anne E. Beall and Robert J. Sternberg, eds., *The Psychology of Gender,* 215–50. New York: Guilford, 1993.

Boles, Janet K. "Political Parties." In Wilma Mankiller, Gwendolyn Mink, Marysa Navarro, Barbara Smith, and Gloria Steinem, eds., *Reader's Companion to U.S. Women's History,* 456–59. Boston: Houghton Mifflin, 1998.

Bonner, Raymond. "A Challenge in India Snarls Foreign Adoptions." *New York Times,* June 23, 2003, A3.

———. "For Poor Families, Selling Baby Girls Was Economic Boon." *New York Times,* June 23, 2003, A3.

Bordo, Susan R. "Beauty (Re)Discovers the Male Body." In Peg Zeglin Brand, ed., *Beauty Matters,* 112–54. Bloomington: Indiana University Press, 2000.

———. *The Flight to Objectivity: Essays on Cartesianism and Culture.* Albany: State University of New York Press, 1987.

———. *Unbearable Weight: Feminism, Western Culture, and the Body.* Berkeley: University of California Press, 1993.

Bourdieu, Pierre. *Masculine Domination.* Translated by Richard Nice. Stanford, Calif.: Stanford University Press, 2001.

Browne, Irene, and Joya Misra. "The Intersection of Gender and Race in the Labor Market." *Annual Review of Sociology,* August 2003, 487–513.

Brownmiller, Susan. *Femininity.* New York: Fawcett Columbine, 1984.

Butler, Judith. *Antigone's Claim.* New York: Columbia University Press, 2000.

———. *Gender Trouble: Feminism and the Subversion of Identity.* New York: Routledge, 1990.

Chodorow, Nancy. "Oedipal Asymmetries and Heterosexual Knots." *Social Problems* 23, no. 4 (1976): 454–58.

———. "The Psychodynamics of Mothering." In *The Reproduction of Mothering: Psychoanalysis and the Sociology of Gender.* Berkeley: University of California Press, 1978.

Chomsky, Noam. "Recent Contributions to the Theory of Innate Ideas." *Synthese,* 1967, 2–11. Reprinted in Robert Cummins and Denise Dellarosa Cummins, eds., *Minds, Brains, and Computers: The Foundations of Cognitive Science,* 452–57. New York: Blackwell, 2000.

Christian, Barbara. "Diminishing Returns: Can Black Feminism(s) Survive the Academy?" In David Theo Goldberg, ed., *Multiculturalismm: A Critical Reader,* 168–77. Cambridge, Mass.: Blackwell, 1994.

———. "The Race for Theory. "*Cultural Critique* 6 (1989). Reprinted in Gloria Anzaldúa, ed., *Making Face, Making Soul/Hacienda Caras: Creative and Critical Perspectives by Women of Color,* 335–45. San Francisco: Aunt Lute.

Cixous, Hélène. "Castration or Decapitation?" *Signs* 7, no. 1 (1981): 41–55. Translated by Annette Kuhn, from "Le sexe ou la tete?" *Les cahiers du GRIF* 23 (1976): 5–15.

———. "The Laugh of Medusa." *Signs* 1, no. 4 (1976): 875–99. Translated by Keith Cohen and Paula Cohen, from "Le Rire de la Meduse." *L'Arc* 61 (1975): 39–54.

Code, Lorraine. "How to Think Globally: Stretching the Limits of Imagination." In Uma Narayan and Sandra Harding, eds., *Decentering the Center: Philosophy for a*

Multicultural, Postcolonial, and Feminist World, 67–79. Bloomington: Indiana University Press, 2000.

Coetzee, J. M. "As a Woman Grows Older." *New York Review of Books,* January 15, 2004, 11–15.

———. *Elizabeth Costello.* New York: Viking, 2003.

Cohen, Morris R., and Ernest Nagel. *Introduction to Logic and Scientific Method.* New York: Harcourt Brace, 1934.

Collins, Patricia Hill. *Black Feminist Thought: Knowledge, Power, and the Politics of Empowerment.* Boston: Unwin Hyman, 1990.

———. *Fighting Words: Black Women and the Search for Justice.* Minneapolis: University of Minnesota Press, 1998.

Combahee River Collective. "A Black Feminist Statement." In Linda J. Nicholson, ed., *The Second Wave: A Reader in Feminist Theory,* 63–70. New York: Routledge, 1997.

Copi, Irving M. *Introduction to Logic.* New York: Macmillan, 1961.

Crenshaw, Kimberle. *Demarginalizing the Intersection of Race and Sex: A Black Feminist Critique of Antidiscrimination Doctrine, Feminist Theory, and Antiracist Politics.* Chicago: University of Chicago Legal Forum, 1989.

Cross, Susan E., and Hazel Rose Karkus. "Gender in Thought, Belief, and Action: A Cognitive Approach." In Anne E. Beall and Robert J. Sternberg, eds., *The Psychology of Gender,* 55–98. New York: Guilford, 1993.

Davis, Angela Y. Interview by George Yancy. In Naomi Zack, ed., *Women of Color and Philosophy,* 135–51. Malden, Mass.: Blackwell, 2000.

———. *Women, Race, and Class.* New York: Random House, 1983.

Delphy, Christine. "The Invention of French Feminism: An Essential Move." *Yale French Studies* 87 (1995): 166–97.

Diers, Peter. "Friendship and Feminist Praxis: Insights from Sartre's *Critique of Dialectical Reason.*" In Julien S. Murphy, ed., *Feminist Interpretations of Jean-Paul Sartre,* 253–71. University Park: Pennsylvania State University Press, 1999.

Di Stephano, Christine. "Masculine Marx." In Mary Lyndon Shanley and Carole Patemean, eds., *Feminist Interpretations and Political Theory,* 146–63. University Park: Pennsylvania State University Press, 1991.

Enloe, Cynthia. *The Morning After: Sexual Politics at the End of the Cold War.* Berkeley: University of California Press, 1993.

Estop, Myrna. *A Theory of Immediate Awareness: Self-Organization and Adaptation in Natural Intelligence.* Dordrecht, Netherlands: Kluwer, 2003.

Fast, Irene. "Aspects of Early Gender Development: A Psychoanalytic Perspective." In Anne E. Beall and Robert J. Sternberg, eds., *The Psychology of Gender,* 173–96. New York: Guilford, 1993.

Ferguson, Ann. "Resisting the Veil of Privilege: Building Bridge Identities as an Ethico-Politics of Global Feminisms." In Uma Narayan and Sandra Harding, eds., *Decentering the Center: Philosophy for a Multicultural, Postcolonial, and Feminist World,* 189–207. Bloomington: Indiana University Press, 2000.

Flax, Jane. *The American Dream in Black and White: The Clarence Thomas Hearings.* Ithaca, N.Y.: Cornell University Press, 1998.

Freud, Sigmund. *The History of the Psychoanalytic Movement.* In *The Basic Writings of Sigmund Freud,* 899–948. Translated and edited by A. A. Brill. New York: Modern Library, 1995.

———. "Infantile Sexuality." In *Three Contributions to the Theory of Sex*. In *The Basic Writings of Sigmund Freud,* 548–71. Translated and edited by A. A. Brill. New York: Modern Library, 1995.

———. *Psychopathology of Everyday Life*. In *The Basic Writings of Sigmund Freud,* 3–148. Translated and edited by A. A. Brill. New York: Modern Library, 1995.

———. *Totem and Taboo*. In *The Basic Writings of Sigmund Freud,* 775–898. Translated and edited by A. A. Brill. New York: Modern Library, 1995.

———. "The Transformations of Puberty." In *Three Contributions to the Theory of Sex*. In *The Basic Writings of Sigmund Freud,* 575–600. Translated and edited by A. A. Brill. New York: Modern Library, 1995.

Frye, Marilyn. "The Necessity of Differences: Constructing a Positive Category of Women." *Signs,* Summer 1996, 991–1010.

Geuss, Raymond. *The Idea of a Critical Theory: Habermas and the Frankfurt School*. New York: Cambridge University Press, 1981.

Gilman, Charlotte Perkins. *The Abridged Diaries of Charlotte Perkins Gilman*. Charlottesville: University Press of Virginia, 1998.

———. *Herland*. In *Herland, The Yellow Wall-Paper, and Selected Writings*. Edited by Denise D. Knight. New York: Penguin, 1999.

Goldstein, Richard. "Neo-Macho Man." *The Nation,* July 24, 2003.

Golombok, Susan, and Robyn Fivush. *Gender Development*. Cambridge: Cambridge University Press, 1994.

Hanson, Jennifer. Introduction to "There are Two Sexes, Not One/Luce Irigaray." In Kelly Oliver, ed., *French Feminism Reader,* 201–6. Lanham, Md.: Rowman & Littlefield, 2000.

Haraway, Donna J. "'Gender' for a Marxist Dictionary." In *Simians, Cyborgs, and Women: The Reinvention of Nature,* 127–48. New York: Routledge, 1991.

Harding, Sandra. "Why Has the Sex/Gender System Become Visible Only Now?" In Sandra Harding and Merrill B. Hintikka, eds., *Discovering Reality: Feminist Perspectives on Epistemology, Metaphysics, Methodology, and Philosophy of Science,* 311–24. Dordrecht, Holland: Reidel, 1983.

Hartmann, Heidi. "The Unhappy Marriage of Marxism and Feminism: Toward a More Progressive Union." In Linda J. Nicholson, ed., *The Second Wave: A Reader in Feminist Theory,* 97–122. New York: Routledge, 1997.

Hensman, Rohini. "The Role of Women in Resistance to Political Authoritarianism in Latin America and South Asia." In Haleh Afshar, ed., *Women and Politics in the Third World,* 48–72. London: Routledge, 1996.

Heyes, Cressida J. *Line Drawings: Defining Women through Feminist Practice*. Ithaca, N.Y.: Cornell University Press, 2000.

Hine, Darlene Clark, ed. *Black Women in America: An Historical Encyclopedia*. 2 vols. Brooklyn: Carlson, 1993.

Hird, Myra J., and Jenz Germon. "The Intersexual Body and the Medical Regulation of Gender." In Kathryn Backett-Milburn and Linda Mckie, eds., *Constructing Gendered Bodies,* 166–78. New York: Palgrave, 2001.

hooks, bell. *Ain't I a Woman? Black Women and Feminism*. Boston: South End, 1981.

Hopkins, Jeffrey. *Cultivating Compassion: A Buddhist Perspective*. New York: Broadway/Random House, 2001.

Horney, Karen. "The Flight from Womanhood: The Masculinity Complex As Viewed by Men and by Women." In Harold Kelman, ed., *Feminine Psychology*, 37–70. New York: Norton, 1967.

Irigaray, Luce. *I Love to You: Sketch of a Possible Felicity in History*. Translated by A. Martin. New York: Routledge, 1994.

———. *Speculum of the Other Woman*. Translated by Gillian C. Gill. Ithaca, N.Y.: Cornell University Press, 1985.

Jacklin, Carol Nagy, and Chandra Reynolds. "Gender and Childhood Socialization." In Anne E. Beall and Robert J. Sternberg, eds., *The Psychology of Gender*, 197–214. New York: Guilford, 1993.

Jaimes, M. Annette. "Some Kind of Indian." In Naomi Zack, ed., *American Mixed Race: The Culture of Microdiversity*, 133–54. Lanham, Md.: Rowman & Littlefield, 1995.

Kessler, Suzanne J. "The Medical Construction of Gender: Case Management of Intersexed Infants." *Signs*, Autumn 1990, 3–26.

Kourany, Janet, ed. *Scientific Knowledge: Basic Issues in the Philosophy of Science*, 176–86. Belmont, Calif.: Wadsworth, 1998.

Kristeva, Julia. *About Chinese Women*. Translated by Anita Barrows. New York: Marion Boyars, 1977.

———. *Powers of Horror*. Translated by Leon Roudiez. New York: Columbia University Press, 1982.

Kruks, Sonia. "Identity Politics and Dialectical Reason: Beyond an Epistemology of Provenance." In Julien S. Murphy, *Feminist Interpretations of Jean-Paul Sartre*, 229–52. University Park: Pennsylvania State University Press, 1999.

Lacan, Jacques. *The Four Fundamental Concepts of Psycho-Analysis*. Edited by Jacques-Alain Miller. Translated by Alan Sheridan. New York: Norton, 1978.

Lacoste, Guillermine de. "The Beauvoir and Levy Interviews: Toward a Feminine Economy." In Julien S. Murphy, *Feminist Interpretations of Jean-Paul Sartre*, 272–79. University Park: Pennsylvania State University Press, 1999.

Locke, John. *Second Treatise of Government*. In John Locke, *Two Treatises of Government*, bk. 2. Edited by Peter Laslett. Cambridge: Cambridge University Press, 1991.

———. *Some Thoughts Concerning Education*. In James A. Axtell, ed., *The Educational Writings of John Locke*. Cambridge: Cambridge University Press, 1968.

Lott, Bernice, and Diane Maluso. "The Social Learning of Gender." In Anne E. Beall and Robert J. Sternberg, eds., *The Psychology of Gender*, 99–126. New York: Guilford, 1993.

Lugones, Maria C., and Elizabeth V. Spelman. "Have We Got a Theory for You." In *Hypatia Reborn: Essays in Feminist Philosophy*. Edited by A. Y. al-Hibri and M. A. Simons. Indianapolis: Indiana University Press, 1990. Reprinted in Naomi Zack, Laurie Shrage, and Crispin Sartwell, eds., *Race, Class, Gender, and Sexuality: The Big Questions*, 374–88. Malden, Mass.: Blackwell, 1998.

Mack, Kenneth W. "A Special History of Everyday Practice: Sadie T. M. Alexander and the Incorporation of Black Women into the American Legal Profession, 1925–1960." In Adrien Katherine Wing, ed., *Critical Race Feminism: A Reader*, 91–100. New York: New York University Press, 2003.

Mann, Bonnie. *Women's Liberation and the Sublime: Kant, Feminism, Postmodernism, Environment*. Malden, Mass.: Oxford University Press, forthcoming.

Martin, Thomas. "Sartre, Sadism, and Female Beauty Ideals." In Julien S. Murphy, ed., *Feminist Interpretations of Jean-Paul Sartre*, 90–104. University Park: Pennsylvania State University Press, 1999.

Marx, Karl. *Capital.* Vol. 1. Translated by Ben Fowkes. London: Penguin, 1990.

Marx, Karl, and Friedrich Engels. *The Communist Manifesto.* In *Karl Marx: Selected Writings.* Edited by Lawrence H. Simon. Indianapolis: Hackett, 1994.

Merchant, Carolyn. *The Death of Nature: Women, Ecology, and the Scientific Revolution.* New York: Harper & Row, 1980.

Merleau-Ponty, Maurice. *The Phenomenology of Perception.* Translated by Colin Smith. New York: Humanities, 1962.

Mills, Charles. *The Racial Contract.* Ithaca, N.Y.: Cornell University Press, 1997.

Moi, Toril. *Sexual Textual Politics: Feminist Literary Theory.* New York: Routledge, 1985.

———. *What Is a Woman?* New York: Oxford University Press, 1999.

Murphy, Julien S. *Feminist Interpretations of Jean-Paul Sartre.* University Park: Pennsylvania State University Press, 1999.

Nagel, Thomas. *What Does It All Mean?* New York: Oxford University Press, 1987.

Neilan, Terence. "High Court in Massachusetts Rules Gays Have Right to Marry." *New York Times*, November 18, 2003, A1.

Nicholson, Linda J. "Feminism and Marx." In *The Second Wave: A Reader in Feminist Theory*, 131–46. New York: Routledge, 1997.

———. *Gender and History.* New York: Columbia University Press, 1986.

Nicholson, Linda J., ed. *Feminism/Postmodernism.* New York: Routledge, 1990.

———. *The Second Wave: A Reader in Feminist Theory.* New York: Routledge, 1997.

Nussbaum, Martha C. *Women and Human Development: The Capabilities Approach.* New York: Cambridge University Press, 2000.

Okin, Susan Moller. "John Rawls: Justice as Fairness—For Whom?" In Mary Lyndon Shanley and Carole Pateman, eds., *Feminist Interpretations and Political Theory.* University Park: Pennsylvania State University Press, 1991.

Oliver, Kelly, ed. *French Feminism Reader.* Lanham, Md.: Rowman & Littlefield, 2000.

Pankhurst, Donna, and Jenny Pearce. "Feminist Perspectives on Democratisation in the South: Engendering or Adding Women In." In Haleh Afshar, ed., *Women and Politics in the Third World,* 40–47. London: Routledge, 1996.

Pateman, Carole. *The Sexual Contract.* Stanford, Calif.: Stanford University Press, 1988.

Popper, Karl. *Conjectures and Refutations: The Growth of Scientific Knowledge* (1965). Sections 1–2, 4–5, 9–10. Reprinted as "Science: Conjectures and Refutations." In Janet A. Kourney, ed., *Scientific Knowledge.* Belmont Calif.: Wadsworth, 1998.

Rai, Shirin. "Women and the State in the Third World." In Haleh Afshar, ed., *Women and Politics in the Third World,* 25–39. London: Routledge, 1996.

Rawls, John. "Fairness to Goodness." *Philosophical Review* 84 (1975): 537.

———. *A Theory of Justice.* Cambridge: Harvard University Press, 1971.

Roopnarine, Jaipaul L., and Nina S. Mounts. "Current Theoretical Issues in Sex Roles and Sex Typing." In Kathryn Backett-Milburn and Linda Mckie, eds., *Constructing Gendered Bodies,* 7–31. New York: Palgrave, 2001.

Rubin, Gayle. "The Traffic in Women: Notes on the 'Political Economy' of Sex." In Rayna R. Reither, ed., *Toward an Anthropology of Women.* New York: Monthly Review Press, 1975. Reprinted in Linda Nicholson, ed., *The Second Wave: A Reader in Feminist Theory*, 27–62. New York: Routledge, 1997.

Ruthven, Ken K. *Feminist Literary Studies: An Introduction.* Cambridge: Cambridge University Press, 1984.

Saletan, William. *Bearing Right: How Conservatives Won the Abortion War.* Berkeley: University of California Press, 2003.

Salkovskis, Paul M., ed. *Frontiers of Cognitive Therapy.* New York: Guilford, 1996.

Sartre, Jean-Paul. *Being and Nothingness.* Translated by Hazel Barnes. New York: Philosophical Library, 1952.

———. *Critique of Dialectical Reason: The Intelligibility of History.* Vol. 2. Edited by Arlette Elkaim-Sartre. Translated by Quintin Hoare. New York: Verso, 1991.

———. *Critique of Dialectical Reason: Theory of Practical Ensembles.* Vol. 1. Translated by Alan Sheridan-Smith. New York: Verso, 1976.

———. "Existentialism Is a Humanism." Translated by Bernard Frechtman. Reprinted in L. Nathan Oaklander, ed., *Existentialist Philosophy: An Introduction,* 310–19. Upper Saddle River, N.J.: Prentice Hall, 1996.

———. *Search for a Method.* Translated by Hazel E. Barnes. New York: Vintage, 1968.

———. *War Diaries: Notebooks from a Phoney War, 1939–40.* Translated by Quintin Hoare. New York: Verso, 1999.

Saussure, Ferdinand de. *Course in General Linguistics.* New York: McGraw-Hill, 1966.

Shanley, Mary Lyndon, and Carole Pateman, eds. *Feminist Interpretations and Political Theory.* University Park: Pennsylvania State University Press, 1991.

Sheets-Johnstone, Maxine. *The Roots of Power: Animate Form and Gendered Bodies.* La Salle, Ill.: Open Court, 1994.

Shrage, Laurie. *Abortion and Social Responsibility: Depolarizing the Debate.* New York: Oxford University Press, 2003.

Skjeie, Hege. "Credo on Difference: Women in Parliament in Norway." Available at www.idea.int (accessed May 2004). First published in International IDEA, *Handbook: Women in Parliament: Beyond Numbers.* Stockholm: International IDEA, 1998.

Spelman, Elizabeth V. *Inessential Woman: Problems of Exclusion in Feminist Thought.* Boston: Beacon, 1988.

Vitousek, Kelly M. "The Current Status of Cognitive-Behavioral Models of Anorexia Nervosa and Bulimia Nervosa." In Paul M. Salkovskis, ed., *Frontiers of Cognitive Therapy,* 383–418. New York: Guilford, 1996.

Waylen, Georgia. "Analyzing Women in the Politics of the Third World." In Haleh Afshar, ed., *Women and Politics in the Third World,* 7–24. London: Routledge, 1996.

Weisner, Merry E. *Women and Gender in Early Modern Europe.* Cambridge: Cambridge University Press, 1993.

Weisser, Susan Ostrov, and Jennifer Fleischner, eds. *Feminist Nightmares: Women at Odds.* New York: New York University Press, 1994.

Wilkinson, Sue, "Still Seeking Transformation: Feminist Challenges to Psychology." In Janet A. Kourany, ed., *The Gender of Science,* 218–27. Upper Saddle River, N.J.: Prentice Hall, 2002.

Willett, Cynthia. *The Soul of Justice: Social Bonds and Racial Hubris.* Ithaca, N.Y.: Cornell University Press, 2001.

Wilson, Robin. "A Kinder, Less Ambitious Professoriate." *Chronicle of Higher Education*, November 8, 2002, 10–11.

Wing, Adrien Katherine, ed. *Critical Race Feminism: A Reader.* 2d ed. New York: New York University Press, 2002.

———. *Global Critical Race Feminism: An International Approach.* New York: New York University Press, 2000.

Woolf, Leonard. *Beginning Again: An Autobiography of the Years 1911–1918.* New York: Harcourt Brace Jovanovich, 1964.

———. *Downhill All the Way: An Autobiography of the Years 1919–1939.* New York: Harcourt Brace Jovanovich, 1967.

Woolf, Virginia. *Three Guineas.* New York: Harcourt, 1938.

Wrangham, Richard, and Dale Peterson. *Demonic Males: Apes and the Origins of Human Violence.* New York: Houghton Mifflin, 1996.

Young, Iris Marion. "Gender as Seriality: Thinking about Women as a Social Collective." In Julien S. Murphy, *Feminist Interpretations of Jean-Paul Sartre,* 200–228. University Park: Pennsylvania State University Press, 1999.

———. *Inclusion and Democracy.* Oxford: Oxford University Press, 2000.

———. "Is Male Gender Identity the Cause of Male Domination?" In *Throwing Like a Girl and Other Essays in Feminist Philosophy and Social Theory,* 36–61. Bloomington: Indiana University Press, 1990.

———. *Justice and the Politics of Difference.* Princeton, N.J.: Princeton University Press, 1990.

———. "Throwing Like a Girl: A Phenomenology of Feminine Body Comportment, Motility, and Spatiality." In *Throwing Like a Girl and Other Essays in Feminist Philosophy and Social Theory,* 141–59. Bloomington: Indiana University Press, 1990. Reprinted from *Human Studies* 3 (1980): 137–56.

Zack, Naomi. "The American Sexualization of Race." In *RACE/SEX: Their Sameness, Difference, and Interplay,* 145–56. New York: Routledge, 1997.

———. *Bachelors of Science: Seventeenth-Century Identity, Then and Now.* Philadelphia: Temple University Press, 1996.

———. *Philosophy of Science and Race.* New York: Routledge, 2002.

———. "Race and Philosophic Meaning." In *RACE/SEX: Their Sameness, Difference, and Interplay,* 29–44. New York: Routledge, 1997.

———. "The Racial Contract according to Charles Mills." In Curtis Stokes and Theresa Melendez, eds., *Racial Liberalism and the Politics of Urban America,* 24–29. East Lansing: Michigan State University Press, 2003.

Zack, Naomi, ed. *Women of Color and Philosophy.* Malden, Mass.: Blackwell, 2000.

Zinn, Maxine Baca, and Bonnie Thornton Dill, eds. *Women of Color in U.S. Society.* Philadelphia: Temple University Press, 1994.

Index

abject, mothers as, 88
abortion, contemporary discussion of, 68–69
Abortion and Social Responsiblity (Shrage), 68
About Chinese Women (Kristeva), 88, 98, 104–5
academic feminism, 1, 3, 7–8, 15–18, 98
Adler, Alfred, 107
adoption, in India, 35–37, 44–48, 52
Ain't I a Woman? (hooks), 3
al-Hibri, Azizah Hahia, 154
Alcoff, Linda, 17–18
Allen, Paula Gunn, 122
The American Dream in Black and White (Flax), 5
androgynization, of women, 145
androgyny, 93
anorexia nervosa, 71–72, 95–96
anthropology, 62
Antigone, family relations of, 171
Antigone's Claim (Butler), 169–71

Bachelors of Science (Zack), 138n6
Bangladesh, women's activism in, 155
Bartky, Sandra Lee, 50–51
beauty, ideals of, 49–50
Beijing Platform for Action 1995, 151

Being and Nothingness (Sartre), 130,134
Belmont, Mrs. O. H. P. 149, 165
Bettelheim, Bruno, 84–85
biological sex, 62
bisexuality: according to Cixous, 88; according to Freud, 84, 100n3
black female gender, as circumstances, 74–75
Black Feminist Thought (Collins), 16
black women: discrimination against, 68; and intersectionality, 4–5; struggle for rights, 5–6
Bodies That Matter (Butler), 21n22
bodily freedom, of women, 47–48, 51
The Body Project (Drumberg), 56n3
bonobos, female social groups in, 167
Bordo, Susan, 71–2, 81n18
Bourdieu, Pierre, 70
Brazil, women's activism in, 155
Brownmiller, Susan, 57n12
bulimia nervosa, 95–96
Butler, Judith, 8, 21n22, 56n3, 167–71

capitalism, 127–29
children, as Other, 35–38
chimpanzees, male aggression of, 167
Chisholm, Shirley, 150
Chodorow, Nancy, 85–86

About the Author

Naomi Zack is professor of philosophy at the University of Oregon. She completed her Ph.D. in philosophy at Columbia University in 1970, with a dissertation on the epistemology of C. I. Lewis. Zack then left academia and philosophy until 1990. She resumed her academic life at the University at Albany, State University of New York, until 2001. She is the author of *Race and Mixed Race* (1993), *Bachelors of Science: Seventeenth-Century Identity, Then and Now* (1996), and *Philosophy of Science and Race* (2002). She has written a textbook, *Thinking About Race* (1997, 2005), as well as numerous articles, and has edited four anthologies, including *American Mixed Race: The Culture of Microdiversity* (1995).